Applied Statistics
and the SAS® Programming Language

Third Edition

Applied Statistics
and the SAS® Programming Language

Third Edition

Ronald P. Cody
University of Medicine and Dentistry of New Jersey
Robert Wood Johnson Medical School

Jeffrey K. Smith
Graduate School of Education
Rutgers University

PRENTICE HALL, Englewood Cliffs, New Jersey 07632

SAS is a registered trademark of SAS Institute Inc., Cary, North Carolina.

ISBN 0-13-500554-X

Prentice-Hall International (UK) Limited, *London*
Prentice-Hall of Australia Pty. Limited, *Sydney*
Prentice-Hall Canada Inc., *Toronto*
Prentice-Hall Hispanoamericana, S. A., *Mexico*
Prentice-Hall of India Private Limited, *New Delhi*
Prentice-Hall of Japan, Inc., *Tokyo*
Simon & Schuster Asia Pte. Ltd., *Singapore*
Editora Prentice-Hall do Brasil, Ltda., *Rio de Janeiro*

This book is dedicated to
Jan, Russell, and Preston Cody
and to
Madelyn, Benjamin, and Leah Smith

CONTENTS

PROGRAMMING SECTION

PREFACE TO THE THIRD EDITION

The second edition of our book was entering its fifth printing when we received a call from our Elsevier editor asking if we thought it was time for a third edition. Although deep down in our hearts we knew it was time, we knew that many hours of hard work lay ahead. It would be far easier to continue to make corrections to the second edition and let it go for a few more years. However, our desire to keep this work current prevailed and this is the result. In the past, we struggled to maintain a compromise among an introductory guide to SAS programming, a statistics book, and a reference work for more advanced SAS programming. In this edition, our resolution to this problem is to split the book into three sections. First, we have written a tutorial section that can serve as an introduction to programming with SAS software. Only very basic statistics are covered in this section. Next, the main part of the book describes common statistical tests, how to run them with SAS software, and how to interpret the results. Finally, a SAS programming section shows common problems in data manipulation and how to solve these problems using SAS software.

When the first edition was written, the SAS system ran only on IBM mainframe computers. One of the main incentives for the second edition was the introduction of PC-SAS which put SAS software in the hands of individual researchers working with desktop computers. The main goal of this third edition is to present a more coherent book that is better suited to a university level course on research methods and statistical programming. Once again, the problem section has been expanded and now includes problems in data manipulation as well as statistical problems. Since the SAS system now runs on so many computer systems (referred to as platforms in computer jargon), it would seem more difficult to write a book on the SAS system. Actually, it has gotten easier, rather than harder, because of the SAS Display Manager which has the same "look and feel" on most of the available platforms. Except for slight differences in how SAS software reads and writes external files, the syntax shown in this book is consistent across platforms.

Learning to program is a skill that is rather difficult to teach. While you will find our examples easy to read and their logic easy to follow, learning to write your own programs is another matter. We know from talking to researchers who use our book, that many people mimic our examples. The best way to break free from this is to practice; our contribution to this is the set of example problems with solutions provided.

To our old friends who have purchased your own third edition, God bless you, our children are nearing college age. To our new friends, we wrote this book to save you time, money, and aggravation. Good luck and don't forget the semicolons.

OVERVIEW

Since you already have this book in your hands, you probably have some idea what the SAS system is. If you haven't, don't panic, you probably have many other wonderful qualities, and we'll explain the system. We like to describe SAS software as a combination of a statistical package, a data base management system, and a high level programming language. Like SPSS, BMDP, SYSTAT, and other statistical packages, SAS software can be used to describe a collection of data and produce a variety of statistical analyses. However, SAS software is much more than just a statistical package. Many companies and educational institutions use SAS software as a high level data management system and programming language. It can be used to organize and transform data and to create reports of all kinds. Also, depending on which portions of the SAS system you have installed on your computer (and depending on what type of computer system you are running), you may be using the SAS system for interactive data entry or an on-line system for order entry or retrieval.

This book will concentrate on the use of the SAS system for the statistical analysis of data and the programming capabilities of SAS software that will be most often used in educational and research applications.

The SAS system is a collection of products, available from the SAS Institute in Cary, North Carolina. The major products available from the SAS Institute are:

Package	Description
Base SAS®	The main SAS module that provides some data manipulation and programming capability and some elementary descriptive statistics
SAS/STAT™	The SAS product that includes all the statistical programs except the elementary ones supplied with the base package

SAS/GRAPH®   A package that provides high quality graphs and maps. Note that "line graphics" (the graphs and charts that are produced by normal character plots), are available in the base and SAS/STAT packages. SAS/GRAPH adds the ability to produce high quality camera-ready graphs, maps and charts.

SAS/FSP®   The initials stand for the Full Screen Product. This package allows you to search, modify, or delete records directly from a SAS data file. It also provides for data entry with sophisticated data checking capabilities. Procedures available with FSP are FSBROWSE, FSEDIT, FSPRINT, FSLIST, and FSLETTER.

SAS/AF®   AF stands for the SAS Applications Facility. This product is used by data processing professionals to create "turn-key" or menu systems for their users. It is also used to create instructional modules relating to the SAS system.

SAS/ETS®   The Econometric and Time Series package. This package contains specialized programs for the analysis of time-series and econometric data.

SAS/OR®   A series of operations research programs.

SAS/QC®   A series of programs for quality control.

SAS/IML™   The Interactive Matrix Language module. The facilities of IML used to be included in PROC MATRIX in the version 5 releases. This very specialized package allows for convenient matrix manipulation for the advanced statistician.

SAS software now runs on a large variety of computers, from personal computers to large multi-million dollar mainframes. The original version of the SAS system was written in a combination of PL/1 and IBM assembly language. Today, SAS software runs under MS-DOS on microcomputers, under UNIX on a large number of minicomputers and workstations, on IBM computers under a variety of operation systems, on Digital Equipment VAX computers, and others too numerous to mention. The major reason for the ability of SAS software to run on such a large variety of machines is that all SAS software was rewritten in C and designed so that most of the code was system independent. The conversion of the entire system to the C programming language was one of the largest (and successful) programming projects ever undertaken. To migrate the SAS system to another computer or operating system, only a small system dependent portion of code needs to be rewritten. The result is that new versions of SAS software are made available for all computers very quickly and the versions of SAS systems from one computer to another look very much alike.

As of this writing, the current mainframe version of the SAS system is version 6.06 and the microcomputer version is 6.04. Although the actual SAS programming statements are system independent, the statements that link a SAS program to external data files and tapes are system dependent. We will discuss these differences but we will use PC-SAS statements in our examples. We have chosen to do this for several reasons. First, PC-SAS uses statements to link to external files that are the same or similar to SAS statements on other systems. Second, PC-SAS is very popular, especially in education and research institutions, the main audience for this book. And third, the authors have the most recent experience with PC-SAS. SAS software running on a medium sized personal computer (an 80386 for example), with sufficient memory and disk storage can create and analyze data sets up to 50,000 observations quite readily. For larger data sets, workstations or minicomputers work well. Finally, for those multi-million observation data sets, a mainframe may be required.

We would like to express our deepest appreciation to Mary Northridge and Lisa Wolf for their careful proofreading of this text. Any remaining errors are the responsibility of the authors. We would also like to thank John Dodge who produced the camera ready copy and never complained about our many revisions.

Ron Cody
Jeffrey Smith
Spring, 1991

Applied Statistics
and the SAS® Programming Language

Third Edition

CHAPTER 1
A SAS® TUTORIAL

A. INTRODUCTION

For the novice, engaging in statistical analysis of data can seem as appealing as going to the dentist. If this pretty much describes your situation, perhaps you can take comfort in the fact that this is the third edition of this book. That means that the first two editions sold pretty well, and this time we may get it right. The purpose of this tutorial is to get you started using SAS software. The key objective is to get one program to run successfully. If you can do that, you can branch out a little bit at a time. Your expertise will grow. Soon, you'll be shopping for plastic pen protectors and neighbors will be asking you to fix their microwaves.

SAS software is a combination of programs originally designed to perform statistical analysis of data. Other programs you may have heard of are SPSS, BMDP, or SYSTAT. If you look at microcomputer magazines in your doctor's office, you might run across other programs, primarily designed to run on microcomputers. Since its inception, the SAS system has grown to where it can perform a fairly impressive array of nonstatistical functions. We'll get into a little of that in later chapters. For now, we want to present the most basic rudiments of the SAS system. If you skipped over it, the Preface to the third edition contains some history of SAS software development and a more complete overview of the capabilities of SAS software.

To begin, SAS software will run on a wide variety of computers and operating systems (computer people call these "platforms"), and we don't know which one you have. The biggest difference concerns whether you are running SAS software on what is called a mainframe, or whether you are running a version designed for microcomputers. Your first guess may be that you are using the microcomputer version since you don't see a mainframe in your office. However, if you are linking from your micro to another computer via a modem, then you are probably running on a mini or mainframe computer. How can you find out? Ask someone. As a matter of fact, right now would be a good time to invite the best computer person you know to lunch. Have this person arrive at your office about an hour before lunch is scheduled so you can go over some basic elements of your system. You need to find out what is necessary on your computer to get the SAS system running. What we can teach you here is how to use the SAS system, and a little bit about how to adapt it to your computer system.

Unfortunately, unless you have remarkable computer aptitude, you'll probably need a little help launching a career in analyzing statistical data.

If you are running on a mainframe (a good source of aerobic exercise while computing), you may well be submitting what are called "batch" jobs. When you run batch jobs, you send your program (across a phone line from your microcomputer or terminal) to the computer. The computer runs your program and holds it until you ask for it or prints out the results on a high speed printer. In order to do this, you need a computer account at the computer center and a terminal or microcomputer with a modem. You need to learn some Job Control Language (which you have to get from your local computer folks), and then you can proceed.

If you are running off a microcomputer or running in what is called "interactive mode" off a minicomputer or mainframe, then you need to learn how to use the SAS Display Manager. This is additional work, but the people who invest the time in learning it are usually glad they did. In all likelihood, you won't have any choice in the matter, so it is best to be happy with whichever mode you have.

Fortunately for you (and us) SAS programs run pretty much the same in both modes and irrespective of what platform you are using. This is the end of the introduction. If you are undaunted, take a deep breath and plunge into the real content in the next section. If you are already daunted, take a minute and get that lunch scheduled, then come back to this.

B. COMPUTING WITH SAS® SOFTWARE: AN ILLUSTRATIVE EXAMPLE

SAS programs communicate with the computer by SAS "statements." There are several kinds of SAS statements, but they share a common feature—they end in a semicolon. **A semicolon in a SAS program is like a period in English.** Probably the most common error found in SAS programs is the omission of the semicolon. This causes the computer to read two statements as a run-on statement and invariably fouls things up.

There are two kinds of SAS statements: **DATA** statements and **PROC** statements. DATA statements tell SAS programs about your data. They are used to indicate where the variables are on data lines, what you want to call the variables, and how to create new variables from existing variables, as well as several other functions we will mention later. PROC statements (pronounced "prock"; this is short for "PROCEDURE") indicate what kind of statistical analyses to perform and provide specifications for those analyses.

SAS programs are like sandwiches. They begin with DATA statements (bread), which tell the program about your data set. Then comes the data (meat). Finally, we have PROC statements (bread), which specify the analyses to be performed. Let's look at an example. Consider this simple data set:

SUBJECT NUMBER	SEX (M OR F)	EXAM 1	EXAM 2	HOMEWORK GRADE
10	M	80	84	A
7	M	85	89	A
4	F	90	86	B
20	M	82	85	B
25	F	94	94	A
14	F	88	84	C

We have 5 variables (SUBJECT NUMBER, SEX, EXAM 1, EXAM 2, and HOMEWORK GRADE) collected on each of 6 subjects. The unit of analysis, people in this example, is called an **observation** in SAS terminology. SAS software uses the term **variable** to represent each piece of information we collect for each observation. Before we can write our SAS program, we need to assign a **variable name** to each variable. We do this so that we can distinguish one variable from another when doing computations or re- questing statistics. SAS variable names must conform to a few simple rules: they must start with a letter, be no more than 8 characters in length, and cannot contain blanks or special characters such as commas, semicolons, etc. Therefore, our column headings of "SUBJECT NUMBER," or "EXAM 1" are not valid SAS variable names. Logical SAS variable names for this collection of data would be:

SUBJECTS   SEX   EXAM1   EXAM2   HWGRADE

It is usually wise to pick variable names that help you remember which name goes with which variable. We could have named our 5 variables VAR1, VAR2, VAR3, VAR4, and VAR5, but we would then have to remem- ber that VAR1 stands for "SUBJECT NUMBER," etc.

To begin, let's say we are interested only in getting the class means for the two exams. In reality it's hardly worth using a computer to add up six numbers, but it does provide a nice example. In order to do this, we could write the following SAS program:

NOTE: The line numbers to the left of the program are not part of the program. They are just there so that we can refer to them in the text.

```
1     DATA TEST;
2     INPUT SUBJECT 1-2 SEX $ 4 EXAM1 6-8 EXAM2 10-12
3     HWGRADE $ 14;
4     CARDS;
5     10 M   80    84 A
6      7 M   85    89 A
7      4 F   90    86 B
8     20 M   82    85 B
9     25 F   94    94 A
10    14 F   88    84 C
11    PROC MEANS;
12    RUN;
```

Lines 1-4 are the DATA statements or DATA paragraph. They begin with the word DATA and end with the word CARDS. Even though SAS programs use a statement called **"CARDS,"** it does not mean that our data have to be on computer cards. (If you don't know what a computer card is, ask an old person.) Rather, CARDS refers to the more general concept "card image," which can be real cards or records on a computer disk. **Line 1** tells the program that we want to create a SAS data set called **TEST**. You have to use a DATA statement, but you don't have to provide a name (you may simply use DATA;). If you do want to give it a name, you must follow the same rules as in naming variables. **Lines 2 and 3** show an **INPUT** statement which gives the program two pieces of information: what to call the variables and where to find them on the data line. The first variable is SUBJECT and can be found in columns 1 and 2 of the data line. The second variable is SEX and can be found in column 4. The dollar sign after SEX means that SEX is an "alphanumeric" variable, that is, a variable that can have letters or numbers as data values. More on this later. EXAM1 is in columns 6-8 etc. **Line 4** says that the DATA statements are done and the next thing the program should look for are the data themselves. Lines 5-10 contain our data.

There is great latitude possible in putting together the data lines. Using a few rules will make life much simpler for you. These are not **laws**, they are just suggestions. First, put each new observation on a new line. Having more than one line per observation is often necessary (and no problem), but don't put two observations on one line (at least for now). Second, line, up your variables. Don't put EXAM1 in columns 6-8 on one line and in columns 9-11 on the next. SAS software can actually handle some degree of sloppiness here, but sooner or later it'll cost you. Third, right-justify your data values. If you have AGE as a variable, record the data as follows:

CORRECT	PROBLEMATIC
87	87
42	42
9	9
26	26
4	4
Right justified	Left justified

Once again, SAS software doesn't care whether you right-justify or not, but other statistical programs will, and right justification is standard. Fourth, use alphanumeric variables sparingly. Take HWGRADE for example. We have HWGRADE recorded alphanumerically. (Normal people call this alphabetically. Computer people don't because letters and/or numbers can be treated as alphanumerics.) But we could have recorded it as 0-4 (0=F, 1=D, etc.). As it stands, we cannot compute a mean grade. Had we coded HWGRADE numerically, we could get an average grade. Enough on how to code data for now.

SAS programs know that the data lines are over when it finds a SAS statement. Usually, the next SAS statement is a PROC statement. PROC says, "Run a procedure," to the program. We specify which procedure right after the word PROC. Line 11 says to run the procedure called MEANS. The MEANS procedure calculates the mean for any variables you specify. **The RUN statement is necessary only when SAS programs are run under the Display Manager.** The RUN statement tells SAS that there are no more statements for the preceding procedure and to go ahead and do the calculations. If we have several PROCs in a row, we only need a single RUN statement at the end of the program. When the lines of SAS code are interpreted, the presence of a PROC statement indicates that there are no more statements associated with the previous PROC and to go ahead and do the computations. However, we recommend that you end each procedure with a RUN statement if you are running SAS software under the Display Manager.

When this program is executed, it produces something called the **SAS LOG** and the **SAS OUTPUT**. The SAS LOG is an annotated copy of your original program (without the data listed). Any SAS error messages will be found there, along with information about the data set that was created. The SAS LOG for this program is shown below:

```
NOTE: Copyright© 1985,86,87 SAS Institute Inc., Cary NC
      27512-8000, U.S.A.
NOTE: SAS® Proprietary Software Release 6.04
      Licensed to UNIVERSITY OF MEDICINE AND DENTISTRY OF
      NJ, Site xxx.
NOTE: AUTOEXEC processing completed.
    1 DATA TEST;
    2 INPUT SUBJECT 1-2 SEX $ 4 EXAM1 6-8 EXAM2 10-12
    3 HWGRADE $ 14;
    4 CARDS;
   11 PROC MEANS;
NOTE:  The data set WORK.TEST has 6 observations and 5
      variables.
NOTE: The DATA statement used 2.00 seconds.
   12 RUN;
NOTE: The PROCEDURE MEANS used 1.00 seconds.
```

The more important part of the output contains the results of the computations and procedures requested by our PROC statements. This portion of the output from the above program is shown next:

N Obs	Variable	N	Minimum	Maximum	Mean	Std Dev
6	SUBJECT	6	4.0000000	25.0000000	13.3333333	7.9916623
	EXAM1	6	80.0000000	94.0000000	86.5000000	5.2057660
	EXAM2	6	84.0000000	94.0000000	87.0000000	3.8987177

If you don't specify which variables you want after the PROC MEANS statement, SAS software will calculate the mean for every numeric variable in the data set. Our program calculated means for SUBJECT, EXAM1, and EXAM2. Since SUBJECT is just an arbitrary ID number assigned to each student, we aren't really interested in its mean. We can avoid getting it (and paying for it) by adding a new statement under PROC MEANS:

```
11   PROC MEANS;
12      VAR EXAM1 EXAM2;
13   RUN;
```

The indentation is only a visual aid. The VAR statement (line 12) specifies on which variables to run PROC MEANS. PROC MEANS not only gives you means, it gives you the number of observations used to compute the mean, the standard deviation, the minimum score found and the maximum score found for each variable. (The specific statistics you get will depend on which version of SAS software you are using and how several options are set.) If you don't want all this information, you can specify just which pieces you want in the PROC MEANS statement. For example:

```
11   PROC MEANS N MEAN STD MAXDEC=1;
12      VAR EXAM1 EXAM2;
13   RUN;
```

will get you just the number of cases (N), mean (MEAN), and standard deviation (STD) for the variables EXAM1 and EXAM2. In addition, the statistics will be rounded to one decimal place (because of the MAXDEC=1 option). Chapter 2 will describe most of the commonly requested options used with PROC MEANS.

C. ENHANCING THE PROGRAM

The program as it is currently written will provide some useful information, but with a little more work, we can put some bells and whistles on it. The bells and whistles version below adds the following features: it computes a final grade for each student, which will be the average of the two exam scores; it lists the students in student number order, showing their exam scores, their final grade and homework grade; it computes the class average for the exams and final grade; and finally, it gives a frequency count for sex and homework grade.

```
 1     DATA EXAMPLE;
 2     INPUT SUBJECT SEX $ EXAM1 EXAM2 HWGRADE $;
 3     FINAL = (EXAM1 + EXAM2)/2.;
 4     CARDS;
 5     10 M 80 84 A
 6      7 M 85 89 A
 7      4 F 90 86 B
 8     20 M 82 85 B
 9     25 F 94 94 A
10     14 F 88 84 C
11     RUN;
12     PROC SORT;
13        BY SUBJECT;
14     RUN;
15     PROC PRINT;
16        TITLE 'ROSTER IN STUDENT NUMBER ORDER';
17        ID SUBJECT;
18        VAR EXAM1 EXAM2 FINAL HWGRADE;
19     RUN;
20     PROC MEANS N MEAN STD MAXDEC=1;
21        TITLE 'DESCRIPTIVE STATISTICS';
22        VAR EXAM1 EXAM2 FINAL;
23     RUN;
24     PROC FREQ;
25        TABLES SEX HWGRADE;
26     RUN;
```

NOTE: Once again, the line numbers to the left are just for reference and are not part of the program.

Lines 1-4 constitute our DATA step or DATA paragraph. **Line 1** is an instruction for the program to create a **data set** whose **data set name** is "EXAMPLE." (Remember that data set names follow the same conventions as variable names.) **Line 2** is an INPUT statement which is different from the one in the previous example. We could have used the same INPUT statement as in the previous example but wanted the opportunity to show you another way that SAS programs can read data. Notice that there are no column numbers following the variable names. This form of an INPUT statement is called "list" input. To use this form of INPUT, the data values must be separated by one or more blanks. The **order** of the variable names in the list correspond to the **order** of the values in the line of data. In this example, the INPUT statement tells the program that the first variable in each line of data represents SUBJECT values, the next variable is SEX, the third EXAM1, and so forth. If your data conform to this "space-between-each-variable" format, then you don't have to specify column numbers for each variable listed in the INPUT statement. You may want to anyway, but it isn't necessary. (You still have to follow alphanumeric variable names with a dollar sign.) If you are going to use the "list directed input," then every variable on your data lines must be listed. Also, since the order of the data values is used to associate values with variables, we have to make special provisions for missing values. Suppose that subject number 10 (the first subject in our example) did not take the first exam. If we listed the data like this:

```
10 M      84 A
```

with the EXAM1 score missing, the 84 would be read as the EXAM1 score, the program would read the letter "A" as a value for EXAM2 (which would cause an error since the program was expecting a number), and a missing value for the homework grade. To hold the place of a missing value when using a "list directed" INPUT statement, use a period to represent the missing value. The period will be interpreted as a missing value by the program and will keep the order of the data values intact. When we specify columns as in the first example, we can use blanks as missing values. Using periods as missing values when we have specified columns in our INPUT statement is also OK but not recommended. The correct way to represent this line of data for list directed input, with the EXAM1 score missing is:

```
10 M . 84 A
```

Since this form of INPUT statement requires one or more blanks between data values, we need at least one blank before and after the period. We may choose to add extra spaces in our data to allow the data values to line up in columns.

Line 3 is a statement assigning the average of EXAM1 and EXAM2 to a variable called FINAL. The variable name "FINAL" must conform to the same naming conventions as the other variable names in the INPUT statement. In this example, FINAL is calculated by adding together the two exam scores and dividing by 2. Notice that we indicate addition with a + sign and division by a / sign. We need the parentheses because, just as with handwritten algebraic expressions, SAS computations are performed according to a hierarchy. Multiplication and division are performed before addition and subtraction. Thus, had we written:

```
FINAL = EXAM1 + EXAM2 / 2.;
```

the FINAL grade would have been the sum of the EXAM1 score and half of the EXAM2 score. The use of parentheses tells the program to add the two exam scores first and then divide by 2. To indicate multiplication, we use an asterisk (*) and to indicate subtraction, we use a - sign. Exponentiation, which is performed before multiplication or division, is indicated by two asterisks (**) followed by the number representing the exponent. As an example, to compute A times the square of B we would write:

```
X = A * B**2;
```

The variable FINAL, although calculated rather than read as data, is equivalent to the other variables for the duration of the program. The "CARDS;" statement in **line 4** indicates that the data step is complete and that the following lines contain data.

Notice that each SAS statement ends with a semicolon. As mentioned before, the semicolon is the logical end of a SAS statement. We could have written lines 1-4 like this:

```
DATA EXAMPLE; INPUT SUBJECT SEX $
EXAM1 EXAM2 HWGRADE $; FINAL =
(EXAM1 + EXAM2)/2.; CARDS;
```

and the program would still run correctly. Using a semicolon as a statement delimiter is convenient since we can write long SAS statements on several lines and simply put a semicolon at the end of the statement. However, if you omit a semicolon at the end of a SAS statement, the program will attempt to read the next statement as part of previous statement. This will not only cause your program to die, it will cause a bizarre error message to come from the SAS system. Omission of one or more semicolons is the most common programming error for novice SAS programmers. **Remember to watch those semicolons!** Notice also that the data lines, since they are not SAS statements, do not end with semicolons.

Lines 5 through 10 contain our data. Remember that if you have data that have been placed in preassigned columns with no spaces between the data values, we must use the form of the INPUT shown earlier, with column specifications after each variable name. This form of data will be discussed further in Chapter 2. The RUN statements in lines 11, 14, 19, 23, and 26 are used when we run SAS program interactively under the Display Manager. Each RUN statement tells the system that we are finished with a section of the program and to do the computations just concluded. For example, when the RUN statement in line 11 is encountered, the data set will be processed. When the RUN statement in line 14 is encountered, the sort will be executed. Even in an interactive SAS session, all the RUN statements except the last one are optional. Without a RUN statement, the program does not know that a procedure is finished until the next PROC statement is processed. Suppose we left out the RUN statement in line 19. The system would not know that there were no more statements following PROC PRINT until the PROC MEANS statement was read. This is OK but it is confusing to see the line PROC MEANS appear in the SAS LOG and the output from PROC PRINT appear in the output window. We feel it is "cleaner" to end each procedure with a RUN statement when we are using SAS interactively. You may find RUN statements present or absent in various problem solutions and examples in this text. Don't worry about it! Remember, when using the Display Manager, only the last RUN statement is absolutely necessary and the others are really only a matter of programming style.

D. SAS® PROCEDURES

Immediately following the data is a series of PROCs. They perform various functions and computations on SAS data sets. Since we want a list of subjects and scores in subject order, we first include a **sort procedure** (lines 12 and 13). Line 13 indicates that we plan to sort our data set; line 13 indicates that the sorting will be by SUBJECT number. Sorting can be multilevel if desired. For example, if we want separate lists of male and female students in subject number order, we will write:

```
PROC SORT;
BY SEX SUBJECT;
```

This multilevel sort indicates that we should first sort by SEX (F's followed by M's—character variables are sorted alphabetically), then in SUBJECT order **within** SEX.

Lines 15 through 18 request a listing of our data (which is now in SUBJECT order). The PRINT procedure is used to list the data values in a SAS data set. We have followed our PROC PRINT statement with three statements that supply information to the procedure. These are the **TITLE**, **ID**, and **VAR** statements. As with all SAS procedures, the supplementary statements following a PROC can be placed in any order. Thus

```
PROC PRINT;
ID SUBJECT;
TITLE 'ROSTER IN STUDENT NUMBER ORDER';
VAR EXAM1 EXAM2 FINAL HWGRADE;
```

is equivalent to

```
PROC PRINT;
TITLE 'ROSTER IN STUDENT NUMBER ORDER';
ID SUBJECT;
VAR EXAM1 EXAM2 FINAL HWGRADE;
```

SAS programs understand the keywords TITLE, ID, and VAR and interpret what follows in the proper context. Notice that each statement ends with its own semicolon. The words following TITLE are placed in single quotes and will be printed across the top of each of the SAS output pages. The ID variable, SUBJECT in this case, will cause the program to print the variable SUBJECT in the first column of the report, omitting the column labeled OBS (observation number) which the program will print when an ID variable is absent. The variables following the keyword VAR indicate which variables, besides the ID variable, we want in our report. The order of these variables in the list also controls the order in which they appear in the report. Finally, lines 24 and 25 request a frequency count for the variables SEX and HWGRADE. That is, what is the number of males and females, the number of A's, B's, etc., as well as the percentages of each category. PROC FREQ will compute frequencies for the variables listed on the TABLES statement. The reason that SAS uses the keyword TABLES instead of VAR for this list of variables is that PROC FREQ can also produce n-way tables (such as 2 X 3 tables).

Partial output from the complete program is shown below:

```
ROSTER IN STUDENT NUMBER ORDER   14:37 Monday, August 27, 1990   1

SUBJECT EXAM1 EXAM2 FINAL HWGRADE
   4     90    86   88.0    B
   7     85    89   87.0    A
  10     80    84   82.0    A
  14     88    84   86.0    C
  20     82    85   83.5    B
  25     94    94   94.0    A


DESCRIPTIVE STATISTICS              14:37 Monday, August 27, 1990   2

VARIABLE            N        MEAN         STANDARD
                                         DEVIATION

EXAM1               6        86.5           5.2
EXAM2               6        87.0           3.9
FINAL               6        86.8           4.2
```

E. OVERVIEW OF THE SAS® DATA STEP

Let's spend a moment to examine what happens when we execute a SAS program. This discussion is a bit technical and can be skipped, but an understanding of how SAS software works will help you when you are doing more advanced programming. When the DATA statement is executed, SAS software allocates a portion of a disk and names the data set "EXAMPLE," our choice for a data set name. The INPUT statement starts out by supplying a missing value for each of our variables. It then reads the first line of data and substitutes the actual data values for the missing values. These data values are not yet written to our SAS data set EXAMPLE but to a place called the **Program Data Vector** (PDV). This is just a "holding" area where data values are stored before they get transferred to the SAS data set. The computation of the final grade comes next (line 3) and the result of this computation is added to the PDV. The CARDS line triggers the end of the data step, at which time the values in the PDV are transferred to the SAS data set. The program then returns control back to the INPUT statement to read the next line of data, compute a final grade, and write the next observation to the SAS data set. This reading, processing, and writing cycle continues until no more observations are left.

F. SYNTAX OF SAS® PROCEDURES

As we have seen above, SAS procedures can have options. In addition, procedures often have statements, like the VAR statement above, which supplies information to the procedure. Finally, statements can also have options. We will show you the general syntax of SAS procedures and then illustrate it with some examples. The syntax of all SAS procedures is:

```
PROC PROCNAME options;
STATEMENTS / statement options;
            .
            .
            .
STATEMENTS / statement options;
```

First, all procedures start with the word PROC followed by the procedure name. If there are any procedure options, they are placed, in any order, between the procedure name and the semicolon, separated by spaces. If we look in a SAS manual under PROC MEANS, we will see a list of options that may be used with the procedure. As we have mentioned, N, MEAN, STD, STDERR, and MAXDEC= are some of the available options. A valid PROC MEANS request with options for N, MEAN, and MAXDEC would be:

```
PROC MEANS N MEAN MAXDEC=1;
```

Next, most procedures need statements to supply more information about what type of analysis to perform. An example would be the VAR statement used with PROC MEANS. Statements follow the procedure, in any order. They each end in a semicolon. So, to run the PROC MEANS statement above, on the variables HEIGHT and WEIGHT, and to supply a title, we would enter:

```
PROC MEANS N MEAN STD MAXDEC=1;
   TITLE 'DESCRIPTIVE STATISTICS ON HEIGHT AND
   WEIGHT DATA';
   VAR HEIGHT WEIGHT;
RUN;
```

The order of the TITLE and VAR statements could have been inter-changed with no change in the results. Finally, some procedure statements also have options. Statement options are placed between the statement and the semicolon, separated from the statement by a slash. To illustrate this, we need to choose a procedure other than PROC MEANS. Let's use PROC FREQ as an example. As we saw, PROC FREQ will usually have one or more TABLES statements following it. There are TABLES options that control which statistics to place in the table. For example, if we do not want the cumulative statistics printed, the statement option NOCUM is used. Since this is a statement option, it is placed between the TABLES statement and the semicolon, separated by a slash. The PROC FREQ request in the earlier example, modified to remove the cumulative statistics would be:

```
PROC FREQ;
    TABLES SEX HWGRADE / NOCUM;
RUN;
```

To demonstrate a procedure with procedure options and statement options, we will use the ORDER= option with PROC FREQ. This useful option controls the order that the values are arranged in our frequency table. One option is ORDER=FREQ. This causes the frequency table to be arranged in frequency order, from the highest frequency to the lowest. The statements to produce such a table and to remove the cumulative statistics from the printout would be:

```
PROC FREQ ORDER=FREQ;
    TABLES SEX HWGRADE / NOCUM;
RUN;
```

G. COMMENT STATEMENTS

Before we leave this chapter, this is a good time to introduce you to one of the most important SAS statements—the comment statement. Yes, we're not kidding! A properly commented program is the sign that a true profes-sional is at work. A comment inserted in a program is one or more lines of text that are ignored by the program—they are there only to help the programmer or researcher when he or she reads the program at a later date.

To insert a comment into a SAS program, begin the comment with an asterisk (*) and end it with a semicolon. Thus,

```
*PROGRAM TO COMPUTE RELIABILITY COEFFICIENTS
RON CODY
SEPTEMBER, 1990
PROGRAM ON THE XYZ COMPUTER STORED IN ACCOUNT
3452323 WITH THE NAME FRED.
CLIENTS PHONE NUMBER IS 123-4567;
```

is a comment statement. Notice how convenient it is to include. Just enter the * and type as many lines as necessary, ending with the semicolon. You may also choose to comment individual lines in one of the following ways:

```
QUES = 6 - QUES;   *TRANSFORM QUES VAR;
X = LOG(X);   *LOG TRANSFORM OF X;
```

or

```
*TRANSFORM THE QUES VARIABLE;
QUES = 6 - QUES;
*TAKE THE LOG OF X;
X = LOG(X);
```

or

```
*
*TRANSFORM THE QUES VARIABLE
*;
QUES = 6 - QUES;
*
*TAKE THE LOG OF X
*;
X = LOG(X);
```

The last method uses more than one asterisk to set off the comment for visual effect. Note however, that each group of three lines is a single comment since it begins with an asterisk and ends with a semicolon.

Let us show you one final, very useful, trick using a comment statement before we conclude this chapter. Suppose you have written a program and run several procedures. Now, you come back to the program and want to run additional procedures. You could edit the program, remove the old procedures and add the new ones. Or, you could "comment them out" by preceding each of the program statements with an asterisk, thereby making them comment statements! As an example, our commented program could look like this:

```
DATA MYPROG;
INPUT X Y Z;
CARDS;
1 2 3
3 4 5
*PROC PRINT;
*    TITLE 'MY TITLE';
*    VAR X Y Z;
PROC CORR;
    VAR X Y Z;
```

The print procedure will not be executed since it will be treated as a comment; the correlation request will be run.

With most computer editor programs, adding or deleting an asterisk at the beginning of each line is very easy to do. Because of this trick (and for other reasons), we recommend that only one SAS statement be placed on a single line. If you had written:

```
PROC MEANS;   VAR X Y Z;
```

on one line, placing an asterisk only at the beginning of the line would cause a syntax error. Please remember to comment your programs.

H. REFERENCES

One of the advantages of SAS software is the variety of procedures that can be performed. We cannot describe them all here nor can we explain every option of the procedures we do describe. You may, therefore, want to obtain one or more of the following manuals available from the SAS Institute Inc., Book Sales Department, SAS Campus Drive, Cary, NC 27513-2414. The SAS Institute also takes phone orders. Their number is (919) 677-8000.

For the MS-DOS and PC-DOS Environments:

SAS Language Guide for Personal Computers, Release 6.03 Edition
SAS Procedures Guide for Personal Computers, Release 6.03 Edition
SAS/STAT User's Guide, Release 6.03 Edition
(You'll want the most current edition when you order)

For the UNIX Environment:

SAS Language Guide, Release 6.03 Edition
SAS Procedures Guide, Release 6.03 Edition
SAS/STAT User's Guide, Release 6.03 Edition

For Mainframe Users:

SAS Procedures Guide, Version 6, First Edition
SAS Language Reference, Version 6, First Edition
SAS/STAT User's Guide, Version 6, Fourth Edition, Vols. 1 & 2

Below are some statistics books which we recommend:

Statistical Principles in Experimental Design, by B.J. Winer (McGraw-Hill, New York, 1971)

Statistical Methods, by Snedecor and Cochran (Iowa State University Press, Iowa, 1980)

Multiple Regression in Behavioral Research: Explanation and Prediction, by Elazar J. Pedhazur (Holt, Rinehart and Winston, New York, 1982)

Experimental Design in Psychology Research, by Edwards (Harper & Row, New York, 1975)

Multivariate Statistics in Behavioral Research, by R. Darrell Bock (McGraw, New York, 1975)

Statistical Methods for Rates and Proportions, by Joseph L. Fleiss (John
Wiley & Sons, New York, 1981)

PROBLEMS

Problems that are considered slightly more challenging are preceded by an asterisk.

1-1. We have collected the following data on 5 subjects:

ID	AGE	SEX	GRADE POINT AVERAGE (GPA)	COLLEGE ENTRANCE EXAM SCORE (CSCORE)
1	18	M	3.7	650
2	18	F	2.0	490
3	19	F	3.3	580
4	23	M	2.8	530
5	21	M	3.5	640

(a) Write the necessary SAS statements to create a SAS data set.

(b) Add the statement(s) necessary to compute the mean grade
point average and mean college entrance exam score.

(c) We want to compute an index for each subject, as follows:

```
INDEX = GPA + 3 x CSCORE/500
```

Modify your program to compute this INDEX for each student and
to print a list of students in order of increasing INDEX. Include in
your listing the student ID, GPA, CSCORE, and INDEX.

1-2. Given the following set of data:

SOCIAL SECURITY NUMBER	ANNUAL SALARY	AGE	RACE
123874414	28,000	35	W
646239182	29,500	37	B
012437652	35,100	40	W
018451357	26,500	31	W

(a) Write a SAS program that will compute the average annual salary and age.

(b) If all subjects were in a 30% tax bracket, compute their taxes (based on gross salary) and print out a list, in social security number order, showing the annual salary and the tax.

1-3. What's wrong with this program?

```
DATA MISTAKE;
    INPUT ID 1-3 TOWN 4-6 REGION 7-9 YEAR 11-12
BUDGET 13-14
    VOTER TURNOUT 16-20
(data cards go here)
PROC MEANS;
    VAR ID REGION VOTER TURNOUT;
    N,STD,MEAN;
```

*1-4. A large corporation is interested in who is buying their product. What the CEO wants is a profile of the "typical buyer." The variables collected on a sample of buyers are: age, sex, race, income, marital status, and homeowner/renter. Set up a layout for the observations and write a SAS program to get the profile of the "typical buyer."

Hints and Comments:

(1) For variables such as "homeowner," it is easier to remember what you have if you let negative responses be 0 and positive responses be 1.

(2) When grouping numerical variables into categories, make sure your grouping fits your needs and your data. For example, if your product was denture cream, the grouping of age (1=<21, 2=22-35, 3=36-50, 4=>50) would be nearly useless. You know these people are mostly over 50. You might want groupings such as (1=<50, 2=50-59, 3=60-69, 4=>69).

√1-5. Given the data set

ID	RACE	SBP	DBP	HR
001	W	130	80	60
002	B	140	90	70
003	W	120	70	64
004	W	150	90	76
005	B	124	86	72

write the SAS statements to produce a report as follows:

RACE AND HEMODYNAMIC VARIABLES

ID	RACE	SBP	DBP
003	W	120	70
005	B	124	86
001	W	130	80
002	B	140	90
004	W	150	90

Note: 1. There is no "OBS" column.
　　　2. Data are in increasing order of SBP.
　　　3. The variable HR is not included in the report.
　　　4. The report has a title.

✓1-6. Given the data set in problem 1-5, modify the program to compute the "average" blood pressure. Average blood pressure (ABP) is computed by taking a weighted average of the systolic and diastolic pressures. It is defined as two-thirds of the diastolic pressure and one-third of the systolic blood pressure. An equivalent expression would be the diastolic pressure plus one-third of the difference between the systolic and diastolic pressures. Using either definition, add APB to the data set.

CHAPTER 2

DESCRIPTIVE STATISTICS

A. DESCRIBING DATA

Even in the most complex statistical analysis, it is important to be able to describe the data in a straightforward, easy-to-comprehend fashion. This is typically accomplished in one of several ways. The first way is through descriptive summary statistics. Probably the most popular way to describe a sample of scores is by reporting: (1) the number of people in the sample (called the sample size and referred to by "n" in statistics books and SAS printouts), (2) the mean (arithmetic average) of the scores and (3) the standard deviation of the scores. The standard deviation is a measure of how widely spread the scores are. Roughly speaking, when the scores form a "bell-shaped" (normal) distribution, we expect to find about 68% of the scores to fall within 1 standard deviation of the mean (plus or minus) and to find about 95% of the scores within 2 standard deviations.

Let's create a SAS data set to introduce some concepts related to descriptive statistics. Suppose we conducted a survey (albeit a very small one) where we recorded the sex, height, and weight of 7 subjects. We collected the following data:

SEX	HEIGHT	WEIGHT
M	68	155
F	61	99
F	63	115
M	70	205
M	69	170
F	65	125
M	72	220

There may be several questions we want to ask about these data. Perhaps we want to count how many males and females are in our sample. We might also want means and standard deviations for the variables HEIGHT and WEIGHT. Finally, we might want to see a frequency distribution of our numeric variables and, perhaps, determine if the data can be considered to have come from a normal distribution. These are fairly simple tasks when only seven people are involved. However, we are rarely interested in such small samples. Once we begin to talk about as many as 20-30 people,

statistical analysis by hand becomes quite tedious. A SAS program to read
these data and to compute some descriptive statistics is shown next:

```
001   DATA HTWT;
002   INPUT SEX $ HEIGHT WEIGHT;
003   CARDS;
004   M 68 155
005   F 61  99
006   F 63 115
007   M 70 205
008   M 69 170
009   F 65 125
010   M 72 220
011   PROC MEANS;
012   RUN;
```

NOTE: The line numbers to the left of the program are not part of the
program but are used for reference.

In this example, our data is placed "in-stream" directly in our program.
For small data sets, this is an appropriate method. For larger data sets, we
usually place our data in a separate file and instruct our SAS program
where to look to find the data. In this program, we have chosen to use the
list form of input where each data value is separated from the next by one
or more spaces. Lines 1-3 define our **data step**. In line 1, we indicated that
we are creating a SAS system file (also known as a SAS data set) called
HTWT. As mentioned in the tutorial, SAS data set names as well as SAS
variables names are from one to eight characters in length. They must start
with a letter or underscore(_). The other characters in SAS data set names
or SAS variable names can, in addition, include the digits 0 through 9. Thus,
our name HTWT meets these criteria and is a valid SAS data set name. Line
2 is the INPUT statement. This statement gives names to the variables we
are going to read. In this form of INPUT where no column numbers or
formats are used, the **order** of the variable names corresponds to the **order**
of the data value. Since our data values are arranged in SEX, HEIGHT, and
WEIGHT order, our INPUT statement lists variables names in the same
order. If we had any missing values in our data, with this form of input, we
would need to use a period (.) to hold the place of a missing value. The $

following the variable name SEX indicates that we are using **character** values for SEX (M and F). Line 3, CARDS, a word that goes back to the days of computer cards, indicates that the lines of data will follow and that the **data step** is finished. Following the data in line 11 is our request for descriptive statistics. PROC MEANS will give us the number of observations used to calculate the descriptive statistics for each of our numeric variables, the mean, standard deviation, and the minimum and maximum values found for those variables. In a moment, we will show you how to request other statistics from PROC MEANS. Let's look at the results of running this program:

```
SAS                                 11:18 Monday, August 13, 1990   1

N Obs  Variable  N      Minimum       Maximum          Mean
-----------------------------------------------------------------
   7   HEIGHT    7     61.0000000    72.0000000     66.8571429
       WEIGHT    7     99.0000000   220.0000000    155.5714286
-----------------------------------------------------------------


N Obs  Variable        Std Dev
---------------------------------
   7   HEIGHT         3.9761192
       WEIGHT        45.7961321
---------------------------------
```

For the variable HEIGHT in our sample, we see that there were seven people (n=7); the shortest person was 61 inches tall and the tallest was 72 inches (from the "minimum value" and "maximum value" columns); their mean height was 66.86 (rounded off); and that the standard deviation was 3.98.

You can specify which statistics you want to compute by indicating **options** for PROC MEANS. Most SAS procedures have **options** which are placed **between the procedure name and the semicolon.** Many of these options are listed in this text; a complete list of options for all SAS procedures can be found in the manuals available from the SAS Institute. As mentioned in the Tutorial section, the option MAXDEC=n will control the number of decimal places for the printed statistics, N will print the number of nonmissing observations, and MEAN will produce the MEAN. So, if you want only the sample size (N) and the MEAN to 3 decimal places, you would write

```
PROC MEANS N MEAN MAXDEC=3;
```

You may also want to specify on which numeric variables in your data set you want to compute descriptive statistics. We make this specification with a **VAR** statement. VAR (short for VARIABLES) is a statement that gives additional information to PROC MEANS (and many other procedures as well). The syntax is the word VAR followed by a list of variable names. So, if we wanted descriptive statistics only on HEIGHT and we wanted the sample size and the mean to 3 decimal places, we would write:

```
PROC MEANS N MEAN MAXDEC=3;
   VAR HEIGHT;
```

The **order** of the options does not matter. A list of the commonly requested options for PROC MEANS is shown next:

OPTION	DESCRIPTION
N	Number of observations on which the statistic was computed
NMISS	Number of missing observations
MEAN	Arithmetic mean
STD	Standard deviation
STDERR	Standard error
MIN	Minimum
MAX	Maximum
SUM	Sum
VAR	Variance
CV	Coefficient of variation
SKEWNESS	Skewness
KURTOSIS	Kurtosis
T	Student's t-tests whether the population mean is zero.
PRT	The probability of obtaining a larger absolute value of t.
MAXDEC=n	Where n specifies the number of decimal places for printed statistics.

As one further example, suppose we wanted the sample size, mean, standard deviation, standard error, and the variance. In addition, we want the statistics rounded to two decimal places. We would write:

```
PROC MEANS MAXDEC=2 N MEAN STD STDERR VAR;
```

Output from this request would look as follows:

```
SAS                            11:18 Monday, August 13, 1990   2

N Obs  Variable  N        Mean      Variance      Std Dev
-------------------------------------------------------------
    7  HEIGHT    7       66.86        15.81         3.98
       WEIGHT    7      155.57      2097.29        45.80
-------------------------------------------------------------


N Obs  Variable     Std Error
----------------------------------
    7  HEIGHT        1.50
       WEIGHT       17.31
----------------------------------
```

The standard error of the mean is used to put a "confidence interval" around the mean. This is useful when our scores represent a sample of scores from some population. For example, if our seven people were a random sample of high school juniors in New Jersey, we could use the sample mean (66.86) as an estimate of the average height of all New Jersey high school juniors. The standard error of the mean tells us how far off this estimate might be. If our population is roughly normally distributed, the sample estimate of the mean (based on a random sample) will fall within one standard error (1.50) of the actual or "true" mean 68% of the time and within 2 standard errors (3.00) of the mean 95% of the time. Therefore, if these scores were a random sample as described, we would be fairly confident that the population mean for New Jersey high school juniors would be between 65.36 and 68.36 (minus and plus 1 standard error) and quite confident that it would fall between 63.86 and 69.86 (minus and plus 2 standard errors). Technically speaking, this is only true when the sample is fairly large (say over 30). For smaller samples, one must use a "t" distribution table to estimate confidence intervals. The variance (listed right after the mean) is the standard deviation squared.

With PROC MEANS as well as many other SAS procedures, when you override the default, you must specify everything you want. In PROC MEANS, if you ask for **any** statistic (Note: MAXDEC= is not a statistic) you will get **only** the statistics you ask for. Therefore, if you decide to override the system defaults and request an additional statistic, you will have to specify **all** you want included. As an example, to **add** a calculation for standard error we would write

```
PROC MEANS N MEAN STD MIN MAX STDERR;
```

B. FREQUENCY DISTRIBUTIONS

Let's look at how to get SAS software to count how many males and females there are in our sample. The following SAS program will do this:

```
001    DATA;
002    INPUT SEX $ HEIGHT WEIGHT;
003    CARDS;
004    M 68 155
005    F 61 99
006    F 63 115
007    M 70 205
008    M 69 170
009    F 65 125
010    M 72 220
011    PROC FREQ;
012       TABLES SEX;
```

This time, instead of PROC MEANS, we are using a procedure (PROC) called FREQ. PROC FREQ is followed by a request for a table of frequencies for the variable SEX. The word TABLES, used with PROC FREQ, is followed by a list of variables for which we want to count occurrences of particular values (e.g., how many males and how many females for the variable SEX). Notice that the last line of the SAS program is indented several spaces from the other lines. The starting column of any SAS statement does not affect the program in any way. The last line was indented only to make it clear to the programmer that the TABLES request is part of PROC FREQ.

The table below is the output from PROC FREQ. The column labeled "FREQUENCY" lists the number of people who are males or females; the column labeled "PERCENT" is the same information expressed as a percent of the total number of people. The "CUM FREQ" and "CUM PERCENT" columns give us the cumulative counts (the number and percentage respectively) for each category of sex.

SEX	FREQUENCY	CUM FREQ	PERCENT	CUM PERCENT
F	3	3	42.857	42.857
M	4	7	57.143	100.000

C. BAR GRAPHS

We have seen the statistics which are produced by running PROC MEANS and PROC FREQ. These are excellent ways to get a summarization of our data. But then, a picture is worth a thousand words (p=1000w) so let's move on to presenting pictures of our data. SAS software can generate a frequency bar chart showing the same information as PROC FREQ, using PROC CHART.

The statements

```
PROC CHART;
    VBAR SEX;
```

were used to generate the frequency bar chart below:

```
FREQUENCY BAR CHART
FREQUENCY
    4 +                     *****
      |                     *****
      |                     *****
      |                     *****
    3 +         *****       *****
      |         *****       *****
      |         *****       *****
      |         *****       *****
    2 +         *****       *****
      |         *****       *****
      |         *****       *****
      |         *****       *****
    1 +         *****       *****
      |         *****       *****
      |         *****       *****
      |         *****       *****
      ---------------------------
               F           M

               SEX
```

The term HBAR in place of VBAR will generate a chart with horizontal bars instead of the vertical bars obtained from VBAR. When HBAR is used, frequency counts and percents are also presented alongside each bar (see below).

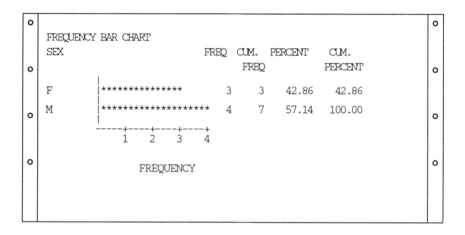

```
FREQUENCY BAR CHART
SEX                            FREQ  CUM.   PERCENT   CUM.
                                     FREQ             PERCENT

F       |***************         3     3    42.86    42.86
        |
M       |*******************     4     7    57.14    100.00
        |
        -----+----+----+----+
             1    2    3    4

            FREQUENCY
```

Now, what about the distribution of heights or weights? If we use PROC FREQ to calculate frequencies of heights, it will compute the number of subjects for **every** value of height (how many people are 60 inches tall, how many are 61 inches tall, etc.). If we use PROC CHART instead, it will automatically place the subjects into height groups (or we can specify options to control how we wanted the data displayed). Since our sample is so small, a frequency distribution of heights or weights would not be very informative. So, to demonstrate how a frequency distribution of a continuous variable like height would be displayed, a larger data set of 1000 subjects was used. The SAS statements

```
PROC CHART;
    VBAR HEIGHT / LEVELS=20;
```

were used to generate the next chart. The option LEVELS=20 is an instruction to group the heights so that there will be 20 equally spaced intervals for the variable HEIGHT. If we leave out any options when we are charting a continuous variable, PROC CHART will use its own grouping algorithm to select the number of levels and the midpoints for the plot.

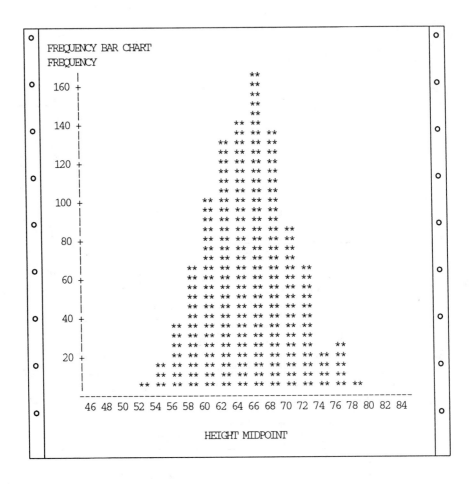

Notice the shape of the distribution. The mean is 65 inches with a standard deviation of 5 inches. If we picture a line drawn connecting the top of each bar, the resulting curve would approximate a normal curve.

Remembering our earlier discussion, approximately 68% of the people in our population would have a height of 65 inches plus or minus 5 inches (one standard deviation). This 68% also represents the proportion of the area under the entire curve from 60 inches to 70 inches.

The VBAR and HBAR statements of PROC CHART have a variety of options. The general form of the VBAR and HBAR statements is

```
VBAR variable(s) / list of options ;
```

An alternative to the LEVELS= option is to provide the procedure with specified midpoints. This is done with the MIDPOINTS option. The form is:

```
MIDPOINTS= lower limit TO upper limit BY interval;
```

An example would be:

```
VBAR HEIGHT / MIDPOINTS=50 TO 80 BY 10;
```

This would produce a histogram with four groups with midpoints at 50, 60, 70, and 80.

There are times when we do not want PROC CHART to divide our numerical variable into intervals. Suppose we had a variable called WEEK that was a numeric variable and represented the day of the week (from 1 to 7). The statement:

```
VBAR WEEK;
```

would most likely produce a chart with midpoints that were not integers. To avoid this and instruct PROC CHART to use the actual values of a variable, the option DISCRETE is added to the option list. To be sure that the frequency chart for WEEK is printed correctly, the statement:

```
VBAR WEEK / DISCRETE;
```

should be used. (Remember that statement options are placed between the statement and the semi-colon, separated by a slash.)

Before we leave PROC CHART, we will demonstrate a few of the other options that are available. To do this, we have constructed another data set which contains the variables DEPT (department), YEAR, QUARTER, and SALES. Each observation contains the amount of sales for a given department by year and quarter. A few observations from this sample data set are shown below:

DEPT	YEAR	QUARTER	SALES
A	1988	1	3000
A	1988	2	4000
A	1988	3	4500
A	1988	4	4700
A	1989	1	3200
etc.			

The statement

```
VBAR DEPT;
```

will produce a simple frequency bar graph as shown below:

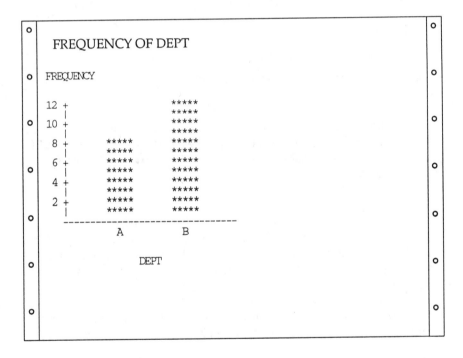

This chart tells us how many A departments and B departments there are in this company.

The statement:

```
VBAR SALES;
```

will produce the following frequency distribution of SALES:

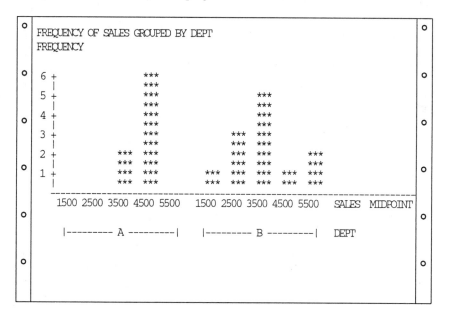

```
FREQUENCY OF SALES
FREQUENCY

   |                              *****     *****
 6 +                              *****     *****
   |                              *****     *****
 4 +                              *****     *****
   |                    *****     *****     *****
 2 +                    *****     *****     *****     *****
   |          *****     *****     *****     *****     *****
   ----------------------------------------------------------------
          1500      2500      3500      4500      5500

                              SALES MIDPOINT
```

To see the sales distributions of each department side-by-side, we can use the GROUP option available with both VBAR and HBAR. The statement:

```
VBAR SALES / GROUP=DEPT;
```

will produce the side-by-side graph like the one below:

```
FREQUENCY OF SALES GROUPED BY DEPT
FREQUENCY

 6 +              ***
   |              ***
 5 +              ***                ***
   |              ***                ***
 4 +              ***                ***
   |              ***                ***
 3 +              ***          ***   ***
   |              ***          ***   ***
 2 +        ***   ***          ***   ***         ***
   |        ***   ***          ***   ***         ***
 1 +        ***   ***    ***   ***   ***   ***   ***
   |        ***   ***    ***   ***   ***   ***   ***
   ----------------------------------------------------------------
      1500 2500 3500 4500 5500   1500 2500 3500 4500 5500   SALES  MIDPOINT

      |--------- A ---------|    |--------- B ---------|   DEPT
```

Another way to display these data would be for the y-axis to represent a sales sum, rather than a frequency or count. This is done by using a SUMVAR option with VBAR or HBAR. The keyword SUMVAR is followed by a variable whose sum we want displayed on the y-axis. We also use the SUMVAR option to display a mean value on the y-axis by adding the keyword TYPE=MEAN to the list of VBAR or HBAR options. We will show you a chart using the SUMVAR and TYPE options. Since we are displaying a sum of sales for each department, the TYPE= option is redundant but is included to remind you that it is available to display other statistics on the y-axis. The statement

```
VBAR DEPT / GROUP=YEAR SUMVAR=SALES TYPE=SUM;
```

produced the graph below:

```
SUM OF SALES BY DEPT GROUPED BY YEAR
SALES SUM

20000 +                                            *****
      |                                            *****
16000 +    *****              *****                *****
      |    *****              *****   *****         *****
12000 +    *****              *****   *****         *****
      |    *****   *****      *****   *****         *****
 8000 +    *****   *****      *****   *****         *****
      |    *****   *****      *****   *****         *****
 4000 +    *****   *****      *****   *****         *****
      |    *****   *****      *****   *****         *****
      ----------------------------------------------------------
           A       B          A       B            A       B    DEPT

           |--- 1988 ---|     |--- 1989 ---|       |--- 1999 ---|  YEAR
```

Other valid values for the TYPE= option are:

OPTION	RESULT
TYPE=FREQ	Frequency count
TYPE=PCT	Percentages
TYPE=CFREQ	Cumulative frequencies
TYPE=CPCT	Cumulative percentages

TYPE=SUM   Totals
TYPE=MEAN   Means

One final option used with VBAR and HBAR is SUBGROUP. The first character of a SUBGROUP variable will be used as the character making up the bars in the bar graph. If we write:

```
VBAR SALES / SUBGROUP=DEPT;
```

the department values (A's and B's) will show us which departments are contributing to the sales frequencies. Please see the chart below for an example:

```
FREQUENCY OF SALES
FREQUENCY

    |                              BBBBB        BBBBB
  6 +                              BBBBB        AAAAA
    |                              BBBBB        AAAAA
  4 +                              BBBBB        AAAAA
    |                   BBBBB      BBBBB        AAAAA
  2 +                   BBBBB      AAAAA        AAAAA        BBBBB
    |        BBBBB      BBBBB      AAAAA        AAAAA        BBBBB
    ------------------------------------------------------------------

           1500       2500       3500         4500         5500


                   SYMBOL DEPT     SYMBOL DEPT

                       A   A          B   B
```

Before we leave PROC CHART, it's hard to resist showing you the fancy three dimensional graphs produced by the BLOCK statement. The BLOCK variable defines the x-axis, the GROUP option defines the y-axis, and the SUMVAR variable (with any of the TYPE= options) defines the z-axis, represented by the heights of the bars. The block chart resulting from the statement

```
PROC CHART;
    BLOCK YEAR / GROUP=DEPT SUMVAR=SALES TYPE=SUM DISCRETE;
```

is shown below:

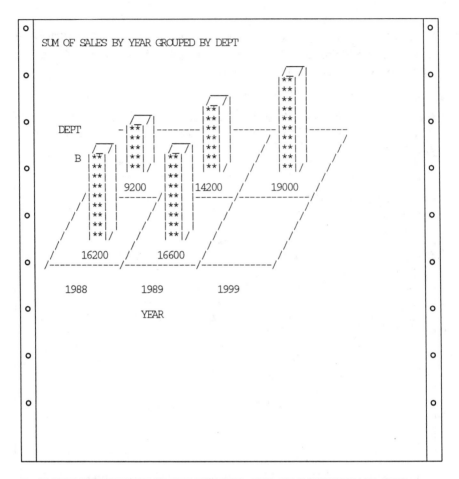

D. MORE DESCRIPTIVE STATISTICS AND FREQUENCY PLOTS

One procedure that can combine **descriptive statistics** with **frequency distributions** is **PROC UNIVARIATE**. This is an extremely useful procedure that can compute, among other things the

1. Number of observations (nonmissing)
2. Mean
3. Standard deviation
4. Variance

5. Skewness
6. Kurtosis
7. Uncorrected and corrected sum of squares
8. Coefficient of variation
9. Standard error of the mean
10. T-test comparing the variable's values against zero
11. Maximum (largest value)
12. Minimum (smallest value)
13. Range
14. Median, upper, and lower quartile ranges
15. Interquartile range
16. Mode
17. 1st, 5th, 10th, 90th, 95th, and 99th percentiles
18. Five highest and five lowest values (useful for data checking)
19. W or D statistic to test whether data are normally distributed
20. Stem and Leaf plot
21. Boxplot
22. Normal probability plot, comparing the cumulative frequency distribution to a normal distribution

To run PROC UNIVARIATE for our variables HEIGHT and WEIGHT, we would write:

```
PROC UNIVARIATE;
    VAR HEIGHT WEIGHT;
```

To request additional options such as Stem and Leaf plots and the test of normality we would add:

```
PROC UNIVARIATE NORMAL PLOT;
    VAR HEIGHT WEIGHT;
```

A portion of the output from the above request is shown next:

```
UNIVARIATE PROCEDURE
Variable=HEIGHT

                        Moments

N                     7   Sum Wgts            7
Mean           66.85714   Sum               468
Std Dev        3.976119   Variance    15.80952
Skewness       -0.32044   Kurtosis    -1.23625
USS               31384   CSS         94.85714
CV             5.947187   Std Mean    1.502832
T:Mean=0       44.48744   Prob|T|       0.0001
Sgn Rank             14   Prob|S|       0.0156
Num ^= 0              7
W:Normal       0.957165   ProbW         0.8052


                     Quantiles(Def=5)

100% Max             72          99%          72
 75% Q3              70          95%          72
 50% Med             68          90%          72
 25% Q1              63          10%          61
  0% Min             61           5%          61
                                  1%          61
Range                11
Q3-Q1                 7
Mode                 61


                       Extremes

   Lowest    Obs      Highest    Obs
       61(     2)         65(      6)
       63(     3)         68(      1)
       65(     6)         69(      5)
       68(     1)         70(      4)
       69(     5)         72(      7)
```

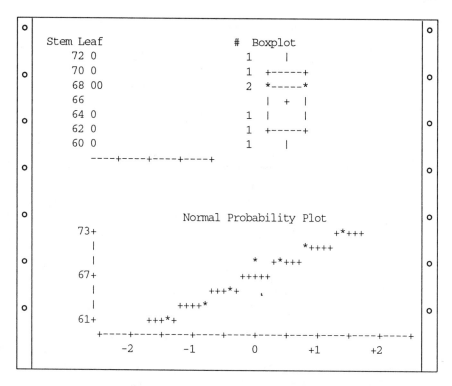

```
    Stem Leaf                    #  Boxplot
       72 0                      1    |
       70 0                      1   +-----+
       68 00                     2   *-----*
       66                            |  +  |
       64 0                      1   |     |
       62 0                      1   +-----+
       60 0                      1    |
          ----+----+----+----+


                    Normal Probability Plot
       73+                                      +*+++
        |                                     *++++
        |                              *    +*+++
       67+                           +++++
        |                       +++*+    .
        |                  ++++*
       61+           +++*+
          +----+----+----+----+----+----+----+----+----+----+
              -2        -1         0        +1        +2
```

There is a lot of information in a PROC UNIVARIATE output. Under the title "Moments" you will see a number of statistics. Though most of them are self explanatory, here is a list with explanations:

N	Number of nonmissing observations
Sum Wgts	Sum of weights (if WEIGHT statement used)
Mean	Arithmetic mean
Sum	Sum of the scores
Std Dev	Standard deviation
Variance	Variance
Skewness	Skewness (measure of the symmetry of the distribution)
Kurtosis	Kurtosis (measure of the flatness of the distribution)
USS	Uncorrected sum of squares (the sum of the scores squared—each score is squared and the squares are added together)

CSS	Corrected sum of squares (sum of squares about the mean)
CV	Coefficient of variation
Std Mean	Standard error of the mean (the standard deviation divided by the square root of n)
T:Mean=0	Student's t-test for testing the hypothesis that the population mean is zero
Prob> |T|	The p-value for the t-statistic (2-tailed)
Sgn Rank	The Wilcoxon signed rank sum (usually used for difference scores)
Prob> |S|	The p-value for the Sign Rank test
Num ^= 0	Number of nonzero observations
W:Normal (D:Normal)	Shapiro-Wilk statistic for a test of normality (SAS will produce the Kolomogorov D:Normal test when n is larger than 2000)
Prob<W (Prob>D)	P-value testing the null hypothesis that the population is normally distributed (when the D:Normal test is done, the statistic is ProbD)

The statistics under the heading "Quantiles(Def=5)" are straightforward. The "Def=5" in the heading indicated that SAS is using definition 5 listed in the SAS Procedures manual. This definition is described as an "empirical distribution function with averaging." We refer those interested in the subtle differences in the five available definitions, to the SAS Procedures manual under PROC UNIVARIATE. The two columns list quantiles from zero (the minimum value) to 100% (the maximum value). In this list, under 50% Med, is the median—the **only** way to have SAS compute a median. (Wouldn't it be a nice option for PROC MEANS?) Below this is the range, the inter-quartile range (Q3-Q1), and the mode.

The list of **Extremes** which comes next is particularly useful. It lists the five lowest and five highest values in the data set. We find this useful for data checking. Obviously incorrect values can be spotted easily. Next to each extreme value is the corresponding observation number. This can be made more useful if an ID statement is used with PROC UNIVARIATE. The ID variable (usually a subject number) will be printed next to each extreme value. That way, when a data error is spotted, it is easier to locate the incorrect value in the data by referring to the ID variable. If we had a variable called SUBJ which represented a subject number, our complete PROC UNIVARIATE request would be:

```
PROC UNIVARIATE NORMAL PLOT;
    VAR HEIGHT WEIGHT;
    ID SUBJ;
```

The next portion of the output from PROC UNIVARIATE is a result of the PLOT option we used. The left side of the page is a Tukey style Stem and Leaf plot. This can be thought of as a sideways histogram. However, instead of using X's to represent the bars, the next digit of the number after the "stem" is used. If we had a height of 72.4 inches, to the right of the 72 in the stem and leaf plot we would find a 4 instead of a 0. Another Tukey invention, the Boxplot is displayed on the right side of the page. The SAS conventions are as follows: the bottom and top of the box represent the sample 25th and 75th percentiles; the median is represented by the dashed line inside the box and the sample mean is shown as a + sign; the vertical lines coming out of the top and bottom of the box are called whiskers and extend as far as the data to a maximum distance of 1.5 times the interquartile range; data values beyond the whiskers but within 3 interquartile ranges of the box boundaries are shown with o's; still more extreme values are shown with an asterisk (*). The Normal Probability Plot shown last, is also a result of the PLOT option and represents a plot of the data compared to a normal distribution. The y-axis displays our data values and the x- axis is related to the inverse of the standard normal function. The asterisks (*) mark the actual data values, the plus signs (+) provide a straight reference line based on the sample mean and standard deviation. The more the sample distribution deviates from normal, the more the asterisks will deviate from the plus signs. You will, no doubt, find the stem and leaf and box plots a more intuitive way to inspect the shape of the distribution.

E. PLOTTING DATA

We would now like to investigate the relationship between height and weight. Our intuition tells us that these two variables are related: the taller a person is, the heavier (in general). The best way to display this relationship is to draw a graph of height versus weight. We can have our SAS program generate this graph by using PROC PLOT. The statements

```
PROC PLOT;
    PLOT WEIGHT*HEIGHT;
```

will generate the graph that follows:

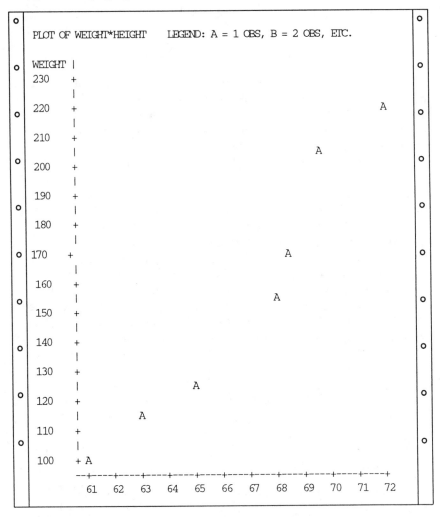

```
PLOT OF WEIGHT*HEIGHT    LEGEND: A = 1 OBS, B = 2 OBS, ETC.

WEIGHT |
  230  +
       |
  220  +                                                      A
       |
  210  +
       |                                          A
  200  +
       |
  190  +
       |
  180  +
       |
  170  +                                  A
       |
  160  +
       |                              A
  150  +
       |
  140  +
       |
  130  +
       |                      A
  120  +
       |              A
  110  +
       |
  100  + A
       --+----+----+----+----+----+----+----+----+----+----+
        61   62   63   64   65   66   67   68   69   70   71   72
```

NOTE: This is a plot using the **original** data set of seven people.

The general form of the plot command is:

```
PROC PLOT;
    PLOT Y variable * X variable;
         (Vertical)     (Horizontal)
```

Notice that SAS software automatically chooses appropriate scales for the X and Y axes. Unless you specify otherwise, PROC PLOT uses letters (A,B,C, etc.) as plotting symbols. Since a computer line printer is restricted to printing characters in discrete locations across or down the page, two data values that are very close to each other would need to be printed in the same location. If **two** data points do occur at one print position, the program prints the letter "**B**"; for **three** data points, the letter "**C**," and so forth.

F. DESCRIBING SUBGROUPS

So far we have looked at descriptive statistics (mean, standard deviation, standard error, etc.) for height and weight, we have counted the number of males and females, and we have seen the relationship between height and weight in a graph. Another useful way of looking at our data comes to mind. Can we calculate descriptive statistics separately for males and females? Can we obtain a plot of height versus weight for males, and one for females? The answer is "yes," and it is quite easy to do. One way is to have the SAS program sort the data by SEX. Once this is done, we can use PROC MEANS and PROC PLOT with a BY statement to produce the desired statistics and graphs.

Our program will look as follows:

```
 1     DATA;
 2     INPUT SEX $ HEIGHT WEIGHT;
 3     CARDS;
 4     M 68 155
 5     F 61 99
 6     F 63 115
 7     M 70 205
 8     M 69 170
 9     F 65 125
10     M 72 220
11     PROC SORT;
12          BY SEX;
13     PROC MEANS;
14          BY SEX;                          (cont.)
```

```
15    PROC PLOT;          (Continued from previous page)
16       BY SEX;
17        PLOT WEIGHT*HEIGHT;
18    RUN;
```

The PROC SORT statements will arrange our data so that they will be grouped by SEX. Once the data set has been sorted, we now have the option to use a **BY** statement with PROC MEANS or PROC PLOT. The result of this program will be separate analyses for males and females. If we omit a BY statement with PROC MEANS or PROC PLOT, the program will ignore the fact that the data set is now sorted by SEX. An alternative to using a BY statement with PROC MEANS is to use a CLASS statement. Briefly, a CLASS variable allows us to compute means for every combination of CLASS variables **without having to sort** the data set first. This will save time and money. The only change to the program above would be to substitute the word CLASS for BY in line 14 and remove the sort statements.

We can generate another graph that will display the data for males and females on a single graph but, instead of the usual plotting symbols of A,B,C, etc., we will use F's and M's (for females and males). The statements

```
PROC PLOT;
    PLOT WEIGHT*HEIGHT=SEX;
```

will accomplish this. The data set does not have to be sorted to use this form of PROC PLOT. The "=SEX" after our plot request specifies that the first letter of each SEX value will be used as plotting symbols. In essence, this allows us to look at 3 variables (height, weight, and sex) simultaneously. The result of running this last procedure is shown below:

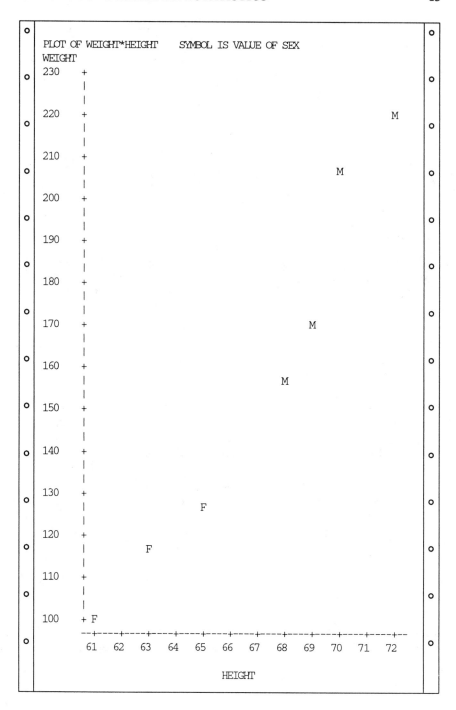

Since we are not using the standard plotting symbols (A, B, C, etc.), multiple observations at a single print location will not be shown on the graph (except in the case of one male and one female, in which case the M and F will overprint if the OVP option is set and you have an output device, such as a lineprinter, that can overprint). The program will print a message indicating the number of "hidden" observations at the bottom of the graph in this case.

If you would like to choose a plotting symbol, instead of the SAS default of A,B, C, etc., you may follow the PLOT request by an equal sign and a plotting symbol of your choice in single quotes. If you wanted an asterisk as your plotting symbol, the plot request would read:

```
PLOT WEIGHT*HEIGHT='*';
```

As with the case of a variable name following the equal sign, choosing a plotting symbol will not allow hidden observations to be displayed and you will see a message to that effect if there are any hidden observations.

PROBLEMS

2-1. Add the necessary statements to compute the number of males and females in Problem 1-1.

2-2. Given the data set from Problem 1-2, use SAS to compute the number of Whites(W) and Blacks(B).

2-3. We have a SAS data set containing variables X, Y, Z, and GROUP.

A. Write the SAS statements to generate a frequency bar chart (histogram) for GROUP (assume GROUP is a categorical variable).

B. Write the SAS statements to generate a plot of Y vs. X (with "Y" on the vertical axis and "X" on the horizontal).

C. Write the SAS statements to generate a separate plot of Y vs. X for each value of the GROUP variables.

2-4. We have recorded the following data from an experiment:

SUBJECT	DOSE	REACT	LIVER_WT	SPLEEN
1	1	5.4	10.2	8.9
2	1	5.9	9.8	7.3
3	1	4.8	12.2	9.1
4	1	6.9	11.8	8.8
5	1	15.8	10.9	9.0
6	2	4.9	13.8	6.6
7	2	5.0	12.0	7.9
8	2	6.7	10.5	8.0
9	2	18.2	11.9	6.9
10	2	5.5	9.9	9.1

Use PROC UNIVARIATE to produce histograms, normal probability plots, and box plots, and test the distributions for normality. Do this for the variables REACT, LIVER_WT, and SPLEEN, first for all subjects and then separately for each of the two DOSES.

2-5. What's wrong with this program?

```
DATA;
     INPUT AGE STATUS PROGNOSIS DOCTOR SEX STATUS2
          STATUS3;
     (data cards)
     PROC CHART BY SEX;
        VBAR STATUS
        VBAR PROGNOSIS;
     PROC PLOT;
        DOCTOR BY PROGNOSIS;
```

2-6. Given the data set

Salesperson	Target company	Number of visits	Number of phone calls	Units sold
Brown	American	3	12	28,000
Johnson	VRW	6	14	33,000
Rivera	Texam	2	6	8,000

Brown	Standard	0	22	0
Brown	Knowles	2	19	12,000
Rivera	Metro	4	8	13,000
Rivera	Uniman	8	7	27,000
Johnson	Oldham	3	16	8,000
Johnson	Rondo	2	14	2,000

(a) Write a SAS program to compare the sales records of the company's three sales people.

(b) Plot the number of visits against the number of phone calls. Use "Salesperson" as the plotting symbol (instead of the usual A, B, C, etc.).

(c) Make a frequency bar chart for each salesperson for the variable "units sold."

*2-7. You have completed an experiment and recorded a subject ID, and values for variables A, B, and C. You want to compute means for A, B, and C but, unfortunately, your lab technician, who didn't know SAS programming, arranged the data like this:

ID	TYPE	SCORE
1	A	44
1	B	9
1	C	03
2	A	50
2	B	7
2	C	88
3	A	39
3	B	9
3	C	34
etc.		

Write a program to read this data set and produce means. (Hint: Remember the power of "BY" variable processing.)

CHAPTER 3

QUESTIONNAIRE DESIGN AND ANALYSIS

A. SURVEY DATA

A common way of collecting certain types of data is with a questionnaire. Although these can be designed in many ways, the following example contains features that make it especially useful when the collected data are to be entered into a computer.

	For office use only
SAMPLE QUESTIONNAIRE	ID ☐☐☐

1. Age in years _____   ☐☐

2. Sex   __1 Male
           __2=Female

3. Race   __1=White
           __2=Black
           __3=Hispanic
           __4=Other   ☐

4. Marital status
           __1=Single
           __2=Married
           __3=Widowed
           __4=Divorced   ☐

5. Education level
           __1=High school or less
           __2=Two year college
           __3=Four year college (B.A. or B.S)
           __4=Post graduate degrees   ☐

For each of the following statements, please place the NUMBER that corresponds with your feelings to the left of the question number. Use the following codes:

1=Strongly disagree 2=Disagree 3=Neutral 4=Agree
5=Strongly agree

___6. The president of the U.S. has been doing a good job.   ☐

___7. The arms budget should be increased.   ☐

___8. There should be more federal aid to big cities.   ☐

Notice that every response on this questionnaire is placed in a box by a coding clerk and that the boxes are all on the right side of the page. This will facilitate the job of transferring the data from the survey instrument to our computer. One should be careful, however, not to ignore the person who is filling out the questionnaire. If the questionnaire confuses the respondent, it will not matter how easy the data are to enter. With this in mind, many experienced questionnaire designers would place the choices for questions 6 through 8 below each of these items and have the respondent check his choice. The typical way of coding data from a questionnaire of this type would be to have the data entered into a computer using a wordprocessor, data entry program, or data-base management system. In the case of the wordprocessor or data entry program, we would probably set aside certain columns for each variable. Where a data base management system is used, the data can either be written to a text file or converted directly to a SAS system file, if the appropriate software is available. (See the section on importing data in chapter 12 for more information on data conversion.) There are also key-to-tape systems for large commercial applications. Another option is the use of an optical mark sense reader for large volume data entry requirements. It is preferable to design the questionnaire so the data can be entered directly from the questionnaire, rather than having to be transcribed first to a coding form.

We might decide to enter our questionnaire data as follows:

COLUMN	DESCRIPTION	VARIABLE NAME
1-3	Subject ID	ID
4-5	Age in years	AGE
6	Sex	SEX
7	Race	RACE
8	Marital status	MARITAL
9	Education level	EDUC
10	President doing good job	PRES
11	Arms budget increased	ARMS
12	Federal aid to cities	CITIES

Typical lines of data would look like this:

```
001091111232
002452222422
```

Notice that we have not left any spaces between the values for each variable. Therefore, we **must** specify the column location for each variable. Our INPUT statement for this questionnaire would be written:

```
INPUT ID 1-3 AGE 4-5 SEX 6 RACE 7 MARITAL 8 EDUC 9
      PRES 10 ARMS 11 CITIES 12;
```

Each variable name is followed by its column designation. A common occurrence with questionnaires is that some people will not answer all the questions. With a **list** INPUT statement (one in which we list only the variable names and not the column designations) we use a **period** to represent **missing values**; with our **column** INPUT statement we leave the column(s) **blank**. We can do this since it is the **columns**, not the order of the data, that determine which variable is being read.

A complete SAS program to (1) calculate the mean age of the respondents and (2) compute frequencies for all the other variables is shown below:

```
DATA;
INPUT ID 1-3 AGE 4-5 SEX 6 RACE 7 MARITAL 8 EDUC 9
      PRES 10 ARMS 11 CITIES 12;
CARDS;
001091111232
002452222422
003351324442
004271111121
005682132333
006651243425
    etc.
PROC MEANS MAXDEC=2 N MEAN STD;
   VAR AGE;
PROC FREQ;
   TABLES SEX RACE MARITAL EDUC PRES ARMS CITIES;
RUN;
```

We have chosen to supply PROC MEANS with options to print statistics to two decimal places and to compute N (the number of nonmissing observations), the mean and standard deviation.

A short-cut method for specifying the variable list in the TABLES statement which would save us some typing is to use the -- notation. The statement:

```
TABLES SEX -- CITIES;
```

is equivalent to the list of variables used in the example above. The convention "variable name -- variable name" means to include all the variables from SEX to CITIES in the order they exist in the data set. In this case, the order is the same as the order on the INPUT statement. As you will see later, such SAS statements as LENGTH, ARRAY, and RETAIN can affect this order. While we are on the topic of variable list notation, ROOTn-ROOTm is used to refer to all variables with the same alphabetic root, from the nth to the mth numeric ending. For example, ABC1-ABC5 is equivalent to: ABC1 ABC2 ABC3 ABC4 ABC5. It is convenient to name certain variables using the same root with a number ending so we can use the single dash notation any time we want to refer to part or all of the list. If we recorded the response to 50 multiple choice questions in a test, convenient variable names would be QUES1, QUES2, ... up to QUES50. Then, if we wanted frequencies on all 50 variables, the tables request:

```
TABLES QUES1-QUES50;
```

would do the trick. It is **not** necessary for the variables to be in any particular order in the data set when this notation is used.

In this questionnaire, we have not requested any statistics for the variable ID. The ID number only serves as an identifier if we want to go back to the original questionnaire to check data values. This is a highly recommended procedure. Without an ID variable of some sort, when we discover an error in the data, it is difficult to find the original questionnaire to check on the correct value. Even if you did not include an ID on the questionnaire, number the questionnaires as they are returned and enter this number in the computer along with the other responses.

A sample of the output from PROC FREQ is shown below:

SEX	FREQUENCY	CUM FREQ	PERCENT	CUM PERCENT
1	4	4	66.667	66.667
2	2	6	33.333	100.000

RACE	FREQUENCY	CUM FREQ	PERCENT	CUM PERCENT
1	3	3	50.000	50.000
2	2	5	33.333	83.333
3	1	6	16.667	100.000

MARITAL	FREQUENCY	CUM FREQ	PERCENT	CUM PERCENT
1	2	2	33.333	33.333
2	2	4	33.333	66.667
3	1	5	16.667	83.333
4	1	6	16.667	100.000

B. ADDING VARIABLE LABELS

We could improve on this output considerably. First, we have to refer to our coding scheme to see the definition of each of the variable names. Some variable names like SEX and RACE need no explanation; others like PRES and CITIES do. We can associate a **VARIABLE LABEL** with each **VARIABLE NAME** by using a **LABEL** statement. These labels will be printed along with the variable name in certain procedures such as PROC FREQ and PROC MEANS. The general form of a LABEL statement is:

```
LABEL variable name='description'
               .
               .
               .
        variable name='description';
```

The "description" can contain up to 40 characters (blanks count as characters) and must be enclosed in single quotes. The LABEL statement can be placed anywhere in the data step. Our program, rewritten to include variable labels, follows:

```
DATA;
INPUT ID 1-3 AGE 4-5 SEX 6 RACE 7 MARITAL 8 EDUC 9
      PRES 10 ARMS 11 CITIES 12;              (cont.)
```

```
                                  (Continued from previous page)
LABEL   MARITAL='MARITAL STATUS'
        EDUC='EDUCATION LEVEL'
        PRES='PRESIDENT DOING A GOOD JOB'
        ARMS='ARMS BUDGET INCREASE'
        CITIES='FEDERAL AID TO CITIES';
CARDS;
001091111232
002452222422
003351324442
004271111121
005682132333
006651243425
RUN;
PROC MEANS MAXDEC=2 N MEAN STD;
   VAR AGE;
RUN;
PROC FREQ;
      TABLES SEX RACE MARITAL EDUC PRES ARMS CITIES;
RUN;
```

Notice that we did not supply a variable label for **all** our variables. The ones you choose to provide with labels are up to you. Now when we run our program, the labels will be printed along with the variable names in our PROC FREQ output. A sample of the output from this program is shown below:

SEX	FREQUENCY	CUM FREQ	PERCENT	CUM PERCENT
1	4	4	66.667	66.667
2	2	6	33.333	100.000

RACE	FREQUENCY	CUM FREQ	PERCENT	CUM PERCENT
1	3	3	50.000	50.000
2	2	5	33.333	83.333
3	1	6	16.667	100.000

```
MARITAL STATUS
MARITAL   FREQUENCY  CUM FREQ    PERCENT  CUM PERCENT

    1         2         2        33.333      33.333
    2         2         4        33.333      66.667
    3         1         5        16.667      83.333
    4         1         6        16.667     100.000

EDUCATION LEVEL
EDUC    FREQUENCY  CUM FREQ    PERCENT  CUM PERCENT

    1         2         2        33.333      33.333
    2         2         4        33.333      66.667
    3         1         5        16.667      83.333
    4         1         6        16.667     100.000

PRESIDENT DOING A GOOD JOB
PRES    FREQUENCY  CUM FREQ    PERCENT  CUM PERCENT

    1         1         1        16.667      16.667
    2         1         2        16.667      33.333
    3         1         3        16.667      50.000
    4         3         6        50.000     100.000

ARMS BUDGET INCREASE
ARMS    FREQUENCY  CUM FREQ    PERCENT  CUM PERCENT

    2         3         3        50.000      50.000
    3         2         5        33.333      83.333
    4         1         6        16.667     100.000

FEDERAL AID TO CITIES
CITIES    FREQUENCY  CUM FREQ    PERCENT  CUM PERCENT

    1         1         1        16.667      16.667
    2         3         4        50.000      66.667
    3         1         5        16.667      83.333
```

C. ADDING VALUE LABELS (FORMATS)

We would like to improve the readability of the output one step further. The remaining problem is that the values for our variables (1=male 2=female etc.) are printed on the output, not the names that we have assigned to these values. We would like the output to show the number of males and females, for example, not the number of 1's and 2's for the variable SEX. We can supply the VALUE LABELS in two steps.

The first step is to define our code values for each variable. For example, 1=male, 2=female will be used for our variable SEX. The codes 1=str disagree, 2=disagree, etc. will be used for three variables: PRES, ARMS, and CITIES. SAS software calls these codes FORMATS and we define the FORMATS in a procedure by that name.

The second step, shown later, will be to associate a FORMAT with one or more variable names. Below is an example of PROC FORMAT used for our questionnaire:

```
PROC FORMAT;
   VALUE SEXFMT 1='MALE' 2='FEMALE';
   VALUE RACE      1='WHITE'  2='BLACK'  3='HISPANIC'
                   4='OTHER';
   VALUE OSCAR   1='SINGLE' 2='MARRIED' 3='WIDOWED'
                   4='DIVORCED';
   VALUE EDUC    1='HIGH SCH OR LESS'
                 2='TWO YR. COLLEGE'
                 3='FOUR YR. COLLEGE'
                 4='GRADUATE DEGREE';
   VALUE LIKERT 1='STR DISAGREE'
                2='DISAGREE'
                3='NEUTRAL'
                4='AGREE'
                5='STR AGREE';
```

The names SEXFMT, RACE, OSCAR, EDUC and LIKERT are format names. (An aside: We chose the name LIKERT since scales such as 1=strongly disagree, 2=disagree, 3=neutral etc. are called Likert scales by psychometricians.) You may choose **any** name (consistent with naming conventions, with the exception that they cannot end in a number) for your formats. It is best to give names that help you remember what the format will be used for. As a matter of fact, **you can use the same name for a format and for a variable** without confusion, as we did with RACE and EDUC. Notice the silly format name OSCAR used to format values of the variable called MARITAL. We did this just to emphasize the fact that format names do not have to be related to the variable names they will be used to format. Format values can be up to 40 characters long but should be restricted to 16 characters since this is the number of characters that will appear in a cross tabulation or frequency table.

Format names for character variables must start with a $ sign. If we had coded SEX as a character variable using M's and F's for Male and Female, a format for this variable could be created with:

```
VALUE $SEX 'M'='MALE'    'F'='FEMALE';
```

Notice that the value to the left of the = sign must also be enclosed in single quotes. If your format value contains any single quotes, enclose it with double quotes.

Once we have defined a set of formats (such as SEXFMT, RACE, LIKERT, etc.), we need to assign the formats to the appropriate variables. Just because we have named a format SEXFMT, for example, does not mean that this format has to be used with the variable we have called SEX. We need another SAS statement that indicates which formats will be used or associated with which variables. Format statements start with the word FORMAT, followed by a single variable or a list of variables, followed by a format name to be used with the preceding variables. The list of variable and format names continues on as many lines as necessary and ends with a semicolon. SAS software knows the difference between our **variable** names and our **format** names since we place a **period after each format name in our format statement**. Format statements can be placed within a **DATA** step or as a statement in a **PROC** step. If we choose to place our format statement in the DATA step, the formatted values will be associated with the assigned variable(s) **for all PROCS** that follow. If we place a format statement in a **PROC** step, the formatted values will be used **only for that procedure**. In this example we will place our format statement in the DATA step. Therefore, we will define our formats with PROC FORMAT **before** we write our DATA step. We will associate the format SEXFMT with the variable SEX, RACE with the variable RACE, and so forth. The variables PRES, ARMS, and CITIES are all "sharing" the LIKERT format. If you look at the completed questionnaire program below, the use of PROC FORMAT and its application in other PROCs should become clear.

```
PROC FORMAT;
   VALUE SEXFMT 1='MALE' 2='FEMALE';
   VALUE RACE   1='WHITE' 2='BLACK' 3='HISPANIC'
                4='OTHER';
   VALUE OSCAR  1='SINGLE' 2='MARRIED' 3='WIDOWED'
                4='DIVORCED';
   VALUE EDUC   1='HIGH SCH OR LESS'
                2='TWO YR. COLLEGE'
                3='FOUR YR. COLLEGE'
                4='GRADUATE DEGREE';
   VALUE LIKERT 1='STR DISAGREE'
                2='DISAGREE'
                3='NEUTRAL'
                4='AGREE'
                5='STR AGREE';
DATA;
INPUT ID 1-3 AGE 4-5 SEX 6 RACE 7 MARITAL 8 EDUC 9
      PRES 10 ARMS 11 CITIES 12;
LABEL  MARITAL='MARITAL STATUS'
       EDUC='EDUCATION LEVEL'
       PRES='PRESIDENT DOING A GOOD JOB'
       ARMS='ARMS BUDGET INCREASE'
       CITIES='FEDERAL AID TO CITIES';
FORMAT SEX SEXFMT. RACE RACE. MARITAL OSCAR.
             EDUC EDUC. PRES ARMS CITIES LIKERT.;
CARDS;
001091111232
002452222422
003351324442
004271111121
005682132333
006651243425
RUN;
PROC MEANS MAXDEC=2;
   VAR AGE;
RUN;
PROC FREQ;
     TABLES SEX RACE MARITAL EDUC PRES ARMS CITIES;
RUN;
```

Output from PROC FREQ in this program is shown below:

```
SEX       FREQUENCY  CUM FREQ    PERCENT   CUM PERCENT

MALE          4          4       66.667      66.667
FEMALE        2          6       33.333     100.000


RACE       FREQUENCY  CUM FREQ    PERCENT   CUM PERCENT

WHITE         3          3       50.000      50.000
BLACK         2          5       33.333      83.333
HISPANIC      1          6       16.667     100.000


MARITAL STATUS
MARITAL    FREQUENCY  CUM FREQ    PERCENT   CUM PERCENT

SINGLE        2          2       33.333      33.333
MARRIED       2          4       33.333      66.667
WIDOWED       1          5       16.667      83.333
DIVORCED      1          6       16.667     100.000


EDUCATION LEVEL
EDUC          FREQUENCY  CUM FREQ   PERCENT   CUM PERCENT

HIGH SCH OR LESS     2        2      33.333      33.333
TWO YR. COLLEGE      2        4      33.333      66.667
FOUR YR. COLLEGE     1        5      16.667      83.333
GRADUATE DEGREE      1        6      16.667     100.000


PRESIDENT DOING A GOOD JOB
PRES          FREQUENCY  CUM FREQ   PERCENT   CUM PERCENT

STR DISAGREE      1          1      16.667      16.667
DISAGREE          1          2      16.667      33.333
NEUTRAL           1          3      16.667      50.000
AGREE             3          6      50.000     100.000


ARMS BUDGET INCREASE
ARMS       FREQUENCY  CUM FREQ    PERCENT   CUM PERCENT

DISAGREE      3          3       50.000      50.000
NEUTRAL       2          5       33.333      83.333
AGREE         1          6       16.667     100.000
```

```
FEDERAL AID TO CITIES
CITIES          FREQUENCY  CUM FREQ   PERCENT  CUM PERCENT

STR DISAGREE        1          1      16.667      16.667
DISAGREE            3          4      50.000      66.667
NEUTRAL             1          5      16.667      83.333
STR AGREE           1          6      16.667     100.000
```

D. RECODING DATA

In the previous questionnaire example, we coded the respondent's actual age in years. What if we want to look at the relationship between age and the questions 6-8 (opinion questions)? It might be convenient to have a variable that indicated an age group rather than the person's actual age. We will look at two ways of accomplishing this.

Look at the following SAS statements:

```
PROC FORMAT;
   VALUE SEXFMT 1='MALE' 2='FEMALE';
        .
        .
        .

   VALUE AGEFMT 1='0-20'  2='21-40'  3='41-60'
                4='GREATER THAN 60';
DATA;
INPUT ID 1-3 AGE 4-5 SEX 6 RACE 7 MARITAL 8 EDUC 9
      PRES 10 ARMS 11 CITIES 12;
IF 0 <= AGE <= 20 THEN AGEGRP=1;
IF 20 < AGE <= 40 THEN AGEGRP=2;
IF 40 < AGE <= 60 THEN AGEGRP=3;
IF AGE > 60 THEN AGEGRP=4;
LABEL  MARITAL='MARITAL STATUS'
        .
        .
        .

        AGEGRP='AGE GROUP';                      (cont.)
```

```
                          (Continued from previous page)
    FORMAT SEX SEXFMT. RACE RACE. MARITAL OSCAR.
                EDUC EDUC. PRES ARMS CITIES LIKERT.
AGEGRP AGEFMT.;
CARDS;
    (data)
PROC FREQ;
    TABLES SEX -- AGEGRP;
RUN;
```

Several new features have been added to the program. The major additions are the four IF statements following the INPUT. With the DATA statement, the program begins to create a data set. When the INPUT step is reached, the program will read a line of data according to the INPUT specifications. Next, each IF statement is evaluated. If the condition is **true**, then the variable AGEGRP will be set to 1,2,3, or 4. Finally, when the CARDS statement is reached, an observation is added to the SAS data set. The variables in the data set will include all the variables listed in the INPUT statement as well as the variable AGEGRP. The variable AGEGRP may be used in any PROC just like any of the other variables. Be sure there are no "gaps" in your recoding ranges. That is, make sure you code your IF statements so that there isn't a value of AGE that is not recoded. If that happens, the variable AGEGRP for that person will have a **missing value**. Notice that the first IF statement is written:

```
IF 0 <= AGE <= 20 THEN AGEGRP=1;
```

and **not** like this:

```
IF AGE <= 20 then AGEGRP=1;
```

The reason is subtle. Since SAS stores missing values as large negative numbers, the above IF statement will be true for missing values as well as the valid ages from 0 to 20. A complete list of the SAS comparison operators is shown below: either the two letter abbreviations or the inequality symbols may be used.

DEFINITION	SYMBOL(S)
Equal to	= or EQ
Greater than	> or GT
Less than	< or LT

DEFINITION	SYMBOL(S)
Greater than or equal to	>= or GE
Less than or equal to	<= or LE
Not equal to	^= or NE

NOTE: the ^ symbol may be ~= or ¬= depending on your keyboard.

A better way to write multiple IF statements is to use an **ELSE** before all but the first IF. The four IF statements would then look like this:

```
IF  0 < AGE <=20 THEN AGEGRP=1;
   ELSE IF 20 < AGE <= 40 THEN AGEGRP=2;
   ELSE IF 40 < AGE <= 60 THEN AGEGRP=3;
   ELSE IF AGE > 60 THEN AGEGRP=4;
```

The effect of the ELSE statements is that when any IF statement is **true**, all the following ELSE statements will be skipped. The advantage is to reduce computer time (since all the IF's do not usually have to be tested) and to avoid the following type of problem. Can you see what will happen with the statements below?

(Assume X can have values of 1,2,3,4, or 5)

```
IF X=1 THEN X=5;
IF X=2 THEN X=4;
IF X=4 THEN X=2;
IF X=5 THEN X=1;
```

What happens when X is 1? The first IF statement is true. This causes X to have a value of 5. The next two IF statements are false but the last IF statement is **true**. X is back to 1! The ELSE statements, besides reducing computer time, prevent the problem above. The correct coding is:

```
IF X=1 THEN X=5;
   ELSE IF X=2 THEN X=4;
   ELSE IF X=4 THEN X=2;
   ELSE IF X=5 THEN X=1;
```

One final note: If all we wanted to do was recode X so that 1=5, 2=4, 3=3, 4=2, and 5=1 the statement

```
X = 6 - X;
```

would be the best way to recode the X values.

Notice that we added a line to the LABEL section and to PROC FORMAT to supply a variable label and a format for our new variable.

There is another way of recoding our AGE variable without creating a new variable. We will use a "trick." By defining a special format, we can have SAS software assign subjects to age categories. We can write

```
PROC FORMAT;
   VALUE AGROUP LOW-20='0-20'
                21-40='21-40'
                41-60='41-60'
                60-HIGH='GREATER THAN 60';
```

As you can see in this example, instead of single values to the left of the = sign, we are supplying a range of values. SAS software will not let us specify overlapping ranges when defining formats. Thus, LOW-20='VERY YOUNG' and 15-30='YOUNG' are not allowed. The special words HIGH and LOW are available to indicate all values under or over a specified value. The term LOW-20 refers to all values from the lowest value up to and including 20. However, the keyword LOW **does not include missing values.** (Note: This was not true in an earlier version of SAS software.)

One additional keyword, OTHER, can be used to match any data value not included in any of the other format ranges. Thus, you can use the form:

```
VALUE AGROUP LOW-20='0-20'
             21-40='21-40'
             41-60='41-60'
             60-HIGH='GREATER THAN 60'
             .='DID NOT ANSWER'
             OTHER='OUT OF RANGE';
```

As you would expect, the .='format label' allows you to supply a label to missing values. A common use of the OTHER= keyword is to supply a format for all values not previously formatted. Suppose we have coded values for 1,2,3,4 and 5. We could then use OTHER='NOT CODED' or something similar to capture any miscoded value. One final form of specifying format values is available. We can code:

```
VALUE RACE 1='WHITE'
           2='BLACK'
           3='NOT SPECIFIED'
           0,4-9='MISCODED'
           OTHER='OUT OF RANGE';
```

A series of values or ranges of values can be separated by commas. In this example, either a 0 or any number from 4 through 9 will be formatted as 'MISCODED'. A good application of this would be to regroup a large number of categories into a smaller number of categories. Suppose we had coded our original questionnaire with five levels of RACE:

```
1=WHITE   2=HISPANIC  3=ORIENTAL  4=BLACK  5=OTHER
```

Now, for a particular analysis, we want to have only three groups — WHITE, BLACK, and OTHER. A quick and easy way to do this is to supply a format like the following:

```
VALUE RACE 1='WHITE'
           4='BLACK'
           2,3,5='OTHER';
```

Once we have defined a format, we can then issue a TABLES request on the original variable (such as AGE). But, by supplying the format information using the format AGROUP for the variable AGE, the new categories will be printed instead of the original AGE values. Notice that we will now place the format statement in the appropriate PROC rather than in the DATA statement since we want to use the recoded values only for PROC FREQ.

Thus, the SAS statements

```
PROC FREQ;
    TABLES AGE;
    FORMAT AGE AGROUP.;
```

will produce the following output:

AGE	FREQUENCY	CUM FREQ	PERCENT	CUM PERCENT
21-40	3	3	50.000	50.000
41-60	1	4	16.667	66.667
GREATER THAN 60	2	6	33.333	100.000

E. TWO-WAY FREQUENCY TABLES

Besides computing frequencies on individual variables, we might have occasion to count occurrences of one variable at each level of another variable. An example will make this clear. Suppose we took a poll of presidential preference and also recorded the sex of the respondent. Sample data might look like this:

SEX	CANDIDATE
M	DEWEY
F	TRUMAN
M	TRUMAN
M	DEWEY
F	TRUMAN
etc.	

We would like to know (1) how many people were for Dewey and how many for Truman, (2) how many males and females were in the sample, and (3) how many males and females were for Dewey and Truman, respectively.

A previous example of PROC FREQ shows how to perform tasks (1) and (2). For (3) we would like a table that looks like this:

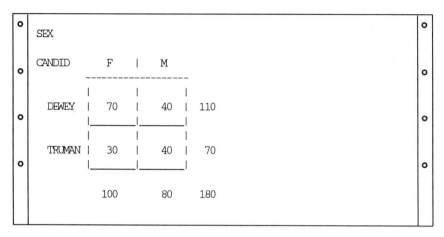

If this were our table, it would show that females favored Dewey over Truman 70 to 30 while males were split evenly. A SAS program to solve all three tasks is given below:

```
DATA;
INPUT SEX $ CANDID $ ;
CARDS;
M DEWEY
F TRUMAN
M TRUMAN
M DEWEY
F TRUMAN
  etc.
PROC FREQ;
   TABLES SEX CANDID;
   TABLES CANDID*SEX;
RUN;
```

Notice that since the variables SEX and CANDID are coded as character values (alphanumeric), we follow each variable name with a $ in the INPUT statement. Another fact that we have not mentioned so far is that the VALUES of our character variables also cannot be longer than eight letters in length when using a list directed input statement unless we modify our INPUT statement to indicate this. So, for the time being, we cannot use this program for the Eisenhower/Stevenson election (without using nicknames).

The first TABLES request is the same type we have seen before; the second, containing the asterisk, is a request for a fourfold or two-by-two table.

What would a table like the one above tell us? If it were based on a random sample of voters, we might conclude that sex affected voting patterns. Before we conclude that this is true of the nation as a whole, it would be nice to see how likely it was that these results were simply due to a quirky sample. A statistic called chi-square will do just this.

Consider the original fourfold table again. There were 180 people in our sample, 110 for Dewey and 70 for Truman, 100 females and 80 males. If there were no sex bias, we would expect the proportion of the population who wanted Dewey (110/180) to be the same for the females and males. Therefore, since there were 100 females, we could expect (110/180) of 100 (approximately 61) females to be for Dewey. Our expectations (in statistics called "**expected values**") for all the other cells can be calculated in a similar manner. Once we have **observed** and **expected** frequencies for each cell (each combination of sex and candidate), the chi-square statistic can be computed. By adding an option for chi-square to our TABLES request, we can have our program compute chi-square and the probability of obtaining a value as large or larger by chance alone. Remembering that **statement** options follow a slash, the request for chi- square is written as:

```
TABLES CANDID*SEX / CHISQ;
```

Output from the above request is shown below:

```
TABLE OF CANDID BY SEX
CANDID          SEX
FREQUENCY|
PERCENT  |
ROW PCT  |
COL PCT  |    F    |    M    |  TOTAL
---------+---------+---------+
DEWEY    |    70   |    40   |   110
         | 38.89   | 22.22   | 61.11
         | 63.64   | 36.36   |
         | 70.00   | 50.00   |
---------+---------+---------+
TRUMAN   |    30   |    40   |    70
         | 16.67   | 22.22   | 38.89
         | 42.86   | 57.14   |
         | 30.00   | 50.00   |
---------+---------+---------+
TOTAL         100       80       180
            55.56     44.44   100.00
```

```
STATISTICS FOR 2-WAY TABLES
CHI-SQUARE                     7.481    DF=  1   PROB=0.0062
PHI                            0.204
CONTINGENCY COEFFICIENT        0.200
CRAMER'S V                     0.204
LIKELIHOOD RATIO CHI-SQUARE    7.493    DF=  1   PROB=0.0062
CONTINUITY ADJ. CHI-SQUARE     6.663    DF=  1   PROB=0.0098
FISHER'S EXACT TEST (1-TAIL)                     PROB=0.0049
                    (2-TAIL)                     PROB=0.0087
```

The key to the table is found in the upper left-hand corner of the table. The first number indicates the FREQUENCY, or the number of subjects in the cell. For example, 70 females favored Dewey for president. The second number in each cell shows the PERCENT of the **total population**. The third number, labeled ROW PCT gives the percent of **each** row. **For example, of all the people for Dewey (row 1),** 70/110 x 100 or 63.64% were female. The last number, COL PCT, is the **column percent.** Of all the **females,** 70% were for Dewey and 30% were for Truman. It is customary to place the variable that we consider the independent variable (SEX in our example) along the columns of the table. In the TABLES request for a two-way cross tabulation, the variable that forms the columns is placed second (e.g., CANDID*SEX). In our statistical requests, rows come first, then columns.

For our example, chi-square equals 7.48 and the probability of obtaining a chi-square this large or larger by chance alone is .006. Therefore, we can say that based on our data, there is a sex bias in presidential preference: there is a tendency for females to show greater preference for Dewey than males do.

The number of degrees of freedom (df) in a chi-square statistic is equal to the number of rows minus one multiplied by the number of columns minus one ((R-1)x(C-1)). Thus, our 2x2 chi-square has 1 df. If there is only one row in the table, then the df are simply the number of cells minus one. Whenever a chi-square table has 1 df and the **expected** value of any cell is less than 5, a "correction for continuity" called Yates' correction should be applied. SAS software prints out a corrected chi-square value and its associated probability beside the heading CONTINUITY ADJ. CHI-SQUARE. An even better alternative when you have small expected values is to use Fisher's exact test, which is included in the list of statistics for the table. Remembering that the chi-square test is non-directional, you will probably want to use the 2-tailed Fisher probability. When the degrees of freedom are greater than 1, no more than 20% of the cells should have **expected** values less than 5. The program will print a warning when this condition occurs. This does not mean that you have to throw your data out if you fall into this situation. Below, we will tell you one alternative if your df are greater than 1. If you are in doubt, consult your local statistician.

For larger tables (more than four cells) the usual alternative when faced with small **expected** cell values is to combine or collapse cells. If we had four categories of age: 0-20, 21-40, 41-60, and over 60, we might combine 0-20 and 21-40 as one group, and 41-60 and 60+ as another. Another example would be combining categories such as "strongly disagree" and "disagree" on an opinion questionnaire. We can use either method of recoding shown in the previous section to accomplish this.

We can use the questionnaire program in the beginning of this chapter to see another example of a two-way table. Suppose we wanted cross tabulations of AGEGRP against the three variables PRES, ARMS, and CITIES. We could write:

```
TABLES (PRES ARMS CITIES)*AGEGRP;
```

This will generate three tables and is a short way of writing:

```
TABLES PRES*AGEGRP ARMS*AGEGRP CITIES*AGEGRP;
```

We can also have multiple column variables in a TABLE request. Thus

```
TABLES (PRES ARMS)*(AGEGRP SEX);
```

would produce four tables — PRES*AGEGRP, PRES*SEX, ARMS*AGEGRP, and ARMS*SEX.

When you use this method, be sure to put the list of variables in parentheses.

One of the tables generated from this program is shown below:

```
TABLE OF PRES BY AGE
PRES        PRESIDENT DOING A GOOD JOB    AGE

FREQUENCY  |
  PERCENT  |
  ROW PCT  |
  COL PCT  |21-40    |41-60     |GREATER  |
           |         |          |THAN 60  |  TOTAL
-------------+--------+--------+--------+
STR DISAGREE |    1 |     0 |     0 |    1
           |  16.67 |  0.00 |  0.00 |  16.67
           | 100.00 |  0.00 |  0.00 |
           |  33.33 |  0.00 |  0.00 |
-------------+--------+--------+--------+
DISAGREE     |    1 |     0 |     0 |    1
           |  16.67 |  0.00 |  0.00 |  16.67
           | 100.00 |  0.00 |  0.00 |
           |  33.33 |  0.00 |  0.00 |
-------------+--------+--------+--------+
NEUTRAL      |    0 |     0 |     1 |    1
           |   0.00 |  0.00 | 16.67 |  16.67
           |   0.00 |  0.00 |100.00 |
           |   0.00 |  0.00 | 50.00 |
-------------+--------+--------+--------+
AGREE        |    1 |     1 |     1 |    3
           |  16.67 | 16.67 | 16.67 |  50.00
           |  33.33 | 33.33 | 33.33 |
           |  33.33 |100.00 | 50.00 |
-------------+--------+--------+--------+
TOTAL             3        1        2       6
              50.00    16.67    33.33  100.00
```

F. COMPUTING CHI-SQUARE FROM FREQUENCY COUNTS

When you already have a contingency table and want to use SAS software to compute a chi-square statistic, there is a WEIGHT statement that will make this task possible. Suppose someone gave you the 2 X 2 table below and wanted to compute chi-square:

GROUP

		Control	Drug
OUTCOME	Dead	20	10
	Alive	80	90

We could code this by reading in values for GROUP, OUTCOME, and the number of subjects, COUNT, in the appropriate cell. Thus we would have:

```
DATA CHISQ;
INPUT GROUP $ OUTCOME $ COUNT;
CARDS;
CONTROL DEAD 20
DRUG DEAD 10
CONTROL ALIVE 80
DRUG ALIVE 90
RUN;
PROC FREQ;
    TABLES OUTCOME*GROUP / CHISQ;
    WEIGHT COUNT;
RUN;
```

The WEIGHT statement tells the procedure how many subjects there are for each combination of OUTCOME and GROUP.

G. "CHECK ALL THAT APPLY" QUESTIONS

A common problem in questionnaire analysis is "check all that apply" questions. For example, suppose we had a question asking respondents which course or courses they were interested in taking. It might be written:

Which course or courses would you like to see offered next semester?

(check ALL that apply)

    __1.Micro-computers   __4.Job Control Language
    __2.Intro to SAS   __5.FORTRAN
    __3.Advanced SAS   __6.PASCAL

As far as our analysis is concerned, this is not one question with up to six answers, but six yes/no questions. Each course offering would be treated as a variable with values of YES or NO (coded as 1 or 0, for example). Our questionnaire would be easier to analyze if it were arranged like this:

Please indicate which of the following courses you would like to see offered next semester:

	(1)yes	(0)no	For office use only
a)Micro-computers	—	—	—
b)Intro to SAS	—	—	—
c)Advanced SAS	—	—	—
d)Job Control Language	—	—	—
e)FORTRAN	—	—	—
f)PASCAL	—	—	—

Our INPUT statement would have six variables (COURSE1-COURSE6 for instance), each to be assigned a value of 1 or 0. A format matching 1=yes and 0=no make the final analysis more readable.

This approach works well when there is a limited number of choices. However, when we are choosing several items from a large number of possible choices, this approach becomes impractical since we need a variable for every possible choice. A common example in the medical field would be the variable "diagnosis" on a patient record. We might have a list of hundreds or even thousands of diagnosis codes and want to consider a maximum of 2 or 3 diagnoses for each patient. Our approach in this case would be to ask for up to 3 diagnoses per patient, using a diagnosis code from a list of standardized codes. Our form might look like this:

Enter up to 3 diagnosis codes for the patient.

diagnosis 1 _____ |_|_|_|

diagnosis 2 _____ |_|_|_|

diagnosis 3 _____ |_|_|_|

Our INPUT statement would be straightforward:

```
DATA DIAG1;
INPUT ID 1-3 . . . DX1 20-22 DX2 23-25 DX3 26-28;
```

Suppose we had the following data:

OBS	ID	DX1	DX2	DX3
1	1	3	4	.
2	2	1	3	7
3	3	5	.	.

Notice that one patient could have a certain diagnosis code as his first diagnosis while another patient might have the same code as his second or third diagnosis. If we want a frequency distribution of diagnosis codes, what can we do? We could try this:

```
PROC FREQ;
   TABLES DX1-DX3;
```

but we would have to add the frequencies from three tables to compute the frequency for each diagnosis code. A better approach would be to create a separate data set that was structured differently. Our goal would be a data set like this:

OBS	ID	DX	
1	1	3	
2	1	4	
3	2	1	(cont.)

4	2	3
5	2	7
6	3	5

The program statements to create the above data set are shown below:

```
001   DATA DIAG2;
002   SET DIAG1;
003   DX=DX1;
004   IF DX NE . THEN OUTPUT;
005   DX=DX2;
006   IF DX NE . THEN OUTPUT;
007   DX=DX3;
008   IF DX NE . THEN OUTPUT;
009   KEEP ID DX;
010   RUN;
```

Each observation from our original data set (DIAG1) will create up to 3 observations in our new data set (DIAG2). The SET statement (line 2) reads an observation from our original data set (DIAG1). The first observation will contain:

ID	AGE	SEX	DX1	DX2	DX3
1	23	M	3	4	.

To these values, we will add a new variable called DX. DX is first set equal to DX1. The Program Data Vector now contains:

ID	AGE	SEX	DX1	DX2	DX3	DX
1	23	M	3	4	.	3

Since DX is not missing, we output (line 4) these values to the first observation in data set DIAG2 (for now, let's ignore the KEEP statement in line 9). Next, DX is set to DX2 and another observation is written to data set DIAG2:

ID	AGE	SEX	DX1	DX2	DX3	DX
1	23	M	3	4	.	3
1	23	M	3	4	.	4

The values for ID, AGE, SEX, DX1, DX2, and DX3 are still the same, only DX has changed. Finally, DX is set equal to DX3, but since DX3, and therefore DX, is missing, no observation is written to DIAG2.

We are now at the bottom of the data step and control is returned to the top of the data step where the SET statement will read another observation from data set DIAG1. This continues until all the observations from DIAG1 have been read. Since we had a KEEP statement in the program, only the variables ID and DX will actually exist in data set DIAG2:

OBS	ID	DX
1	1	3
2	1	4
3	2	1
4	2	3
5	2	7
6	3	5

We can now count the frequencies of DX codes using PROC FREQ with DX as the TABLE variable.

This program can be made more compact by using an ARRAY and a DO loop. (See chapter 13 for a more detailed explanation of ARRAYS.)

```
DATA DIAG2;
SET DIAG1;
ARRAY D{*} DX1-DX3;
DO I = 1 TO 3;
   DX=D{I};
   IF D{I} NE . THEN OUTPUT;
   END;
KEEP ID DX;
```

PROBLEMS

3-1. Suppose we have a variable called GROUP that has numeric values of 1,2, or 3. Group 1 is a control group, group 2 is given aspirin, and group 3 is given Tylenol. Create a format to be assigned to the variable GROUP.

3-2. A survey was conducted and data were collected and coded. The data layout is shown below (all values are numeric):

VARIABLE	DESCRIPTION	COLUMNS	CODING VALUES
ID	Subject identifier	1-3	
SEX		4	1=Male 2=Female
PARTY	Political party	5	1=Republican 2=Democrat 3=Not registered
VOTE	Did you vote in the last election?	6	0=No 1=Yes
FOREIGN	Do you agree with the government's foreign policy?	7	0=No 1=Yes
SPEND	Should we increase domestic spending?	8	0=No 1=Yes

Collected data are shown below:

```
00711110
01322101
13721001
117 1111
42813110
01723101
03712101
```

(a) Create a SAS data set, complete with **labels** and **formats**, for this questionnaire.

(b) Generate frequency counts for the variables SEX, PARTY, VOTE, FOREIGN, and SPEND.

(c) Test if there is a relationship between voting in the last election and agreement with spending and foreign policy. (Have SAS compute chi-square for these relationships.)

3-3. We have a SAS data set containing the variables WEIGHT, HEIGHT, SEX, and RACE. We want to recode WEIGHT and HEIGHT as follows:

```
WEIGHT    0-100    = 1
          101-150  = 2
          151-200  = 3
            >200   = 4

HEIGHT    0-70     = 1
            >70    = 2
```

We then want to generate a table of WEIGHT categories (rows) by HEIGHT categories (columns). Recode these variables in two ways: First, with "IF" statements; second, with format statements. Then write the necessary statements to generate the table.

*3-4. A physical exam was given to a group of patients. Each patient was diagnosed to have none, 1, 2, or 3 problems from the code list below:

CODE	PROBLEM DESCRIPTION
1	Cold
2	Flu
3	Trouble sleeping
4	Chest pain
5	Muscle pain
6	Headaches
7	Overweight
8	High blood pressure
9	Hearing loss

The coding scheme is as follows:

VARIABLE	DESCRIPTION	COLUMN(S)
SUBJ	Subject number	1-2
PROB1	Problem 1	3
PROB2	" 2	4
PROB3	" 3	5
HR	Heart rate	6-8
SBP	Systolic blood pressure	9-11
DBP	Diastolic blood pressure	12-14

Using the sample data below:

COLUMNS	12345678901234
	11127 78130 80
	1787 82180110
	031 62120 78
	4261 68130 80
	89 58120 76
	9948 82178100

(a) Compute the mean HR, SBP, and DBP.

(b) Generate frequency counts for each of the nine medical problems.

3-5. What's wrong with this program?

```
1      DATA IGOOFED;
2      INPUT #1 ID 1-3 SEX 4 AGE 5-6 RACE 7
          (QUES1-QUES10) (1.)
          #2 @4 (QUES11-QUES25) (1.);
3      FORMAT SEX SEX. RACE RACE. QUES1-QUES25 YESNO.;
4      CARDS;
       00112311010011101
          1100111001101011
       002244210111011100
          0111011101111010
              etc.                           (cont.)
```

```
                            (Continued from previous page)
5      PROC FORMAT;
6          VALUE SEX 1='MALE' 2='FEMALE';
7          VALUE RACE 1='WHITE' 2='BLACK' 3='HISPANIC';
8          VALUE YESNO 0='NO' 1='YES';
9      PROC FREQ;
10         VAR SEX RACE QUES1-QUES25 / CHISQ;
11     PROC MEANS MAXDEC=2 N MEAN STD MIN MAX;
12         BY RACE;
13         VAR AGE;
```

Hints and comments: The INPUT statement is correct. The pointers (@ and # signs) and format lists (1.) are described in Chapter 10. There are 4 errors.

CHAPTER 4

WORKING WITH DATE AND LONGITUDINAL DATA

A. PROCESSING DATE VARIABLES

Suppose you wanted to read the following information into a SAS data set:

ID	DOB	ADMITTING DATE	DISCHARGE DATE	DX	FEE
001	102150	091090	091390	8	3000
002	050540	090190	090590	7	5000

We could arrange our data in columns like this:

Variable Name	Description	Column(s)
ID	Patient ID	1-3
DOB	Date of Birth	5-10
ADMIT	Date of Admission	12-17
DISCHRG	Discharge Date	18-23
DX	Diagnosis	25
FEE	Hospital Fee	26-30

You might be tempted to write an input statement like this:

```
INPUT ID 1-3 DOB 5-10 ADMIT 12-17 DISCHRG 18-23
      DX 25 FEE 26-30;
```

However, the 6 digits of the date values have no meaning when read as a six digit number. SAS software includes extensive provisions for working with date and time variables. The first step in reading date values is to tell the program what style our date value uses. Common examples are:

EXAMPLE	EXPLANATION
102150	Month - Day - Year
10/21/50	Month - Day - Year (Separated by slashes)
211050	Day - Month - Year (European style)
501021	Year - Month - Day
21OCT50	2-digit Day, 3-character Month, 2-digit Year

OCT50   3-character Month and 2-digit Year only
10211950   2-digit Month, 2-digit Day, 4-digit Year
10/21/1950   2-digit Month, 2-digit Day, 4-digit Year
               (Separated by slashes)

SAS programs can read any of these examples, providing we use a date format to tell the program how to interpret the digits in the date field. Once SAS knows it's reading a date, it converts it to the number of days from a fixed point in time: January 1, 1960. It doesn't matter if your date comes before or after this date. Therefore, we can subtract any two dates to find the number of days in between. We can also convert the SAS internal date value back to any of the allowable SAS date formats for reporting purposes. As we saw in the last chapter, we can associate formats with variables. We can also use formats in our INPUT statement (more technically called INFORMATS) to give the program instructions on how to read the date. The SAS date format MMDDYY6., for example, is used to read dates in month-day-year order. The 6 in the format refers to the number of columns occupied by the date. The format MMDDYY8. would be used for dates in the form 10/21/50 or 10-21-50. So far, we have used space-between-the-numbers and columns to instruct SAS how to read our data values. To use a format in an INPUT statement, we first tell the program what column to start reading, then the variable name we want to assign, followed by the format we want to use. Using our column assignments above, a valid INPUT statement would be:

```
INPUT ID 1-3 @5 DOB MMDDYY6. @12 ADMIT MMDDYY6.
      @18 DISCHRG MMDDYY6. DX 25 FEE 26-30;
```

The @ signs, referred to as pointers, tell SAS at which column to start reading the next data value. Our three dates are all in the form MMDDYY (month-day-year) and occupy 6 columns, so the MMDDYY6. format is used. Remember that all of our formats end with periods when used in format statements. The same is true here. Since the date of admission ends in column 17 and the discharge date starts in column 18, the pointer @18 is redundant since, after reading columns 12-17, the program is ready to read column 18 next anyway. (See chapter 10 for more details on how to use the INPUT statement.)

Let's calculate two new variables from these data. First, we will compute our subject's age at the time of admission. Next, we will compute the length of stay in the hospital. All we have to do is subtract any two dates to get the number of days in between. Therefore, our completed program looks like the one below:

```
DATA HOSPITAL;
INPUT ID 1-3 @5 DOB MMDDYY6. @12 ADMIT MMDDYY6.
@18 DISCHRG MMDDYY6. DX 25 FEE 26-30;
AGE = ADMIT - DOB;
LEN_STAY = DISCHRG - ADMIT;
CARDS;
(data lines)
```

So far so good, but we now have the subject's age in days! We could convert this to years by dividing by 365.25 (approximately correct since there is a leap year every 4 years). This would give us:

```
AGE = (ADMIT - DOB) / 365.25;
```

We may want to define age so that a person is not considered, say 18 years old, until his 18th birthday. That is, we want to drop any fractional portion of his age in years. A SAS function that does this is the FLOOR function. We can write:

```
AGE = FLOOR((ADMIT - DOB) / 365.25);
```

The FLOOR function, like all SAS functions, has an argument in parentheses after the function name. If we wanted to round the age to the nearest tenth of a year, we would use the ROUND function. This function has two arguments, the number to be rounded, and the roundoff unit. To round to the nearest tenth of a year, we would use:

```
AGE = ROUND (((ADMIT - DOB) / 365.25),.1);
```

To the nearest year, the function would be:

```
AGE = ROUND (((ADMIT - DOB) / 365.25),1);
```

It is important to remember that once SAS has converted our dates into the number of days from January 1, 1960, it is stored just like any other numeric value. Therefore, if we print it out (with PROC PRINT for example), the result will not look like a date. We need to supply SAS with a format to use when printing our dates. This format does not have to be the same one we used to read the date in the first place. Some useful date formats and their results are shown in the table below:

The date 10/21/50 Printed with Different Date Format

FORMAT	RESULT
MMDDYY6.	102150
MMDDYY8.	10/21/50
DATE7.	21OCT50
WORDDATE.	OCTOBER 21, 1950

The formats listed here may also be used in the INPUT statement. In the age calculation above, what age would be computed for a person born on January 1, 1899 who was admitted on January 1, 1990? If we entered his date of birth as 01/01/99, the computer would assume he was born in 1999, not 1899 and compute an age of -9 years. A person born in 1880, admitted on the same date would be listed as 10 years old. Clearly, we need a way to include century data for people born before 1900. We can do this in several ways. First, if we provide a variable that indicates the century, we can include it in our calculation. Suppose a variable called CENTURY has values of 18 or 19 to indicate if the subject was born in the 1800's or the 1900's. One way to compute his age would be:

```
AGE = (ADMIT - DOB) / 365.25;
      IF CENTURY=18 THEN AGE=AGE+100;
```

A more compact equation would be:

```
AGE = (ADMIT - DOB) / 365.25 + 100 * (CENTURY=18);
```

Notice the expression (CENTURY=18). This is called a logical expression. It is the first time we have combined a **logical** expression in a calculation. The result of the logical expression (CENTURY=18) is evaluated. A **true** value equals 1 and a **false** value equals 0. So, if a subject was born in the 1800's, we would add 100 to his age. This is a good place to point out that the two line computation of age is perfectly fine. Only a compulsive programmer (like one of the authors) would feel the need to write a more elegant, one line expression. There are times when more lengthy, straightforward approaches are best. They are less likely to contain errors, are easier for other people to understand, and finally, are easier for the original programmer to modify or debug at a later date.

Another approach to this problem is to code the original date in a form such as:

```
01/01/1899        or        01011899
```

We could read the first date with the MMDDYY10. format and the second with the MMDDYY8. format. You might recall that MMDDYY8. is also used to read a date such as:

```
10/21/50
```

However, the system is smart enough to realize that an eight digit date without slashes must be using a 4 digit year. One practical comment on dates. If you know something about your data and know, for example, that there will not be subjects over 100 years old, you could just check if any ages are negative (subjects born before 1900) and add 100. However, if your data base could conceivably contain 2 year olds and 102 year olds, you must include the century in your calculations.

B. LONGITUDINAL DATA

There is a type of data, often referred to as longitudinal data, that needs special attention. Longitudinal data are collected on a group of subjects over time. Caution: this portion of the chapter is difficult and may be hazardous to your health!

To examine the special techniques needed to analyze longitudinal data, let's follow a simple example. Suppose we are collecting data on a group of patients. (The same scheme would be applicable to periodic data in business or data in the social sciences with repeated measures.) Each time they come in for a visit, we will fill out an encounter form. The data items we collect will be:

```
PATIENT ID
DATE OF VISIT (Month Day Year)
HEART RATE
SYSTOLIC BLOOD PRESSURE
DIASTOLIC BLOOD PRESSURE
DIAGNOSIS CODE
DOCTOR FEE
LAB FEE
```

Now, suppose each patient comes in a maximum of 4 times a year. One way to arrange our SAS data set is like this (each visit will be on a separate line):

```
DATA PATIENTS;
INPUT #1 ID1 1-3 DATE1 MMDDYY6. HR1 10-12 SBP1 13-15
         DBP1 16-18 DX1 19-21 DOCFEE1 22-25 LABFEE1 26-29
      #2 ID2 1-3 DATE2 MMDDYY6. HR2 10-12 SBP2 13-15
         DBP2 16-18 DX2 19-21 DOCFEE2 22-25 LABFEE2 26-29
      #3 ID3 1-3 DATE3 MMDDYY6. HR3 10-12 SBP3 13-15
         DBP3 16-18 DX3 19-21 DOCFEE3 22-25 LABFEE3 26-29
      #4 ID4 1-3 DATE4 MMDDYY6. HR4 10-12 SBP4 13-15
         DBP4 16-18 DX4 19-21 DOCFEE4 22-25 LABFEE4 26-29;
FORMAT DATE1-DATE4 MMDDYY8.;
CARDS;
007102183070120080014004000150
007120183072130090020005000200
007
007
009090383066110070137003000000
009
009
009
005070583074140082013009000000
005011582080180096014020001500
005061882070170084014008000400
005070383064140084014008000200
```

The number signs (#) in the INPUT statement signify multiple lines per subject. Since our date is in the form Month - Day - Year, we will use the MMDDYY6. format. We also included an **output** format for our dates with a **FORMAT** statement. This FORMAT statement uses the same syntax as the earlier examples in this chapter where we created our own formats. The output format MMDDYY8. specifies that the date variables be printed in month/day/year format.

With this method of one line per patient visit, we would need to insert BLANK lines of data for any patient who had less than four visits, to fill out 4 lines per subject. This is not only clumsy but occupies a lot of unnecessary space. If we wanted to compute within-subject means, we would continue (before the CARDS statement)

```
AVEHR = MEAN (OF HR1-HR4);
AVESBP = MEAN (OF SBP1-SBP4);
AVEDBP = MEAN (OF DBP1-DBP4);
          etc.
```

where "MEAN" is one of the SAS built-in functions that will compute the mean of all the variables listed in parentheses. (Note: If any of the variables listed as arguments of the MEAN function have missing values, the result will be the mean of the **nonmissing** values.) A much better approach would be to treat **each visit as a separate observation**. Our program would then look like this:

```
DATA PATIENTS;
INPUT ID 1-3 DATE MMDDYY6. HR 10-12 SBP 13-15
 DBP 16-18 DX 19-21 DOCFEE 22-25 LABFEE 26-29;
FORMAT DATE MMDDYY8.;
CARDS;
```

Now, we need to include only as many lines of data as there are patient visits; blank lines to fill out 4 lines per subject are not needed. Our variable names are also simpler since we do not need to keep track of HR1, HR2, etc. How do we analyze this data set? A simple PROC MEANS on a variable such as HR,SBP, or DOCFEE will not be particularly useful since we are averaging 1 to 4 values per patient together. Perhaps the average of DOC-FEE would be useful since it represents the average doctor fee **per** PATIENT VISIT, but statistics for heart rate or blood pressure would be a weighted average, the weight depending on how many visits we had from each patient. How do we compute the average heart rate or blood pressure PER PATIENT? The key is to use **ID as a BY variable.**

Here is our program (with sample data):

```
DATA PATIENTS;
INPUT ID 1-3 DATE MMDDYY6. HR 10-12 SBP 13-15
      DBP 16-18 DX 19-21 DOCFEE 22-25 LABFEE 26-29;
FORMAT DATE MMDDYY8.;
CARDS;
0071021830701200800140040015O
0071201830721300900200050020O
0090903830661100701370030000O
0050705830741400820130090000O
0050115820801800960140200150O
0050618820701700840140080040O
0050703830641400840140080020O
RUN;
PROC SORT;
   BY ID DATE;
RUN;
PROC MEANS NOPRINT;
   BY ID;
   VAR HR -- DBP DOCFEE LABFEE;
   OUTPUT OUT=STATS MEAN=HR SBP DBP DOCFEE LABFEE;
RUN;
```

What have we done here? The PROC SORT statement assures us that
the data set is in patient-date order. We can now use ID as a BY variable
with PROC MEANS. The result is the mean HR, SBP, etc. per patient, which
is placed in a new data set STATS, created with the **OUTPUT** statement of
PROC MEANS. Each variable listed after "MEAN=" in the OUTPUT
statement will be the **mean** of the variables listed in the **VAR** statement, in
the **order** they appear. Thus, HR in the data set STATS will be the mean HR
in the data set PATIENTS. The variable names you choose following
"MEAN=" are arbitrary; they do **not** have to be the same as the names in
the VAR list. You may also leave out the list of variable names after the
MEAN= statement and SAS will use the same names that you listed in the
VAR statement. If you use this notation, the OUTPUT line would be
written:

```
OUTPUT OUT=STATS MEAN=;
```

It is the **order** of the variable names corresponding to the **order** of the VAR list that is important. Because of the **BY** variable, the mean HR etc. will be computed for **each subject**. The **NOPRINT** option simply says to create the new data set **STATS** without printing the PROC MEANS statistics in our output. (This output, had we omitted the NOPRINT option, would be the mean HR etc. for EACH patient.) In this example, the data set STATS would look like this (we can always test this with a PROC PRINT statement).

```
OBS  ID   HR      SBP     DBP    DOCFEE   LABFEE

 1    5  71.33   157.50   86.5   112.5    525.
 2    7  71.00   125.00   85.0    45.0    175.
 3    9  66.00   110.00   70.0    30.0      0.
```

This data set contains the mean HR, SBP, etc. **per** patient. We could analyze this data set with additional SAS procedures to investigate relationships between variables or compute descriptive statistics where each data value corresponds to a single value (the MEAN) from each patient.

An alternative to sorting the data set and using a BY statement with PROC MEANS is to use a CLASS statement. Using a CLASS statement is similar to using a BY statement except for two important differences. First, you do **not have to sort the data set**. For large data sets, this can mean a large saving of CPU time (and money). Secondly, the output data set will contain some extra variables that may prove to be extremely useful. On the down side, use of a CLASS statement will require considerably more **memory** than a BY statement, especially if there are several CLASS variables and many levels of each. In general, try using a CLASS statement first and resort to using a BY statement only if memory limitations force you to. Let's run this procedure with a CLASS statement and examine the output data set. The MEANS procedure we will run is:

```
PROC MEANS NOPRINT;
   CLASS ID;
   VAR HR -- DBP DOCFEE LABFEE;
   OUTPUT OUT=STATS MEAN=;
RUN;
```

The output is shown below:

```
Output from PROC MEANS with a CLASS statement

OBS  ID  _TYPE_  _FREQ_    HR       SBP      DBP     DOCFEE  LABFEE

 1   .     0       7     70.8571  141.429  83.7143  81.429    350
 2   5     1       4     72.0000  157.500  86.5000  112.500   525
 3   7     1       2     71.0000  125.000  85.0000  45.000    175
 4   9     1       1     66.0000  110.000  70.0000  30.000     0
```

There are several things to notice about this data set. First, there are two new variables, _TYPE_ and _FREQ_. The variable _TYPE_ has values that depend on the number of CLASS variables we have used. In this example there was a single CLASS variable. _TYPE_ equal to 0 represents the mean of all subjects, or the **grand mean** in statistical jargon. Since there is only one CLASS variable (ID), the _TYPE_ = 1 observations represent the means for each subject (the same as we had when we used a BY statement). The _FREQ_ variable should be clear now. _FREQ_ represents the number of observations that were used to compute the mean. Subject 5 had 4 visits, subject 7 had 2 visits, etc. In order for this data set to be useful, we would most likely want to eliminate the observation which contained the grand mean. There are two choices here. One, we could create a new data set from this one, which does not contain this observation. The other choice would be to use the NWAY option of PROC MEANS which is an instruction to keep only the observations with the largest _TYPE_ value. When there is only one CLASS variable, this would be the _TYPE_ equals 1 observations. The way to create a new observation from an old one is to use a SET statement in the data step. Here is an example:

```
DATA IDMEANS;
SET STATS;
IF _TYPE_ = 1;
RUN;
```

The SET statement can be thought of like an INPUT statement except that observations are read from a SAS data set instead of raw data. This program will read each observation from the data set STATS (created from PROC MEANS). Before the observation is added to the new data set,

IDMEANS, the subsetting IF statement is evaluated. This rather strange looking IF statement has no THEN clause—it is implied. When the IF statement is **true**, observations will be added to the new IDMEANS data set. You may want to see the section on subsetting data sets in Chapter 14 for a more complete explanation. A much simpler and more efficient way is to use the NWAY option of PROC MEANS. This provides only cell means. The PROC statement would read:

```
PROC MEANS NOPRINT NWAY;
```

C. USING PROC MEANS WITH MORE THAN ONE CLASS VARIABLE

When there is more than one CLASS variable, the interpretation of the _TYPE_ variable becomes more complicated. Suppose we have a data set with the variables RACE, SEX, and SCORE. If we want the mean SCORE for each combination of RACE and SEX and we want these means in a new data set, we can write:

```
PROC MEANS NWAY NOPRINT;
   CLASS RACE SEX;
   VAR SCORE;
   OUTPUT OUT=MEANOUT MEAN= ;
RUN;
```

The resulting data set will have as many observations as there are combinations of RACE and SEX. If we leave out the NWAY option, we will have additional observations in the output data set. First, for _TYPE_ = 0 we will have the mean for all sexes and all races (the grand mean). The _TYPE_ = 1 observations will be the mean SCORE for each SEX; the _TYPE_ = 2 observations will be the mean SCORE for each RACE; and the _TYPE_ = 3 observations will be the means for each combination of RACE and SEX. An "easy" way to figure this out is to write the _TYPE_ values in **binary**. We have:

TYPE	BINARY
0	00
1	01
2	10
3	11

Remembering the CLASS variables are RACE and SEX, we first line up the binary digits with the CLASS variables (in the order they are listed). A '1' underneath a variable indicates we are computing means for each level of this variable. The chart below should help clarify this:

TYPE	RACE	SEX	INTERPRETATION
0	0	0	Mean over all RACES and SEXES
1	0	1	Mean for each value of SEX
2	1	0	Mean for each value of RACE
3	1	1	Mean for each combination of RACE and SEX (cell means)

We can easily extend this method for more CLASS variables. Since this is such a difficult topic for beginning SAS users, a sample OUTPUT data set from PROC MEANS where the NWAY option was **not** used is shown: (Had NWAY been used, only the _TYPE_ = 3 observations would have been included.)

RACE	SEX	_TYPE_	_FREQ_	SCORE
		0	8	5.875
	F	1	4	6.000
	M	1	4	5.750
B		2	4	6.000
W		2	4	5.750
B	F	3	2	5.000
B	M	3	2	7.000
W	F	3	2	7.000
W	M	3	2	4.500

D. OUTPUTTING STATISTICS OTHER THAN MEANS

We saw that PROC MEANS can create an output data set, using an OUTPUT statement, which contains means for each variable in the VAR list for each level of the variables in the CLASS or BY statement. We used the keyword MEAN= to indicate that we wanted to output means. Any of the options that are available to be used with PROC MEANS (see chapter 2) can also be used to create variables in the data set created by PROC MEANS. For example, if we wanted our new data set to contain the mean, standard deviation, and maximum value, we would write:

```
PROC MEANS NOPRINT;
   CLASS ID;
   VAR HR SBP DBP DOCFEE LABFEE;
   OUTPUT OUT=STATS MEAN=MHR MSBP MDBP MDOCFEE MLABFEE
        STD=SDHR SDSBP SDDBP SDDOCFEE SDLABFEE
        MAX=MXHR MXSBP MXDBP MXDOCFEE MXLABFEE;
RUN;
```

Notice that we included a list of variables after the keywords MEAN=, STD=, and MAX=, since we need to have a **different** variable name for each of these statistics. The resulting data set (STATS) will include the variable ID as well as the variables representing the mean, standard deviation, maximum, and the two variables _TYPE_ and _FREQ_ created by the procedure. There will be as many observations in this data set as there are subjects.

E. MOST RECENT (OR LAST) VISIT PER PATIENT

What if we want to analyze the most recent visit for each patient? The data set PATIENTS in our previous example was sorted in patient-date order. The most recent visit would be the last observation for each patient ID. We can extract these observations with the following SAS program:

```
001   DATA PATIENTS;
002   INPUT ID 1-3 DATE MMDDYY6.  HR 10-12 SBP 13-15
003   DBP 16-18 DX 19-21 DOCFEE 22-25 LABFEE 26-29
004   FORMAT DATE MMDDYY8. ;
005   CARDS;
006   (data cards)
007   RUN;
008   PROC SORT;
009      BY ID DATE;
010   RUN;
011   DATA RECENT;
012   SET PATIENTS;
013      BY ID;
014   IF LAST.ID;
015   RUN;
```

Line 11 creates a new data set called RECENT. As we discussed previously, the SET statement in line 12 acts like an INPUT statement except that observations are read one by one from the SAS data set PATIENTS instead of our original data.

We are permitted to use a BY variable following our SET statement providing our data set has been previously sorted by the same variable (it has). The effect of adding the BY statement permits the use of the special **FIRST.** and **LAST.** internal SAS logical variables. Since ID was our BY variable, FIRST.ID will be a logical variable (i.e., true or false: 1 or 0) that will be part of each observation as it is being processed but will not remain with the final data set RECENT. FIRST.ID will be **TRUE** (or 1) whenever we are reading a **new ID**; LAST.ID will be **TRUE** whenever **we are reading the** last **observation for a given ID. To clarify this,** here are our observations and the value of FIRST.ID and LAST.ID in each **case:**

OBS	ID	DATE	HR	SBP	DBP	DX	DOCFEE	LABFEE	FIRST.ID	LAST.ID
1	5	01/15/82	80	180	96	14	200	1500	1	0
2	5	06/18/82	70	170	84	14	80	400	0	0
3	5	07/03/83	64	140	84	14	80	200	0	0
4	5	07/05/83	74	140	82	13	90	0	0	1
5	7	10/21/83	70	120	80	14	40	150	1	0
6	7	12/01/83	72	130	90	20	50	200	0	1
7	9	09/03/83	66	110	70	137	30	0	1	1

By adding the IF statement in line 14, we can select the last visit for each patient (in this case, observations 4, 6, and 7). By the way, this IF statement may also look strange—there is no logical expression following it. Since the value of FIRST. and LAST. variables are true (1) or false (0), they can be placed directly in an if statement without the more traditional form:

```
IF LAST.ID = 1;
```

which is what you would normally expect to see with a subsetting IF statement. We could also select the **first** visit for each patient with the statement:

```
IF FIRST.ID;
```

F. COMPUTING FREQUENCIES ON LONGITUDINAL DATA SETS

To compute frequencies for our diagnoses, we would use PROC FREQ on our original data set (PATIENTS). We would write

```
PROC FREQ DATA=PATIENTS ORDER=FREQ;
   TITLE 'DIAGNOSES IN DECREASING FREQUENCY ORDER';
   TABLES DX;
```

Notice we use the DATA= option on the PROC FREQ statement to make sure we were counting frequencies from our original data set. The ORDER= option allows us to control the order of the categories in a PROC FREQ output. Normally, the diagnosis categories would be listed in numerical order. The ORDER=FREQ option lists the diagnoses in frequency order from the most common diagnosis to the least. While we are on the subject, another useful ORDER= option is ORDER=FORMATTED. This will order the diagnoses alphabetically by the diagnosis formats (if we had them). Remember that executing a PROC FREQ procedure on our original data set (the one with multiple visits per patient) will have the effect of counting the number of times each diagnosis was made. That is, if a patient came in for three visits, each with the same diagnosis, we would add 3 to the frequency count for that diagnosis. If, for some reason, we want to count a diagnosis only once for a given patient, even if this diagnosis is made on subsequent visits, we can **sort our data set by ID and DX**. We then have a data set such as the following:

ID	DX	FIRST.ID	FIRST.DX
5	13	1	1
5	14	0	1
5	14	0	0
5	14	0	0
7	14	1	1
7	20	0	1
9	137	1	1

If we now use the logical FIRST.DX and FIRST.ID variables, we can accomplish our goal of counting a diagnosis only once for a given patient. The logical variable FIRST.DX will be **true** each time a new ID- diagnosis combination is encountered. The data set and procedure would look as follows (assume we have previously sorted by ID and DX):

```
DATA DIAG;
SET PATIENTS;
    BY ID DX;
IF FIRST.DX;
RUN;
PROC FREQ ORDER=FREQ;
    TABLES DX;
RUN;
```

We have accomplished our goal of counting a diagnosis code only once per patient. As you can see, the SAS internal variables FIRST. and LAST. are extremely useful. Think of using them anytime you need to do something special for the first or last occurrence of a variable.

PROBLEMS

4-1. We have collected data on a questionnaire as follows:

Variable	Starting Column	Length	Description
ID	1	3	Subject ID
DOB	5	6	Date of Birth in MMDDYY format
ST_DATE	11	6	Start Date in MMDDYY format
END_DATE	17	6	Ending Date in MMDDYY format
SALES	23	4	Total Sales

Here is some sample data:

```
001 1021461112801228887343
002 0913550202800204908123
005 0606400312810312855000
003 0705441115801113909544
```

(a) Write a SAS program to read these data.

(b) Compute age (in years) at the time work was started and the length of time between ST_DATE and END_DATE (also in years).

(c) Compute the sales per year of work.

(d) Print out a report showing:

ID   DOB   AGE   LENGTH   SALES_YR

where LENGTH is the time at work computed in (b) and SALES_YR is the sales per year computed in (c). Use the MMDDYY8. format to print the DOB.

(e) Modify the program to compute AGE as of the last birthday and sales per year rounded to the nearest 10 dollars. Try using the DOLLAR6. format for SALES_YR.

4-2. For each of eight mice, the date of birth, date of disease, and date of death was recoded. In addition, the mice were placed into one of two groups (A or B). Given the data below, compute the time from birth to disease, the time from disease to death, and age at death. All times can be in days. Compute the mean, standard deviation, and standard error of these three times for each of the two groups.

Here are the data:

RAT_NO	DOB	DISEASE	DEATH	GROUP
1	23MAY90	23JUN90	28JUN90	A
2	21MAY90	27JUN90	05JUL90	A
3	23MAY90	25JUN90	01JUL90	A
4	27MAY90	07JUL90	15JUL90	A
5	22MAY90	29JUN90	22JUL90	B
6	26MAY90	03JUL90	03AUG90	B
7	24MAY90	01JUL90	29JUL90	B
8	29MAY90	15JUL90	18AUG90	B

Arrange these data in any columns you wish. Hint: Use the DATE7. format to read dates in this form.

*4-3. Using the data set (PATIENTS) described in section E, write the necessary SAS statements to create a data set in which we compute the mean HR, SBP, and DBP for each patient, **omitting the first visit** from the calculations. (Patient 9 with only one visit will be eliminated.)

*4-4. Write a program similar to 4-3 except include all the data for each patient (**unless** a patient has had only one visit).

*4-5. We have a data set that contains from 1 to 20 observations per subject. Each observation contains the variables ID, GROUP, TIME, WBC (white blood cell count), and RBC (red blood cell count). We want to create a data set that contains the **mean** WBC and RBC for each subject. This new data set should contain the variables ID, GROUP, WBC, and RBC, where WBC and RBC are the mean values for the subject. Finally, we want to **exclude** any subjects from this data set that have 5 or fewer observations in the original data set. Hint: We will want to use PROC MEANS with a CLASS statement. Since we want both ID and GROUP in the new data set, they will both have to be CLASS variables. Also, remember the _FREQ_ variable that PROC MEANS creates. It will be useful in creating a data set that meets the last condition of excluding subjects with 5 or fewer observations.

4-6. Modify the program in 4-5 to include the standard deviation of WBC and RBC for each subject.

CHAPTER 5

CORRELATION AND REGRESSION

A. CORRELATION

A common statistic to show the strength of a relationship that exists between two continuous variables is called the **Pearson correlation coefficient** or just correlation coefficient (there are other **types** of correlation coefficients). The correlation coefficient is a number that ranges from -1 to +1. A positive correlation means that as values of one variable increase, values of the other variable also tend to increase. A small or zero correlation coefficient would tell us that the two variables are not linearly related. Finally, a negative correlation coefficient shows an inverse relationship between the variables: as one goes up, the other goes down. Before we discuss correlations any further, we should calculate the correlation coefficient between height and weight in one of our earlier examples. The entire program would look as follows:

```
DATA HTWT;
INPUT SEX $ HEIGHT WEIGHT;
CARDS;
M 68 155
F 61  99
F 63 115
M 70 205
M 69 170
F 65 125
M 72 220
RUN;
PROC CORR;
    VAR HEIGHT WEIGHT;
RUN;
```

In the example above, a correlation coefficient of 0.97165 was computed between the variables HEIGHT and WEIGHT. We will discuss the meaning of this in a moment.

The general form of PROC CORR is:

```
PROC CORR options;
   VAR  variables;
```

where "variables" is replaced with a list of variable names, separated by spaces. If no options are selected, a Pearson correlation coefficient is computed. As we will discuss later, a nonparametric correlation coefficient also exists (the Spearman coefficient). The option SPEARMAN will produce Spearman rank correlations. If you use the SPEARMAN option, you must use the PEARSON option as well if you also want Pearson correlations to be computed.

The CORR procedure will compute correlation coefficients between all pairs of variables in the VAR list. If the list of variables is large, this will result in a very large number of coefficients. If all you want is a number of correlations between one or more variables against another set of variables, a WITH statement is available. PROC CORR will then compute a correlation coefficient between every variable in the WITH list against every variable in the VAR list. For example, suppose we had the variables IQ and GPA (grade point average). We also recorded a student score on ten tests (TEST1-TEST10). If we only want to see the correlation between the IQ and GPA versus each of the ten tests, the syntax is:

```
PROC CORR;
   VAR IQ GPA;
   WITH TEST1-TEST10;
```

This notation can save considerable computation time as well as many trees!

Many people will ask, "How large a correlation coefficient do I need to show that two variables are correlated?" Each time PROC CORR prints a correlation coefficient, it also prints a probability associated with the coefficient. This number gives the probability of obtaining a sample correlation coefficient as large as or larger than the one obtained **by chance alone** (that is, when the variables in question actually have zero correlation). We see below the output from PROC CORR:

```
CORRELATION ANALYSIS

  2 'VAR' Variables:  HEIGHT   WEIGHT


                       Simple Statistics

  Variable              N          Mean      Std Dev          Sum

  HEIGHT                7       66.85714      3.97612     468.00000
  WEIGHT                7      155.57143     45.79613          1089

              Simple Statistics

  Variable      Minimum         Maximum

  HEIGHT       61.00000        72.00000
  WEIGHT       99.00000       220.00000

Pearson Correlation Coefficients / Prob > |R| under Ho: Rho=0 / N = 7

                     HEIGHT          WEIGHT

  HEIGHT            1.00000         0.97165
                    0.0             0.0003

  WEIGHT            0.97165         1.00000
                    0.0003          0.0
```

In this listing, we see that the correlation between height and weight is .97165 and the significance level is .0003. This small p-value indicates that it is unlikely to have obtained a correlation this large, by chance, if the sample of 7 subjects was taken from a population whose correlation was zero. Remember that this is just an example. Correlations this large are quite rare in social science data.

B. SIGNIFICANCE OF A CORRELATION COEFFICIENT

The significance of a correlation coefficient is a function of the magnitude of the correlation and the sample size. With a large number of data points, even a small correlation coefficient can be significant. For example, with 10 data points, a correlation coefficient of .63 or larger is significant (at the .05

Unix Quik Reference

File commands

To	Type
Change a filename	mv oldname newname
Copy a file	cp source destination
Delete a file	rm filename
List the files in the current directory	ls
List all files including dot files	ls -a
List files with access codes	ls -l
Print a file	lpr filename
View the print queue	lpq
View a file on-screen	more filename

Directory commands

To	Type
Create a directory	mkdir directoryname
Delete a directory	rmdir directoryname
(note all files in the directory must be deleted before you delete the directory)	
Copy a directory	cp -r sourcename destination
(note you must create the destination directory before you copy to it.)	
Change to another directory	cd directorypath
Print your working directory	pwd
Return to your home directory	cd

Filename suffixes

File type	Suffix
Assembler program source	.s
C program source	.c
F77 program source	.f
Object file	.o
Pascal program source	.p

Compilers and languages

Compiler	Command
C Compiler	cc filename
F77 Compiler	f77 filename
Vax assembler	as filename
Pascal interpreter	pi filename
Pascal program executor	px filename
Pascal interpreter and executor	pix filename
Pascal compiler	pc filename

Miscellaneous Unix commands

To	Type
Change the mode of a file	chmod mode filename
Change your password	passwd
Check your disk usage	du
Get the manual entry for a command	man command
List manual entries about keyword	man -k word
Print the date	date
Read or send mail	mail
See who is on the system	who
Send a message to another user	write username
Set terminal options	stty option ...

Vi Editor
(remember that Vi command mode will not echo most commands)

Movement commands

To Move the cursor	Type
To line number n	nG
Up one screen	B (ctrl-B)
Up one-half screen	U (ctrl-U)
Up one line	k
To the start of a line	0 (zero)
Back one word	b
Back one character	h
Forward one character	l
Forward one word	w
The end of a line	$
Down one line	j
Down one-half screen	D (ctrl-D)
Down one screen	F (ctrl-F)

Insertion commands
(use ESC to exit insert mode)

To insert	Type
Before the cursor	i
At the start of a line	I
After the Cursor	a
At the end of a line	A
On a new line below	o
On a new line above	O

Search Commands

To search	Type
Forward for string	/string
Backward for string	?string
search and replace n times	:s/old/new/n

Deletion Commands

To Delete	Type
The current character	x
The current line	dd
N words	dnw
N lines	dNd
To the end of a line	D

Change Commands
(Use ESC when finished)

To change	Type
One character	r
Characters	R
N words	cNw
N lines	cNc
To the end of a line	C

Miscellaneous Commands
(: commands end with RETURN)

To	Type
Display line numbers	:se nu
Issue a Unix command from within vi	:!command
Join two lines	J
Quit without writing	:q!
Read a file into vi	:r file
Redraw the screen	z
Repeat last command	.
Save and quit	ZZ
Undo the last command	u
Write file named new	:w'new'
Write and quit	:wq

level); with 100 data points, a correlation of .195 would be significant. Note that a negative correlation shows an equally strong relationship as a positive correlation (although the relationship is inverse). A correlation of - .40 is just as strong as one of +.40. It is important to remember that correlation indicates only the strength of a relationship—it **does not necessarily imply causality.** For example, we would probably find a high positive correlation between the number of hospitals in each of the 50 states versus the number of household pets in each state. Does this mean that pets make people sick and therefore make more hospitals necessary? Doubtful. A more plausible explanation would be that both variables (number of pets and number of hospitals) are related to population size.

Being **SIGNIFICANT** is not the same as being **IMPORTANT** or **STRONG**. That is, knowing the significance of the correlation coefficient does not tell us very much by itself. Once we know that our correlation coefficient is significantly different from zero, we need to look further to interpret the importance of this correlation. Let us digress a moment to ask what we mean by the significance of a correlation coefficient. Suppose we had a population of x and y values in which the correlation was zero. We could imagine a plot of this population as shown below:

Suppose further that we choose a small sample of 10 points from this population. In the plot below, the o's represent the x,y pairs we choose "at random" from our population.

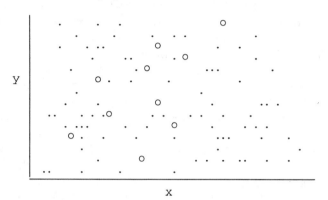

Notice that "by chance alone," we can wind up with a nonzero correlation coefficient. However, as our sample size increases, it becomes more and more **unlikely** to choose a sample at random that would have a large correlation coefficient. The lesson here is: Whenever we compute a correlation coefficient, we must find the probability of obtaining a correlation this large or larger by chance alone.

C. HOW TO INTERPRET A CORRELATION COEFFICIENT

One of the best ways of interpreting a correlation coefficient (r) is to look at the square of the coefficient (r-squared). R-squared can be interpreted as the proportion of variance in one of the variables that can be explained by variation in the other variable. As an example, our height/weight correlation is .97. Thus, r-squared is .94. We can say that 94% of the variation in weight can be explained by variation in height (or vice versa). Also, (1 - .94) or 6% of the variance of weight is due to factors other than height variation. With this interpretation in mind, if we examine a correlation coefficient of .4, we see that only .16 or 16% of the variance of one variable is explained by variation in the other.

Another consideration in the interpretation of correlation coefficients is this: **Be sure to look at a scatter plot of the data** (using PROC PLOT). It often turns out that one or two extreme data points can exert undue influence on the correlation coefficient and cause it to be much larger or smaller than expected.

An important assumption concerning correlation coefficients is that each pair of x,y data points is independent of any other pair. That is, each pair of points has to come from a different subject. Suppose we had 20 subjects and we measured two variables (say blood pressure and heart rate) on each of the 20 subjects. We could then calculate a correlation coefficient using 20 pairs of data points. Suppose instead that we made 10 measurements of blood pressure and heart rate on each subject. We cannot compute a valid correlation coefficient using all 200 data points (10 points for each of 20 subjects) because the 10 points for each subject are not independent. The best method would be to compute the mean blood pressure and heart rate for each subject and use the mean values to compute the correlation coefficient. Having done so, we'll keep in mind that we correlated mean values when we are interpreting the results.

D. LINEAR REGRESSION

Given a person's height, what would be their predicted weight? How can we best define the relationship between height and weight? By looking at the graph below we see that the relationship is approximately linear. That is, we can imagine drawing a straight line on the graph with most of the data points being only a short distance from the line. **The vertical distance from each data point to this line is called a residual.**

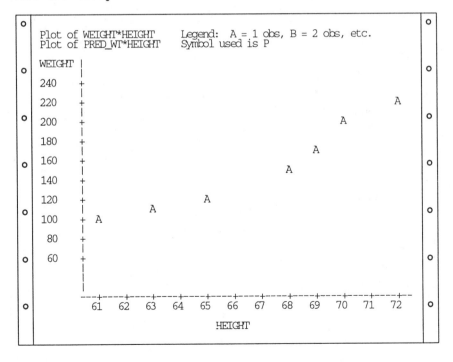

How do we determine the "**best**" straight line to fit our height/weight data? The method of **least squares** is commonly used. This method finds the line (called the **regression line**) that minimizes the **sum** of the **squared residuals**. A residual is the difference between a subject's predicted score and his/her actual score.

Using our height/weight program, we add the following PROC to give us the equation for the regression line:

```
PROC REG;
   TITLE 'REGRESSION LINE FOR HT/WT DATA';
   MODEL WEIGHT=HEIGHT;
RUN;
```

PROC REG (short for regression) has the general form

```
PROC REG;
   MODEL  dependent variable(s) = independent
   variable;
```

The output from the above procedure is shown below:

```
Model: MODEL1
Dependent Variable: WEIGHT

Analysis of Variance

                    Sum of         Mean
Source       DF    Squares        Square      F Value    Prob>F

Model        1    11880.32724   11880.32724    84.451    0.0003
Error        5      703.38705     140.67741
C Total      6    12583.71429

       Root MSE      11.86075    R-square     0.9441
       Dep Mean     155.57143    Adj R-sq     0.9329
       C.V.           7.62399
```

```
o                                                                          o
     Parameter Estimates

                      Parameter      Standard      T for H0:
o    Variable  DF     Estimate         Error     Parameter=0    Prob > |T|   o
     INTERCEP   1    -592.644578    81.54217462      -7.268        0.0008
     HEIGHT     1      11.191265     1.21780334       9.190        0.0003
```

Look first at the bottom few lines. There is an estimate for two parameters, INTERCEPT and HEIGHT. The general equation for a straight line can be written as

```
y = mx + b
```

where

```
m = slope
b = intercept.
```

(Statisticians often use **a** or b_0 for the intercept and **b** or b_1 for the slope.)

We can write the equation for the "best" straight line defined by our height/weight data as:

```
WEIGHT = (11.19)(HEIGHT) + (-592.64)
       = (11.19)(HEIGHT) - 592.64
```

Given any height, we can now predict the weight. For example, the predicted weight of a 70-inch-tall person would be:

```
WEIGHT = (11.19)(70) - 592.64 = 190.66 LBS.
```

To the right of the parameter estimates, we see columns labeled Standard Error, T for H0:Parameter=0, and Prob > |T|. The T values and the associated probabilities (Prob > |T|) test the hypothesis that the parameter is actually zero. That is, if the true slope and intercept were zero, what would the probability be of obtaining, by chance alone, a value as large as or larger than the one actually obtained? The standard error can be thought of in much the same way as the standard error of the mean. It reflects the accuracy with which we know the true slope and intercept.

In our case, the slope is 11.19 and the standard error of the slope is 1.22. We can therefore form a 95% confidence interval for the slope by taking two (approximately) standard errors above and below the mean. The 95%

confidence interval for our slope is 8.75 to 13.63. Actually, since the number of points in our example is small (n=7) we really should go to a t-table to find the number of standard errors above and below the mean for a 95% confidence interval. (This is recommended when n is less than 30.) Going to a t-table, we look under degrees of freedom (df) equal to n-1 and the level of significance (two-tail) equal to .05. The value of t for df=6, and p=.05 is 2.45. Our 95% confidence interval is then 11.19 plus or minus (2.45)(1.22)=2.99.

Inspecting the indented portion of the output, we see values for Root MSE, R-square, Dep Mean, Adj R-sq and C.V. Root MSE is the square root of the error variance. That is, it is the standard deviation of the residuals. R-square is the square of the generalized correlation coefficient. Since we have only one independent variable (HEIGHT), R- square is the square of the Pearson correlation coefficient between HEIGHT and WEIGHT and, as we discussed in the previous section, the square of the correlation coefficient tells us how much variation in the dependent variable can be accounted for by variation in the independent variable. When there is more than one independent variable, R-square will reflect the variation in the dependent variable accounted for by a linear combination of all the independent variables (see Chapter 9 for a more complete discussion). The Dep Mean is the mean of the dependent variable (WEIGHT in this case). C.V. is the coefficient of variation discussed in Chapter 2. Finally, Adj R-sq is the squared correlation coefficient corrected for the number of independent variables in the equation. This adjustment has the effect of **decreasing** the value of R^2. The difference is typically small but becomes larger and more important when dealing with multiple independent variables (see Chapter 9).

E. PARTITIONING THE TOTAL SUM OF SQUARES

The top portion of the printout presents what is called the analysis of variance table for the regression. It takes the variation in the dependent variable and breaks it out into various sources. To understand this table, think about an individual weight. This weight can be thought of as the mean weight for all individuals plus (or minus) a certain amount because the individual is taller (or shorter) than average. The regression tells us that taller people are heavier. Finally, there is a piece attributable to the fact that the prediction is less than perfect. So we start at the mean, move up or down due to the regression, and then up or down again due to error (or residual). The analysis of variance table breaks these components apart and looks at the contribution of each through the sum of squares.

The **total sum of squares** is the sum of squared deviations of each person's weight from the grand mean. This total sum of squares (SS) can be divided into the two portions; the sum of squares due to regression (or model), and the sum of squares error (sometimes called residual). The first portion reflects deviations between the PREDICTED values and the MEAN. This is called the Sum of Squares due to the **MODEL** in the output. The other portion, called the **Sum of Squares** (ERROR) in the output, reflects the deviation of each weight from the PREDICTED weight. The column labeled **Mean Square** is the **Sum of Squares** divided by the **degrees of freedom**. In our case, there are seven data points. The **total** degrees of freedom is equal to n-1 or 6. The **model** has two parameters and has 1 df. The error degrees of freedom is the **total** df minus the **model** df which gives us 5. We can think of the **Mean Square** as the respective variance (square of the standard deviation) of each of these two portions of variation. Our intuition tells us that if the deviations about the regression line are small (Error Mean Square) compared to the deviation between the predicted values and the mean (Model Mean Square) then we have a good regression line. To compare these mean squares, the ratio

$$F = \frac{\text{MEAN SQUARE MODEL}}{\text{MEAN SQUARE ERROR}}$$

is formed. The larger this ratio, the better the fit (for a given number of data points). The program prints this F value and the probability of obtaining an F this large or larger by chance alone. In the case where there is only one independent variable, the probability of the F statistic is exactly the same as the probability associated with testing for the significance of the correlation coefficient. If this probability is "large" (over .05) then our linear model is not doing a good job of describing the relationship between the variables.

F. PLOTTING THE POINTS ON THE REGRESSION LINE

To plot out height/weight data, we can use PROC PLOT as follows:

```
PROC PLOT;
   PLOT WEIGHT*HEIGHT;
```

However, we would have to draw in the regression line by hand, using the slope and intercept from PROC REG. It would be desirable to have SAS software plot the regression line (actually, the regression predicted values) for us. From SAS version 6.03 on, PROC REG allows the use of a PLOT **statement**. The form is:

```
PLOT y_variable * x_variable = symbol / options;
```

where y_variable and x_variable are the names of the variables to be plotted on the y- and x-axes respectively. The symbol can be either a single character in single quotes or a variable name whose value is to be the plotting symbol (as in PROC PLOT). There are some special "variable names" that can be used with a PLOT statement. In particular, the names PREDICTED. and RESIDUAL. (Note: the periods are part of the keyword) are used to plot predicted and residual values. A common option is OVER-LAY which is used to plot more than one graph on a single set of axes. Suppose we want to see a plot of WEIGHT versus HEIGHT in the above PROC REG example. In addition, we want to see the points on the regression line. We want the plotting symbols for the WEIGHT versus HEIGHT graph to be asterisks (*) and the symbols showing the predicted values (the regression line) to be the letter 'P'. The procedure, complete with the PLOT statement is shown next, followed by the plot:

```
PROC REG;
   MODEL WEIGHT = HEIGHT;
   PLOT PREDICTED.*HEIGHT = 'P'  WEIGHT*HEIGHT='*'
   / OVERLAY;
RUN;
```

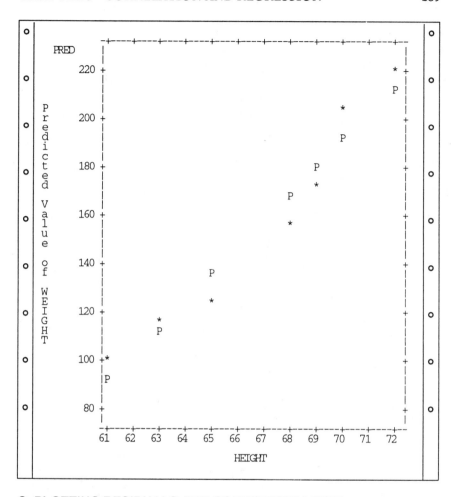

G. PLOTTING RESIDUALS AND CONFIDENCE LIMITS

Before we leave this section, we should mention that SAS software has the ability to **PLOT** several computed values other than the PREDICTED value of the dependent variable. The most useful statistics besides the predicted values are:

RESIDUAL.   The RESIDUAL (i.e., difference
                        between actual and predicted
                        values for each observation).

L95.   The Lower or Upper 95% confi-
U95.   dence limit for an individual
                             predicted value. (i.e., 95% of
                             the dependent data values would
                             be expected to be between these
                             two limits).

L95M.   The Lower or Upper 95% confi-
U95M.   dence limit for the mean of the
                             dependent variable for a given
                             value of the independent variable.

    To demonstrate some of these options in action, we will produce the
following:

    (a) A plot of the original data, predicted values, and the upper and
    lower 95% confidence limits for the mean weight.

    (b) A plot of residuals versus HEIGHT. Note: If this plot shows some
    systematic pattern (rather than random points), one could try to
    improve the original model.

Here is the program to accomplish the above requests:

```
PROC REG;
MODEL WEIGHT = HEIGHT;
      PLOT PREDICTED.*HEIGHT = 'P'
U95M.*HEIGHT='-' L95M.*HEIGHT='-'
      WEIGHT*HEIGHT='*' / OVERLAY;
PLOT RESIDUAL.*HEIGHT='o';
RUN;
```

The two graphs are shown below:

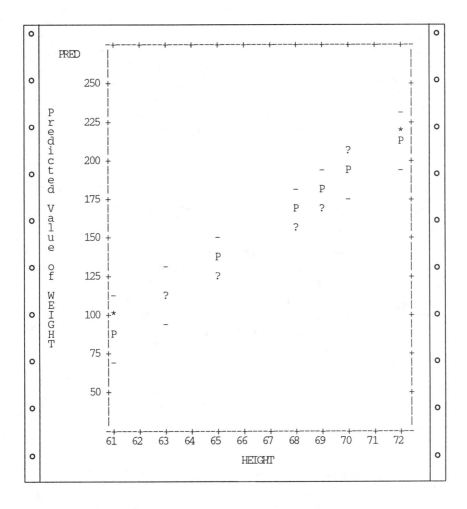

In this graph, the *'s are the original data points, the P's represent the predicted values, the -'s the upper and lower 95 percent confidence intervals about the mean weight for a given height. The question marks represent multiple observations (perhaps a raw data value and a predicted value were very close together). The next graph is discussed in the following section.

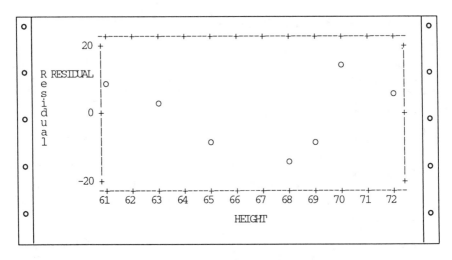

H. ADDING A QUADRATIC TERM TO THE REGRESSION EQUATION

The plot of residuals above suggests that a second order term (height squared) might improve the model since the points do not seem random, but rather, form a curve that could be fit by a second order equation. Although this chapter deals mostly with **linear** regression, let us show you quickly how you might explore this possible quadratic relationship between height and weight. First, we need to add a line in the original data step to compute a variable that represents the height squared. After the INPUT statement, include a line such as the following:

```
HEIGHT2 = HEIGHT * HEIGHT;
```

Next, write your MODEL and PLOT statements:

```
PROC REG;
   MODEL WEIGHT = HEIGHT HEIGHT2;
   PLOT RESIDUAL.*HEIGHT='o';
RUN;
```

When you run this model, you will get an r-squared of .9743, an improvement over the .9441 obtained with the linear model. A look at the residual plot below shows that the distribution of the residuals is more random than the earlier plot. A caution or two is in order here. First, remember that this is an example with a very small data set and that the original correlation is quite high. Second, although it is possible to also enter cubic terms, etc., one should keep in mind that results need to be interpretable. Sometimes, a simple model is preferred even though the "fit" may not be quite as good as one with more (possibly uninterpretabel) terms.

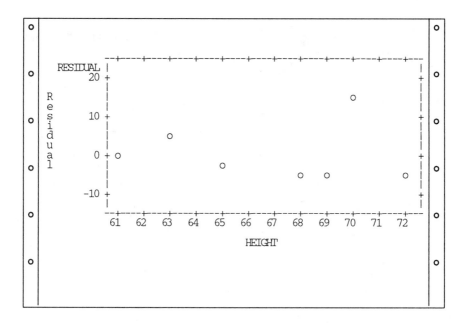

I. TRANSFORMING DATA

Another regression example is given here to demonstrate some additional steps that may be necessary when doing regression. Shown below are data that were collected on 10 people:

SUBJECT	DRUG DOSE	HEART RATE
1	2	60
2	2	58
3	4	63
4	4	62
5	8	67
6	8	65
7	16	70
8	16	70
9	32	74
10	32	73

Let's write a SAS program to define this collection of data and to plot drug dose by heart rate.

```
DATA;
INPUT DOSE HR;
CARDS;
2 60
    .
    .
    .
32 73
RUN;
PROC PLOT;
    PLOT HR*DOSE;
RUN;
PROC REG;
    MODEL HR = DOSE;
RUN;
```

The resulting graph and the PROC REG output are shown below:

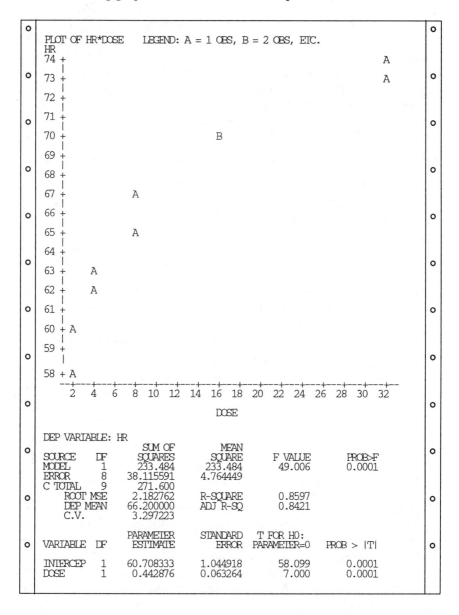

```
PLOT OF HR*DOSE    LEGEND: A = 1 OBS, B = 2 OBS, ETC.
HR
74 +                                              A
   |
73 +                                              A
   |
72 +
   |
71 +
   |
70 +                        B
   |
69 +
   |
68 +
   |
67 +        A
   |
66 +
   |
65 +        A
   |
64 +
   |
63 +    A
   |
62 +    A
   |
61 +
   |
60 + A
   |
59 +
   |
58 + A
   --+---+---+---+---+---+---+---+---+---+---+---+---+---+---+---+-
     2   4   6   8   10  12  14  16  18  20  22  24  26  28  30  32
                                DOSE
```

```
DEP VARIABLE: HR
                  SUM OF          MEAN
SOURCE    DF      SQUARES         SQUARE     F VALUE      PROB>F
MODEL     1       233.484         233.484    49.006       0.0001
ERROR     8       38.115591       4.764449
C TOTAL   9       271.600
      ROOT MSE    2.182762        R-SQUARE   0.8597
      DEP MEAN    66.200000       ADJ R-SQ   0.8421
      C.V.        3.297223

                  PARAMETER       STANDARD   T FOR H0:
VARIABLE  DF      ESTIMATE        ERROR      PARAMETER=0   PROB > |T|

INTERCEP  1       60.708333       1.044918   58.099        0.0001
DOSE      1       0.442876        0.063264   7.000         0.0001
```

Either by clinical judgment or by careful inspection of the graph, we decide that the relationship is not linear. We see an approximately equal increase in heart rate each time the dose is doubled. Therefore, if we plot log dose against heart rate we can expect a linear relationship. SAS software has a number of built-in functions such as logarithms and trigonometric functions. These functions are described in the **SAS Language: Reference, Version 6,** and in the **SAS Language Guide for Personal Computers,** Version 6.03. We can write mathematical equations to define new variables by placing these statements between the INPUT and CARDS statements. In SAS programs, we represent addition, subtraction, multiplication, and division by the symbols +,-,*, and /, respectively. Exponentiation is written as **. To create a new variable which is the log of dose, we write

```
DATA;
INPUT DOSE HR;
LDOSE = LOG(DOSE);
CARDS;
```

where LOG is a SAS function that yields the natural (base e) logarithm of whatever value is in the parentheses.

We can now plot log dose versus heart rate and compute a new regression line.

```
PROC PLOT;
   PLOT HR*LDOSE;
PROC REG;
   MODEL HR=LDOSE;
```

Output from the above statements is shown on the following page. Approach transforming variables with caution. Keep in mind that when a variable is transformed, one should not refer to the variable as in the untransformed state. That is, don't refer to the "log of dosage" as "dosage." Some variables are frequently transformed: income, sizes of groups, and magnitudes of earthquakes are usually presented as logs, or in some other transformation.

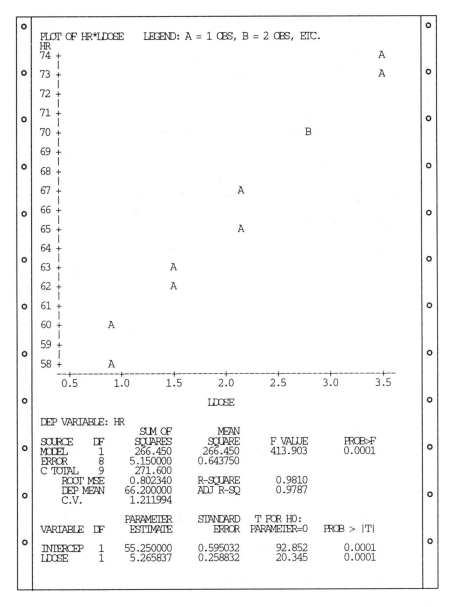

```
PLOT OF HR*LDOSE    LEGEND: A = 1 OBS, B = 2 OBS, ETC.
HR
74 +                                                       A
   |
73 +                                                       A
   |
72 +
   |
71 +
   |
70 +                                          B
   |
69 +
   |
68 +
   |
67 +                              A
   |
66 +
   |
65 +                              A
   |
64 +
   |
63 +                  A
   |
62 +                  A
   |
61 +
   |
60 +          A
   |
59 +
   |
58 +          A
   --+---------+---------+---------+---------+---------+---------+--
     0.5       1.0       1.5       2.0       2.5       3.0       3.5
                                  LDOSE
```

DEP VARIABLE: HR

SOURCE	DF	SUM OF SQUARES	MEAN SQUARE	F VALUE	PROB>F
MODEL	1	266.450	266.450	413.903	0.0001
ERROR	8	5.150000	0.643750		
C TOTAL	9	271.600			
ROOT MSE		0.802340	R-SQUARE	0.9810	
DEP MEAN		66.200000	ADJ R-SQ	0.9787	
C.V.		1.211994			

VARIABLE	DF	PARAMETER ESTIMATE	STANDARD ERROR	T FOR H0: PARAMETER=0	PROB > |T|
INTERCEP	1	55.250000	0.595032	92.852	0.0001
LDOSE	1	5.265837	0.258832	20.345	0.0001

Notice that the data points are now closer to the regression line. The MEAN SQUARE ERROR term is smaller and R-SQUARE is larger, confirming our conclusion that dose versus heart rate fits a logarithmic curve better than a linear one.

J. COMPUTING WITHIN-SUBJECT SLOPES

There are times when we need to compute slopes for each subject (on multiple measurements) or slopes for a subset of the entire population. An example would be a study where each subject was assigned to group A or group B. We then measured his or her performance on a test three times and the rate of learning (the slope of the score versus time curve) was compared between the two groups. Prior to version 6, this was a difficult problem to solve. Thanks to the response of the SAS Institute to user requests, we can now output a data set containing slopes with PROC REG. The procedure option, OUTEST=datasetname, will create a data set containing all variables in the BY statement as well as the slopes (coefficients) of each of the independent variables in the model. To illustrate, here is a program to analyze the study design just described:

```
DATA TEST;
INPUT ID GROUP $ TIME SCORE;
CARDS;
1 A 1 2
1 A 2 5
1 A 3 7
2 A 1 4
2 A 2 6
2 A 3 9
3 B 1 8
3 B 2 6
3 B 3 2
4 B 1 8
4 B 2 7
4 B 3 3
RUN;
PROC REG OUTEST=SLOPES DATA=TEST;
   BY ID GROUP;
   MODEL SCORE = TIME / NOPRINT;
RUN;
PROC TTEST DATA=SLOPES;
   CLASS GROUP;
   VAR TIME;
RUN;
```

```
                               Data Set SLOPES

    ID  GROUP  _MODEL_    _TYPE_    _DEPVAR_    _RMSE_    INTERCEP   TIME  SCORE

     1   A     MODEL1     PARMS      SCORE      0.40825   -0.3333    2.5   -1
     2   A     MODEL1     PARMS      SCORE      0.40825    1.3333    2.5   -1
     3   B     MODEL1     PARMS      SCORE      0.81650   11.3333   -3.0   -1
     4   B     MODEL1     PARMS      SCORE      1.22474   11.0000   -2.5   -1

    TTEST PROCEDURE

    Variable: TIME

    GROUP   N         Mean       Std Dev    Std Error     Minimum        Maximum
    ---------------------------------------------------------------------------
    A       2   2.50000000   0.00000000   0.00000000    2.50000000     2.50000000
    B       2  -2.75000000   0.35355339   0.25000000   -3.00000000    -2.50000000

    Variances         T        DF     Prob>|T|
    ---------------------------------------------
    Unequal      21.0000      1.0      0.0303
    Equal        21.0000      2.0      0.0023

    For H0: Variances are equal, F' = 9999.99  DF = (1,1)  Prob>F' = 0.0001
```

The data set SLOPES, produced by PROC REG, and the results from the t-test are shown above. The variable TIME represents the slope of the SCORE by TIME graph (i.e., the coefficient of TIME). The reason that the GROUP variable was included in the BY statement was to include it in the output data set. One could also include other variables where each subject can have only one value (such as SEX). Since slope in this example is a computation over observations for an individual, any other variable which could have different values for an individual cannot be used. The dependent variable in each model is given a value of -1.

PROBLEMS

5-1. Given the following data:

X	Y	Z
1	3	15
7	13	7
8	12	5
3	4	14
4	7	10

(a) Write a SAS program and compute the Pearson correlation coefficient between X and Y; X and Z. What is the significance of each?

(b) Change the correlation request to produce a correlation matrix, i.e., the correlation coefficient between each variable against every other variable.

5-2 Given the following data:

AGE	SYSTOLIC BLOOD PRESSURE
15	116
20	120
25	130
30	132
40	150
50	148

How much of the variance of SBP (systolic blood pressure) can be explained by the fact that there is variability in AGE? (Use SAS to compute the correlation between SBP and AGE.)

5-3. From the data for X and Y in Problem 5-1:

(a) Use SAS to compute a regression line (Y on X). (b) What is the slope and intercept? (c) Are they significantly different from zero?

5-4. Using the data from 5-1, compute three new variables LX, LY, and LZ, which are the natural logs of the original values. Compute a correlation matrix for the three new variables.

5-5. Generate:

(a) a plot of Y vs. X (data from 5-1);

(b) a plot of the regression line and the original data on the same set of axes.

5-6. Given the data set:

COUNTY	POP	HOSPITAL	FIRE_CO	RURAL
1	35	1	2	YES
2	88	5	8	NO
3	5	0	1	YES
4	55	3	3	YES
5	75	4	5	NO
6	125	5	8	NO
7	225	7	9	YES
8	500	10	11	NO

(a) Write a SAS program to create a SAS data set of the above data.

(b) Run PROC UNIVARIATE to check the distributions for the variables POP, HOSPITAL, and FIRE_CO.

(c) Compute a correlation matrix for the variables POP, HOSPITAL, and FIRE_CO. Produce both Pearson and Spearman correlations. Which is more appropriate? Why?

(d) Recode POP, HOSPITAL, and FIRE_CO so that they each have two levels (use a median cut or a value somewhere near the 50th percentile). Compute crosstabulations between the variable RURAL and the recoded variables.

5-7. What's wrong with this program?

```
1       DATA MANY-ERR;
2       INPUT X Y Z;
3       IF X LE 0 THEN X=1;
4       IF Y LE 0 THEN Y=1;
5       IF Z LE 0 THEN Z=1;
6       LOGX=LOG(X);
7       LOGY=LOG(Y);
8       LOGZ=LOG(Z);
9       CARDS;
        1 2 3
        . 7 8
        4 . 10
        7 8 11
10      PROC CORR / PEARSON SPEARMAN;
11         VAR X-LOGZ;
```

CHAPTER 6

T-TESTS AND NONPARAMETRIC COMPARISONS

A. T-TEST: TESTING DIFFERENCES BETWEEN TWO MEANS

A common experimental design is to randomly assign subjects to a treatment or a control group and then measure one or more variables that would be hypothesized to be affected by the treatment. In order to determine whether the means of the treatment and control groups are significantly different, we set up what is called a **"null hypothesis"** (H_0). It states that the treatment and control groups would have the same mean if we repeated the experiment a large (infinite) number of times and that the differences in any one trial are attributable to the luck of the draw in assigning subjects to treatment and control groups. An alternative hypotheses (H_A) to the null hypothesis are that one particular mean will be greater than the other (called a 1-tailed test) **or** that the two means will be different, but the researcher cannot say *a priori* which will be greater (called a 2-tailed test). The researcher can specify either of these two alternative hypotheses. When the data have been collected, a procedure called the t-test is used to determine the probability that the difference in the means that is observed is due to chance. The lower the likelihood that the difference is due to chance, the greater the likelihood that the difference is due to there being real differences between treatment and control groups. The following example will demonstrate a SAS program that performs a t-test.

Students are randomly assigned to a control or treatment group (where a drug is administered). Their response times to a stimulus is then measured. The times are as follows:

(Response time in milliseconds)

CONTROL	TREATMENT
80	100
93	103
83	104
89	99
98	102

Is the mean of the treatment group significantly different from the mean of the control group? A quick calculation shows the mean of the control group to be 89.8 and the mean of the treatment group to be 101.6. You may recall the discussion in Chapter 2 about the standard error of the mean. When we use a sample to estimate the population mean, the standard error of the mean reflects how accurately we can estimate the population mean. As you will see when we write a SAS program to analyze this experiment, the standard error of the control mean is .97 and the standard error of the treatment mean is .93. Since the means are 11.8 units apart, even if each mean is several standard errors away from its true population mean, they would still be significantly different from each other. There are some assumptions that must be met before we can apply this test. First, the two groups must be independent. This will be ensured with our method of random assignment. Second, the theoretical distribution of sampling means should be normally distributed (this will be ensured if the sample size is sufficiently large). And third, the variances of the two groups should be approximately equal. This last assumption is checked automatically each time a t-test is computed by the SAS system. The SAS t-test output contains t-values and probabilities for both the case of equal group variances and unequal group variances. We will see later how to test whether the data are normally distributed. Finally, when the t-test assumptions are not met, there are other procedures that can be used. These will be demonstrated later in this chapter.

It's time now to write a program to describe our data and to request a t-test. What are our variables? What information have we collected on each subject? We know which group each person belongs to and what his response time is. The program can thus be written as follows:

```
DATA;
INPUT GROUP $ TIME;
CARDS;
C  80
C  93
C  83
C  89
C  98
T  100
T  103
T  104
T  99
T  102                                          (cont.)
```

```
RUN;                    (Continued from previous page)
PROC TTEST;
    CLASS GROUP;
    VAR TIME;
RUN;
```

PROC TTEST has two parts. Following the word CLASS is the **independent** variable—the variable that identifies the two groups of subjects. In our case, the variable GROUP has values of C (for the control group) and T (for the treatment group).

The variable or variable list that follows the word VAR identifies the **dependent** variable(s), in our case, TIME. When more than one **dependent** variable is listed, a **separate** t-test is computed for each dependent variable in the list.

Look at the TTEST output below:

```
TTEST PROCEDURE

Variable: TIME

GROUP   N         Mean     Std Dev    Std Error       Minimum        Maximum
----------------------------------------------------------------------------
C       5   88.6000000  7.30068490  3.26496554   80.00000000    98.0000000
T       5  101.6000000  2.07364414  0.92736185   99.00000000   104.0000000

Variances        T       DF     Prob|T|
------------------------------------------
Unequal     -3.8302     4.6      0.0145
Equal       -3.8302     8.0      0.0050

For H0: Variances are equal, F' = 12.40  DF = (4,4)  ProbF' = 0.0318
```

We see the mean value of TIME for the control and treatment groups, along with their corresponding standard deviations and standard errors. Below this are two sets of t-values, degrees of freedom, and probabilities. One is valid if we have equal variances, the other if we have unequal variances. You will usually find these values very close unless the variances differ widely. The bottom line gives us the probability that the variances are unequal due to chance. If this probability is small (say less than .05) then we are going to reject the hypothesis that the variances are equal. We then use the t-value and probability labeled UNEQUAL. If the PROB F' value is greater than .05, use the t-value and probability for equal variances.

In this example, we look at the bottom of the t-test output and see that the F ratio (larger variance divided by the smaller variance) is 12.40. The probability of obtaining a ratio this large or larger by chance alone is 0.0318. That is, if the two samples came from populations with equal variance, there is a small probability (.0318) of obtaining a ratio of our sample variances of 12.40 or larger by chance. We should therefore use the t-value appropriate for groups with unequal variance. The rule of thumb here is to use the t-value, df, and probability labeled **unequal** if the probability from the F-test is **less** than .05.

B. RANDOM ASSIGNMENT OF SUBJECTS

In our discussion of t-tests, we said that we randomly assigned subjects to either a treatment or control group. This is actually a very important step in our experiment and we can use SAS software to provide us with a method for doing this.

We could take our volunteers one by one, flip a coin, and decide to place all the "heads" in our treatment group and the "tails" in our control group. This is acceptable, but we would prefer a method that ensures an equal number of subjects in each group. One method would be to place all the subjects' names in a hat, mix them up, and pull out half the names for treatment subjects and the others for controls. This is essentially what we will do in our SAS program. The key to the program is the SAS random number function.

The function UNIFORM(0) will generate a pseudorandom number in the interval from 0 to 1. The zero argument of the UNIFORM function is called the **seed**. This is a number that is used the first time the function is called, to start the random number series. A zero argument instructs the SAS program to use a value from the internal **time clock** as the seed. Using the time clock as a seed will generate a different series of random numbers each time you run the program. You may want to supply your own seed instead. It should be a five-, six, or seven-digit odd number. Each time you run the program with your own seed, you will generate the **same series of random numbers**. This is sometimes desirable, but as a rule, use a zero seed unless you have a specific need for a repeatable series of random numbers. SAS software has another uniform random number function called RANUNI which is used in the same way as UNIFORM except that the restrictions for the **seed** do not apply. The SAS manuals prefer RANUNI over UNIFORM; however, either will do for the type of applications shown here. We will create a SAS data set with our subjects' names (or we could use subject numbers instead) and assign a random number to each subject. We can then split the group in half (or in any number of subgroups) using a special feature of PROC RANK. Here is the program:

```
PROC FORMAT;
   VALUE GRPFMT 0='CONTROL' 1='TREATMENT';
DATA RANDOM;
INPUT SUBJ NAME $20.;
GROUP=UNIFORM(0);
CARDS;
1 CODY
2 SMITH
3 HELM
4 BERNHOLC
   etc.
PROC RANK GROUPS=2;
   VAR GROUP;
RUN;
PROC SORT;
   BY NAME;
RUN;
PROC PRINT;
   TITLE 'SUBJECT GROUP ASSIGNMENTS';
   ID NAME;
   VAR SUBJ GROUP;
   FORMAT GROUP GRPFMT.;
RUN;
```

The key to this program is the UNIFORM function, which assigns a random number from 0 to 1 to each subject. The GROUPS=2 option of PROC RANK divides the subjects into two groups (0 and 1), depending on the value of the random variable GROUP. Values below the median become

0; those above the median become 1. The GRPFMT format assigns the labels "CONTROL" and "TREATMENT" using values of 0 and 1, respectively. We can use this program to assign our subjects to any number of groups by changing the "GROUPS=" option of PROC RANK to indicate the desired number of groups. Sample output from this program is shown below:

```
SUBJECT GROUP ASSIGNMENTS

   NAME    SUBJ GROUP

BERNHOLC   4   CONTROL
CODY       1   CONTROL
HELM       3   TREATMENT
SMITH      2   TREATMENT
```

Although this may seem like a lot of work just to make random assignments of subjects, we recommend that this or an equivalent procedure be used for assigning subjects to groups. Other methods such as assigning every other person to the treatment group can result in unsuspected bias.

C. TWO INDEPENDENT SAMPLES: DISTRIBUTION FREE TESTS

There are times when the assumptions for using a t-test are not met. One common problem is that the data are not normally distributed. For example, suppose we collected the following numbers in a psychology experiment that measured the response to a stimulus:

0 6 0 5 7 6 9 4 8 0 7 0 5 6 6 0 0

A frequency distribution would look like this:

```
X
X
X      X
X      X
X      XXX
X      XXXXXX
----------------------
0123456789
```

What we are seeing is probably due to a threshold effect. The response is either zero (the stimulus is not detected) or, once the stimulus is detected, the average response is about 6. Data of this sort would artificially inflate the standard deviation (and thus the standard error) of the sample and make the t-test more conservative. However, a nonparametric test (a test that does not assume a normal distribution of data) would be safer to use.

Another common problem is that the data values may only represent ordered categories. Scales like 1=very mild, 2=mild, 3=moderate, 4=strong, 5=severe, etc. reflect the strength of a response, but we cannot say that a score of 4 (strong) is worth twice the score of 2 (mild). Scales like these are referred to as **ordinal** scales. (Most of the scales we have been using until now have been **interval** or **ratio** **scales**.) We will need a nonparametric test to analyze differences in central tendencies for ordinal data. Finally, for very small samples, nonparametric tests are often more appropriate since assumptions concerning distributions are hard to determine.

SAS software provides us with several nonparametric two-sample tests. Among these are the Wilcoxon rank-sum test (equivalent to the Mann-Whitney U-test) for two samples.

Consider the following experiment. We have two groups, A and B. Group B has been treated with a drug to prevent tumor formation. Both groups are exposed to a chemical that will encourage tumor growth. The masses (in grams) of tumors in groups A and B are

```
A: 3.1 2.2 1.7 2.7 2.5
B: 0.0 0.0 1.0 2.3
```

Are there any differences in tumor mass between groups A and B? We will choose a nonparametric test for this experiment because of the absence of a normal distribution and the small sample sizes involved. The Wilcoxon test first puts all the data (groups A and B) in increasing order (with special provisions for ties), retaining the group identity. In our experiment we have:

```
MASS     0.0 0.0 1.0 1.7 2.2 2.3 2.5 2.7 3.1
GROUP     B   B   B   A   A   B   A   A   A
RANK     1.5 1.5  3   4   5   6   7   8   9
```

The sums of ranks for the A's and B's are then computed. We have:

```
SUM RANKS A = 4+5+7+8+9 = 33
SUM RANKS B = 1.5+1.5+3+6 = 12
```

If there were smaller tumors in group B, we would expect the B's to be at the lower end of the rank ordering and therefore have a smaller sum of ranks than the A's. Is the sum of ranks for group A sufficiently larger than the sum of ranks for group B, so that the probability of the difference occurring by chance alone is small (less than .05)? The Wilcoxon test gives us the probability that the difference in rank sums that we obtained occurred by chance.

For even moderate sample sizes, the Wilcoxon test is almost as powerful as its parametric equivalent, the t-test. Thus, if there is a question concerning distributions or if the data are really ordinal, you should not hesitate to use the Wilcoxon test instead of the t-test.

The program to analyze this experiment using the Wilcoxon test is shown below:

```
DATA;
INPUT GROUP $ MASS @@;
CARDS;
A 3.1 A 2.2 A 1.7 A 2.7 A 2.5
B 0.0 B 0.0 B 1.0 B 2.3
PROC NPAR1WAY WILCOXON;
   CLASS GROUP;
   VAR MASS;
RUN;
```

First, we have introduced a new feature of the INPUT statement. Normally, when a SAS program has finished reading an observation, it goes to a new line of data for the next observation. The two '@' signs at the end of the INPUT statement instruct the program to "**hold the line**" and not automatically go to a new line of data for the next observation. This way, we can put data from several observations on one line. By the way, a single @ sign will hold the line for another INPUT statement but will go to the next line when the CARDS statement is encountered. See chapter 10 for more details on the use of single and double trailing @ signs.

PROC NPAR1WAY performs the nonparametric tests. The options WILCOXON and MEDIAN request these particular tests. Our example above shows a request for a Wilcoxon rank sum test. The CLASS and VAR statements are identical to the CLASS and VAR statements of the t-test procedure.

The output from the NPAR1WAY procedure follows:

```
N P A R 1 W A Y   P R O C E D U R E

Wilcoxon Scores (Rank Sums) for Variable MASS
Classified by Variable GROUP

                          Sum of      Expected      Std Dev        Mean
        GROUP      N      Scores      Under H0      Under H0       Score

        A          5       33.0         25.0      4.06543697    6.60000000
        B          4       12.0         20.0      4.06543697    3.00000000
Average Scores were used for Ties
Wilcoxon 2-Sample Test (Normal Approximation)
(with Continuity Correction of .5)

S= 12.0000         Z= -1.84482          Prob |Z| =    0.0651

T-Test approx. Significance =      0.1023

Kruskal-Wallis Test (Chi-Square Approximation)
CHISQ=  3.8723           DF=  1          Prob CHISQ=       0.0491
```

The sum of ranks for groups A and B are shown, as well as their expected values. The probability that the medians differ by chance alone is .0651.

D. ONE-TAILED VERSUS TWO-TAILED TESTS

When we conduct an experiment like the tumor example in Section B, we have a choice in the way we state the alternate hypothesis. In our example, the null hypothesis was that the mass of tumors was the same for groups A and B. The alternative hypothesis was that groups A and B were not the same. We would reject the null hypothesis if A>B or B>A. This type of hypothesis requires a two-tailed test. If we were using a t-test, we would have to consider absolute values of t greater than the critical value. If our alpha level is .05 then we have .025 from each **tail** of the t-distribution.

In many research studies, the researcher has a reasonable expectation of the results. If we are testing a new drug against a placebo, we **expect** the drug to be better. If we are testing whether people prefer blue widgets to red widgets, then we probably do **not** have an expectation either way. Whenever a directional alternative hypothesis (e.g., B>A) can be justified from the **substantive issues** in the study, then a one-tailed test can be used. With a one-tailed test, the 5% of the curve associated with the .05 alpha level can all be located in one tail, which increases the power of the study (i.e., makes it more likely to find a significant difference when, in fact, one exists.) If our tumor example had been stated as a one-tailed test, we could have divided the p-value by 2, giving p=.0331 for the Wilcoxon test probability. **The decision to do a one-tailed test should be based on an understanding of the theoretical considerations of the study and not as a method of reducing the p-value below the .05 level.**

E. PAIRED T-TESTS (RELATED SAMPLES)

Our t-test example in section A had subjects randomly assigned to a control or treatment group. Therefore, the groups could be considered to be independent.

There are many experimental situations where each subject receives both treatments. For example, each subject in the earlier example could have been measured in the absence of the drug (control value) and after having received the drug (treatment value). The response times for the control and treatment groups would no longer be independent. We would expect a person with a very short response time in the control situation to also have a short response time after taking the drug (compared to the other people who took the drug). We would expect a positive correlation between the control and treatment values.

Our regular t-test cannot be used here since the groups are no longer independent. A variety of the t-test referred to as a **paired t-test** is used instead. The differences between the treatment and control times are computed for each subject. If most of the differences are positive, we suspect that the drug lengthens reaction time. If most are about zero, the drug has no effect. The paired t-test computes a mean and standard error of the **differences** and determines the probability that the absolute value of the mean difference was greater than zero by chance alone.

Before we program this problem, it should be mentioned that this would be a very poor experiment. What if the response time increased because the subjects became tired? If each subject were measured twice, without being given a drug, would the second value be different because of factors other than the treatment? One way to control for this problem is to take half of the subjects and measure their drug response time first and the control value later, after the drug has worn off. We will see a better way to devise experiments to handle this problem in Chapter 8 (Repeated Measures Designs).

Experiments that measure the same subject under different conditions are sometimes called repeated measures experiments. They do have the problem just stated: one measurement might affect the next. However, if this can be controlled, it is much easier to show treatment effects with smaller samples, compared to a regular t-test.

If we took two independent groups of people, we would find that within the control group or the treatment group there would be variation in response times because of individual differences. However, if we measure the same subject under two conditions, even if that person has much longer or shorter response times than the other subjects, the **difference** between the scores should approximate the difference for other subjects. Thus, each subject acts as his own control and therefore controls some of the natural variation between subjects.

The SAS system does not include a paired t-test as part of PROC TTEST. We will need to compute the difference scores ourselves and then use PROC MEANS to compute the probability that the difference is significantly different from zero.

Our data are arranged like this:

SUBJECT	CONTROL VALUE	TREATMENT VALUE
1	90	95
2	87	92
3	100	104
4	80	89
5	95	101
6	90	105

NOTE: Subjects 1-3 were measured in control/treatment order, subjects 4-6 were measured in treatment/control order.

The program is written as follows:

```
DATA;
INPUT CTIME TTIME;
DIFF=TTIME-CTIME;                                    (cont.)
```

```
CARDS;                    (Continued from previous page)
90  95
87  92
100 104
80  89
95  101
90  105
PROC MEANS N MEAN STDERR T PRT;
    VAR DIFF;
RUN;
```

The variable names CTIME and TTIME were chosen to represent the response times in the control and treatment conditions, respectively. For each observation, we are calculating the difference between the treatment and control times, by creating a new variable called DIFF.

PROC MEANS is followed by a list of options. N, MEAN, and STDERR cause the number of subjects, the mean, and the standard error of the mean to be printed. In our case, these statistics will be computed for the variable DIFF. The options T and PRT will give us the t-value and its associated probability, testing if the variable (DIFF) is significantly different from zero. The output is shown below:

```
Analysis Variable : DIFF

N Obs  N       Mean      Std Error            T  Prob|T|
-----------------------------------------------------------
   6   6   7.3333333   1.6865481    4.3481318   0.0074
-----------------------------------------------------------
```

In this example, the mean difference is positive (7.3) and the probability of the difference occurring by chance is .0074. We can state that response times are longer under the drug treatment compared to the control values. Had the mean difference been negative, we would state that response times were shorter under the drug treatment, because DIFF was computed as treatment time minus control time.

PROBLEMS:

6-1. The following table shows the time (in minutes) for subjects to feel relief from headache pain:

(Cure time in minutes)

ASPIRIN	TYLENOL
40	35
42	37
48	42
35	22
62	38
35	29

Write a SAS program to read these data and perform a t-test. Is either product significantly quicker than the other (at the .05 level)?

6-2. Using the same data as 6-1, perform a Wilcoxon rank-sum test.

6-3. In another study, 4 subjects are given Drug A for the first occurence of headache and then Drug B the next time they have a headache. Four other subjects are given Drug B first, and Drug A for their second headache. Again, the "cure" time is recorded. What type of test will you use to test if one drug is faster than the other? Below are some made-up data. Write the SAS statements to run the appropriate analysis.

SUBJECT	DRUG A	DRUG B
1	20	18
2	40	36
3	30	30
4	45	46
5	19	15
6	27	22
7	32	29
8	26	25

*6-4. A researcher wants to randomly assign 30 patients to one of three treatment groups. Each subject has a unique subject number (SUBJ). Write a SAS program to assign these subjects to a treatment group.

6-5. What's wrong with this program?

```
1      DATA DRUGSTDY;
2      INPUT SUBJ 1-3 DRUG 4 HEARTRATE 5-7 SBP 8-10
3          DBP 11-13;
4      AVEBP=DBP + (SBP-DBP)/3;
5      CARDS;
        0011064130080
        0021068120076
        0031070156090
        0042080140080
        0052088180092
        0062098178094
6      PROC NPAR1WAY WILCOXON MEDIAN;
7          TITLE 'MY DRUG STUDY';
8          CLASS DRUG;
9          VAR HEARTRATE SBP DBP AVEBP;
10     PROC T-TEST;
11         CLASS DRUG;
12         VAR HEARTRATE SBP DBP AVEBP;
13         RUN;
```

CHAPTER 7

ANALYSIS OF VARIANCE

A. ONE-WAY ANALYSIS OF VARIANCE

We have analyzed experiments with two groups (control and treatment) using a t-test. Now, what if we have more than two groups? Take the situation where we have three treatment groups: A, B, and C. It was once the practice to use t-tests with this design, comparing A with B, A with C, and B with C. With four groups (ABCD) we would have comparisons AB, AC, AD, BC, BD, and CD. As the number of groups increases, the number of possible comparisons grows rapidly. What is wrong with this procedure of multiple comparisons? Any time we show the means of two groups to be significantly different, we state a probability that the difference occurred by chance alone. Suppose we make 20 multiple comparisons and each comparison is made at the .05 level. Even if there are no **real** differences between the groups, we expect to find one comparison significant at the .05 level. (The actual probability of at least one significant difference by chance alone is .64.) The more comparisons that are made, the greater the likelihood of finding a pair of means significantly different by chance alone.

The method used today for comparisons of three or more groups is called Analysis of Variance (**ANOVA**). This method has the advantage of testing whether there are **any** differences between the groups with a single probability associated with the test. The hypothesis tested is that **all** groups have the same mean. Before we present an example, we should note that there are several **assumptions** that should be met before an analysis of variance is used. Essentially, the same assumptions for a t-test need to be met when conducting an ANOVA. That is, we must have **independence** between groups (unless a **repeated measures design** is used); the sampling distributions of sample means must be **normally distributed**; and the groups should have nearly equal variances (called **homogeneity of variance**). The analysis of variance technique is said to be **robust**. This is a term used by statisticians which means that the assumptions can be violated somewhat and the technique can still be used. So, if the distributions are not perfectly normal or if the variances are unequal, we may still use analysis of variance. The judgment of how serious a violation to permit is subjective, and, if in doubt, see your local statistician. Winer has an excellent discussion of the effect of homogeneity of variance violations and the use of analysis of variance. Balanced designs (those with the same number of subjects under each of the experimental conditions) are preferred over unbalanced designs, especially when the group variances are unequal.

Consider the following experiment:

We randomly assign 15 subjects to three treatment groups X,Y, and Z (with 5 subjects per treatment). Each of the three groups has received a different method of speed reading instruction. A reading test is given and the number of words per minute is recorded for each subject. The following data are collected:

X	Y	Z
700	480	500
850	460	550
820	500	480
640	570	600
920	580	610

The null hypothesis is that mean(X) = mean(Y) = mean(Z). The alternative hypothesis is that the means are not all equal. The means of groups X,Y, and Z are 786, 518, and 548, respectively. How do we know if the means obtained are different because of differences in the reading programs or because of random sampling error? By chance, the five subjects we choose for group X might be faster readers than those chosen for groups Y and Z.

In our example, the mean reading speed of all 15 subjects (called the GRAND MEAN) is 617.33. Now, we normally think of a subject's score as whatever it happens to be; 580 is 580. But we could also think of 580 as being 37.33 points lower than the grand mean (580-617.33 = -37.33).

We might now ask the question, "What causes scores to vary from the grand mean?" In this example, there are two possible sources of variation. The first source of variation is the training method (X,Y, or Z). If X is a far superior method, then we would expect subjects in X to have higher scores, in general, than subjects in Y or Z. When we say "higher scores in general" we mean something quite specific. We mean that being a member of group X causes one's score to increase by so many points.

The second source of variation is due to differences among individuals. Therefore, within each group there will be variation. We can think of a formula to represent each person's score:

| THE PERSON'S SCORE | = | THE GRAND MEAN | + | AN ADDITION OR SUBTRACTION FROM THE GRAND MEAN DEPENDING ON WHICH GROUP THE PERSON IS IN. | + | AN ADDITION OR SUBTRACTION DEPENDING ON THE INDIVIDUAL'S VARIABILITY. |

Now that we have the ideas down, let's return briefly to the mathematics.

It turns out that the mathematics are simplified if, instead of looking at differences in scores from the grand mean, we look instead at the square of the differences. The sum of all the squared deviations is called the total SUM OF SQUARES or **SS total**.

To be sure this is clear, we will calculate the total SS in our example. Subtracting the grand mean (617.33) from each score, squaring the differences (usually called **deviations**), and adding up all the results, we have:

$$\text{SS total} = (700\text{-}617.33)^2 + (850\text{-}617.33)^2 + \ldots + (610\text{-}617.33)^2$$

As we mentioned earlier, we can separate the total variation into two parts: one due to differences in the reading methods (often called SUM OF SQUARES BETWEEN (groups)) and the other due to the normal variations between subjects (often called the SUM OF SQUARES ERROR). Note that the word ERROR here is not the same as "mistake." It simply means that there is variation in the scores that we cannot attribute to a specific variable. Some statisticians call this **residual** instead of **error**.

Our intuition tells us that if there is a large variation between the group means compared to variation within each group, then the means could be considered to be different because of differences in the reading methods. If we take the "average" sum of squares due to group differences (MEAN SQUARE between) divided by the "average" sum of squares due to subject differences (MEAN SQUARE error), the result is called an F ratio.

$$F = \frac{MS \text{ between}}{MS \text{ error}} = \frac{SS \text{ between}/(k\text{-}1)}{SS \text{ error}/(N\text{-}k)}$$

N = # of subjects(total),
k = # of groups

If the variation **between** the groups is large compared to the variation within the groups, this ratio will be large. If the null hypothesis is true, the F statistic will be equal to 1.00 on the average. Just how far away from 1.00 is **too** far away to be attributable to chance is a function of the number of groups and the number of subjects in each group. SAS analysis of variance procedures will give us the F ratio and the probability of obtaining a value of F this large or larger by chance alone.   .

The box on the following page contains a more detailed explanation of how an F ratio is computed along with an example. You may wish to skip the box for now.

We can write the following program (using our reading speed data):

```
DATA;
INPUT GROUP $ WORDS;
CARDS;
X 700
X 850

  .

  .

Z 610
PROC ANOVA;
    TITLE 'ANALYSIS OF READING DATA';
    CLASSES GROUP;
    MODEL WORDS = GROUP;
    MEANS GROUP;
RUN;
```

Look at the section of the program beginning with the statement, "PROC ANOVA." The first thing we want to indicate is which variable(s) is going to be the **independent** variable. We do this with a "**CLASSES**" statement. We are using the variable named GROUP as our independent variable. It could have been SEX, or TREATMENT, or any other variable in the SAS data set. It is almost always the case that the independent variable(s) in an ANOVA will have a relatively small number of possible values. Next, we want to specify what our MODEL is for the analysis. Basically, we are

Consider a one-way ANOVA with three groups (A, B, C) and three subjects within each group. The design is shown below:

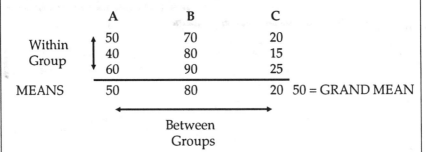

	A	B	C
Within Group	50	70	20
	40	80	15
	60	90	25
MEANS	50	80	20 50 = GRAND MEAN

Between
Groups

If we want to estimate the within-group variance (also called ERROR variance), we take the deviation of each score from the group mean, square the result, and add up the squared deviations for each of the groups and divide the result by the degrees of freedom. (The number of degrees of freedom is N-k, where N is the total number of subjects and k is the number of groups.) In the example above, the within group variance is equal to

$$[(50\text{-}50)^2 + (40\text{-}50)^2 + (60\text{-}50)^2 + (70\text{-}80)^2 + ...$$
$$+ (25\text{-}20)^2]/6 = 450/6 = 75.0$$

This within-group variance estimate (75.0) can be compared to the between-group variance. The between-group variance is obtained by taking the squared deviations of each group mean from the grand mean, multiplying each deviation by the number of subjects in a group, and dividing by the degrees of freedom (k-1). In our example the between-group variance is

$$[3(50\text{-}50)^2 + 3(80\text{-}50)^2 + 3(20\text{-}50)^2]/2 = 2700$$

If the null hypothesis is true, the between-group variance estimate will be close to the within-group variance and the ratio

$$F = \frac{\text{BETWEEN GROUP VARIANCE}}{\text{WITHIN GROUP VARIANCE}}$$

will be close to 1. In our example, $F = 2700/75 = 36.0$ with a probability of .0005 of obtaining a ratio this large or larger by chance alone.

saying what the dependent and independent variables are for this analysis. Following the word MODEL, is our dependent variable or a list of dependent variables, separated by spaces. When we have more than one dependent variable, a separate analysis of variance will be performed on each of them. For a one-way ANOVA, following the dependent variable(s) is an equal sign, followed by the independent variable. You must be sure to list any of the independent variables in the MODEL statement in the previous CLASSES statement. In the next line, MEANS GROUP will give us the mean value of the dependent variable (WORDS) for each level of GROUP. Output from this program is shown below:

```
ANALYSIS OF READING DATA
ANALYSIS OF VARIANCE PROCEDURE
CLASS LEVEL INFORMATION
CLASS      LEVELS    VALUES
GROUP        3        X Y Z

NUMBER OF OBSERVATIONS IN DATA SET = 15
DEPENDENT VARIABLE: WORDS
SOURCE                DF      SUM OF SQUARES        MEAN SQUARE
MODEL                  2      215613.33333333      107806.66666667
ERROR                 12       77080.00000000        6423.33333333
CORRECTED TOTAL       14      292693.33333333
MODEL F =            16.78                           PR > F = 0.0003

R-SQUARE              C.V.           STD DEV            WORDS MEAN
0.736653           12.9826         80.14570065        617.33333333

SOURCE                DF           ANOVA SS     F VALUE     PR > F
GROUP                  2      215613.33333333    16.78      0.0003

MEANS
GROUP         N         WORDS
X             5       786.000000
Y             5       518.000000
Z             5       548.000000
```

The output begins by recapitulating the details of the analysis. Pay attention to the levels of each CLASS variable to be sure that there were not any data errors, resulting in extraneous levels of one or more CLASS variables. Then we are given the number of cases (observations) in the data set and the name of the dependent variable. Next comes the stuff of the analysis. There are usually two sections here: an analysis for the MODEL as a whole and a breakdown according to the contribution of each independent variable. Where the ANOVA only has one independent variable (a "one-way ANOVA") these two sections are quite similar. Let's look at the top section first. We see the terms "SOURCE," "DF," "SUM OF SQUARES," "MEAN SQUARE," "MODEL F=," and "PR > F =." SOURCE tells us what aspect of the analysis we are considering. We have "MODEL," "ERROR," and "CORRECTED TOTAL" as categories here. MODEL means all of the independent variables and their interactions added together. ERROR means the residual variation after the MODEL variation has been removed. In our one-way ANOVA, we have only GROUP to consider. It has 2 degrees of freedom (DF). The sum of squares is 215613.33. The mean square (SS/DF) is 107806.67. The next row contains the same information for the error term. There we see the DF and SUM OF SQUARES for the CORRECTED TOTAL (which just means the sum of squares deviated from the Grand Mean). The next line contains the F statistic and the probability of it having occurred by chance. Below this we find the R- SQUARE for the Model, the coefficient of variation (C.V.) and the mean and standard deviation for the dependent variable.

The next section uses the same terms described above only now each independent variable or interaction is listed separately. Since we only have one independent variable, the results look identical to the ones above. In this example, we would therefore reject the null hypothesis since our F (with 2 and 12 degrees of freedom) is 16.78 and the p-value is .0003 and conclude that the reading instruction methods were not all equivalent.

Now that we know the reading methods are different, we want to know what the differences are. Is X better than Y or Z? Are the means of groups Y and Z so close that we cannot consider them different? In general, methods used to find group differences after the null hypothesis has been rejected are called **post hoc** or **a posteriori** tests. SAS software provides us with a variety of these tests to investigate differences between levels of our independent variable. These include **Duncan's multiple-range test,** the **Student-Newman-Keuls' multiple range test, least significant difference test, Tukey's studentized range test, Scheffe's multiple-comparison procedure,** and others. To request a post hoc test, place the SAS option name for the test you want, following a slash (/) on the MEANS statement. The

SAS names for the post hoc tests previously listed are DUNCAN, SNK, LSD, TUKEY, and SCHEFFE, respectively. In practice, it is easier to include the request for a post hoc test at the same time we request the analysis of variance. If the analysis of variance is not significant, **WE SHOULD NOT LOOK FURTHER AT THE POST HOC TEST RESULTS.** Our examples will use Duncan's multiple-range test for post hoc comparisons. You may use any of the available methods in the same manner. Winer (see Chapter 1) is an excellent reference for analysis of variance and experimental design. A discussion of most of these post hoc tests can be found there.

For our example we have:

```
MEANS GROUP / DUNCAN;
```

Unless we specify otherwise, the differences between groups are evaluated at the .05 level. Alpha levels of .1 or .01 may be specified by following the post hoc option name with ALPHA=.1 or ALPHA=.01. For example, to specify an alpha level of .1 for a Scheffe test, we would have

```
MEANS GROUP / SCHEFFE ALPHA=.1;
```

Here is the output from the Duncan procedure in our example:

```
DUNCAN'S MULTIPLE RANGE TEST FOR VARIABLE WORDS
MEANS WITH THE SAME LETTER ARE NOT SIGNIFICANTLY DIFFERENT.
ALPHA LEVEL=.05        DF=12        MS=6423.33

        GROUPING            MEAN        N    GROUP
            A             786.000000    5    X

            B             548.000000    5    Z
            B
            B             518.000000    5    Y
```

The Duncan procedure uses the following method to show group differences:

On the right are the group identifications. The order is determined by the group means, from highest to lowest. At the far left is a column labeled "GROUPING." Any groups that are not significantly different from one another will have the same letter in the GROUPING column. In our example, the Y and Z groups both have the letter 'B' in the GROUPING column and are therefore not significantly different. The letter 'B' between GROUP Z and GROUP Y is there for visual effect. It helps us realize that groups Y and Z are not significantly different (at the .05 level). Group X has an A in the grouping column and is therefore significantly different (p < .05) from the Y and Z groups.

From this Duncan's test we conclude that

1. Method X is superior to both methods Y and Z.
2. Methods Y and Z are not significantly different.

How would we describe the statistics used and the results of this experiment in a journal article? Although there is no "standard" format, we will suggest one approach here. The key is clarity. Here is our suggestion:

METHOD

We compared three reading methods: (1) Smith's Speed Reading Course, (2) Standard Method, and (3) Evelyn Tree's Institute. Fifteen subjects were randomly assigned to one of the three methods. At the conclusion of training, a standard reading test (Cody Count the Words Test version 2.1) was administered.

RESULTS

The mean reading speed for the three methods was

METHOD	READING SPEED (Words per minute)
(1) Smith's	786
(2) Standard	518
(3) Tree's	548

A one-way analysis of variance was performed. The F-value was 16.78 (df=2,12, p=.0003). A Duncan multiple range test (p=.05) showed that Smith's method was significantly superior to either Tree's or the Standard method. Tree's and the Standard method were not significantly different from each other.

The results of the Duncan multiple range test can easily be described in words when there are only three groups. With four or more groups, especially if the results are complicated, we can use another method. Consider the following results of a Duncan test on an experiment with 4 treatment groups:

GROUPING		MEAN	N	GROUP
A		80	10	1
A				
A	B	75	10	3
	B			
	B	72	10	2
C		60	10	4

We see that groups 1 and 3 are not significantly different. (They both have the letter "A" in the GROUPING column). Neither are groups 2 and 3. But 1 and 2 are! Remember that **"not significantly different"** does not mean **"equal."** Finally, group 4 is significantly different from all the other groups ($p < .05$). We can describe these results in a journal article like this:

GROUP

	1	3	2	4
MEAN	80	75	72	60

DUNCAN MULTIPLE RANGE TEST EXAMPLE

Any two groups with a common underscore are not significantly different ($p < .05$).

B. ANALYSIS OF VARIANCE: TWO INDEPENDENT VARIABLES

Suppose we ran the same experiment comparing reading methods, using 15 male subjects and 15 female subjects. In addition to comparing reading instruction methods, we could compare male vs. female reading speeds. Finally, we might want to see if the effects of the reading methods are the same for males and females.

This experimental design is called a two-way analysis of variance. The "two" refers to the fact that we have two independent variables: GROUP and SEX. We can picture this experiment as follows:

GROUP

		X	Y	Z
		700	480	500
		850	460	550
	MALE	820	500	480
		640	570	600
		920	580	610
SEX				
		900	590	520
		880	540	660
	FEMALE	899	560	525
		780	570	610
		899	555	645

In this design we have each of the three reading instruction methods for each level of SEX (male/female). Designs of this sort are called **factorial** designs. The combination of GROUP and SEX is called a cell. For this example, males in group X constitute a cell. In general, the number of cells in a factorial design would be the number of levels of one independent variable times the number of levels of the other independent variable. Three levels of GROUP times two levels of SEX = 6 cells in our case.

The total sum of squares is now divided or partitioned into four components. We have the sum of squares due to GROUP differences and the sum of squares due to SEX differences. The combination of GROUP and SEX provides us with another source of variation (called an interaction), and finally, the remaining sum of squares is attributed to error. We will discuss the interaction term later in this chapter.

Since there are the same number of subjects in each cell, the design is said to be "balanced" (some statisticians call this "orthogonal"). When we have **more than one independent variable** in our model, we **cannot** use PROC ANOVA if our design is **unbalanced**. For unbalanced designs, PROC GLM (general linear model) is used instead. The programming of our balanced design experiment is similar to the one-way analysis of variance.

Here is the program:

```
DATA;
INPUT GROUP $ SEX $ WORDS;
CARDS;
X M 700
   .
   .
   .
Z F 645
PROC ANOVA;
   TITLE 'ANALYSIS OF READING DATA';
   CLASSES GROUP SEX;
   MODEL WORDS = GROUP|SEX;
   MEANS GROUP|SEX / DUNCAN;
RUN;
```

As before, following the word CLASSES is a list of independent variables. The vertical line between GROUP and SEX in the MODEL and MEANS statements indicates that we have a factorial design (also called a crossed design). Some computer terminals may not have the "|" symbol on the keyboard. In this simple case, the term GROUP | SEX can be written as

```
GROUP SEX GROUP*SEX
```

The "|" symbol is especially useful when we have higher-order factorial designs such as GROUP | SEX | DOSE. Written out the long way, this would be

```
GROUP SEX DOSE GROUP*SEX GROUP*DOSE
SEX*DOSE GROUP*SEX*DOSE
```

That is, each variable, and every two- and three-way interaction term is specified.

Let's study the output of the previous example carefully to see what conclusions we can draw about our experiment. The first portion of the output is shown below:

ANALYSIS OF READING DATA

Analysis of Variance Procedure

Class Level Information

Class	Levels	Values
GROUP	3	X Y Z
SEX	2	F M

Number of observations in data set = 30

Dependent Variable: WORDS

Source	DF	Sum of Squares	Mean Square	F Value	Pr > F
Model	5	531436.17	106287.23	23.92	0.0001
Error	24	106659.20	4444.13		
Corrected Total	29	638095.37			

R-Square	C.V.	Root MSE	WORDS Mean
0.832848	10.31264	66.664	646.4333

Source	DF	Anova SS	Mean Square	F Value	Pr > F
GROUP	2	503215.27	251607.63	56.62	0.0001
SEX	1	25404.30	25404.30	5.72	0.0250
GROUP*SEX	2	2816.60	1408.30	0.32	0.7314

The top portion labeled "CLASS LEVEL INFORMATION" indicated our two independent variables and the levels of each. The analysis of variance table shows us the SUM OF SQUARES and MEAN SQUARE for the entire model and the error. This overall F value (23.92) and the probability p=.0001 shows us how well the model (as a whole) explains the variation about the grand mean. This could be very important in certain types of studies where we want to create a general predictive model. In this case, we are more interested in the detailed sources of variation (GROUP, SEX, and GROUP*SEX).

Each source of variation in the table has an F value and the probability of obtaining a value of F this large or larger by chance. In our example, the GROUP variable was significant at .0001 and SEX at .0250. Since there are only two levels of SEX, we do not need the Duncan test to claim that males and females are significantly different with respect to reading speed (p=.025).

In a two-way analysis of variance, when we look at GROUP effects, we are comparing GROUP levels without regard to SEX. That is, when the groups are compared, we combine the data over males and females. Conversely, when we compare males to females, we combine data from the three treatment groups.

The term GROUP*SEX is called an **interaction** term. If group differences were **not** the same for males and females, we would have a significant interaction. For example, if males did better with method A compared to method B while females did better with B compared to A, we would expect a significant interaction. In our example, the interaction between GROUP and SEX was not significant (p=.73). (Our next example will show a case where there is a significant interaction.)

The portion of the output resulting from the "MEANS GROUP | SEX / DUNCAN" request is shown next:

```
DUNCAN'S MULTIPLE RANGE TEST FOR VARIABLE WORDS

NOTE: This test controls the type I comparisonwise error rate, not the
      experimentwise error rate

Alpha= 0.05  df= 24  MSE= 4444.133

Number of Means    2    3
Critical Range  61.47 64.58

Means with the same letter are not significantly different.

Duncan Grouping          Mean     N  GROUP

              A          828.80   10  X

              B          570.00   10  Z
              B
              B          540.50   10  Y

Duncan's Multiple Range Test for variable: WORDS

NOTE: This test controls the type I comparisonwise error rate, not the
      experimentwise error rate

Alpha= 0.05  df= 24  MSE= 4444.133

Number of Means    2
Critical Range  50.19

Means with the same letter are not significantly different.

Duncan Grouping          Mean     N  SEX

              A          675.53   15  F

              B          617.33   15  M
```

```
 o                                                                            o
     Level of   Level of          ------------WORDS------------
     GROUP      SEX        N         Mean                SD
     X          F          5      871.600000          51.887378
 o   X          M          5      786.000000         113.929803          o
     Y          F          5      563.000000          18.574176
     Y          M          5      518.000000          54.037024
     Z          F          5      592.000000          66.011363
```

The first comparison shows group X to be significantly different ($p < .05$) from Y and Z. The second table shows that females have significantly higher reading speeds than males. We already know this because SEX was a significant main effect ($p=.025$) and there are only two levels of SEX. Following the two Duncan tests are the mean reading speeds (and standard deviations) for each combination of GROUP and SEX. These values are the means of the 6 cells in our experimental design.

C. INTERPRETING SIGNIFICANT INTERACTIONS

We will now discuss an example that has a significant interaction term. We have two groups of children. One group is considered normal, the other, hyperactive. Each group of children is randomly divided, with one half receiving a placebo and the other a drug called ritalin. A measure of activity is determined for each of the children. The following data are collected:

	PLACEBO	RITALIN
	50	67
	45	60
NORMAL	55	58
	52	65
	70	51
HYPERACTIVE	72	57
	68	48
	75	55

We will name the variables in this study GROUP (NORM or HYPER), DRUG (PLACEBO or RITALIN), and ACTIVITY (activity score). Since the design is balanced (same number of subjects per cell), we can use PROC ANOVA. The PROC statements are written like this:

```
PROC ANOVA;
    TITLE 'ACTIVITY STUDY';
    CLASSES GROUP DRUG;
    MODEL ACTIVITY = GROUP|DRUG;
    MEANS GROUP|DRUG;
RUN;
```

This is a two-way analysis of variance factorial design just like the last example. Again, the vertical bar between GROUP and DRUG in the MODEL and MEANS statements indicates that we have a factorial design and GROUP and DRUG are crossed. Notice that we do not need to request a Duncan test since there are only two levels of each independent variable.

A portion of the output is shown below:

SOURCE	DF	ANOVA SS	F VALUE	PR F
GROUP	1	121.00000000	8.00	0.0152
DRUG	1	42.25000000	2.79	0.1205
GROUP*DRUG	1	930.25000000	61.50	0.0001

The first thing to notice is that there is a strong GROUP*DRUG interaction term (p=.0001). When this occurs, we must be careful about interpreting any of the main effects (GROUP and DRUG in our example). That is, we must first understand the nature of the interactions before we look at main effects.

By looking more closely at the interaction between GROUP and DRUG, we will see why the main effects shown in the analysis of variance table can be misleading. The best way of explaining a two-way interaction is to take the cell means and plot them. These means can be found in the portion of the output from the MEANS request. The portion of the output containing the cell means is shown below:

Level of GROUP	Level of DRUG	N	----------ACTIVITY---------- Mean	SD
HYPER	PLACEBO	4	71.2500000	2.98607881
HYPER	RITALIN	4	52.7500000	4.03112887
NORM	PLACEBO	4	50.5000000	4.20317340
NORM	RITALIN	4	62.5000000	4.20317340

We can use this set of means to plot an interaction graph. We pick one of the independent variables (we will choose DRUG) to go on the x-axis and then plot means for each level of the other independent variable (GROUP) on the y-axis. We can either do this by hand or have SAS plot it for us. To have SAS plot the interaction graph, we first have to use PROC MEANS to create a data set containing the cell means. The SAS statements to create a data set of cell means is shown next:

```
PROC MEANS NWAY NOPRINT;
   CLASS GROUP DRUG;
   VAR ACTIVITY;
   OUTPUT OUT=MEANS MEAN=;
RUN;
```

Notice that we use GROUP and DRUG as CLASS variables and the NWAY option of PROC MEANS, since this will restrict the output data set to the highest order interaction (the cell means). Next, we use PROC PLOT to plot the interaction graph. We can choose to place either of the independent variables on the x-axis and plot a separate graph for each level of the other independent variable. We will choose DRUG to be the x-axis variable and plot a separate graph for each level of GROUP. A shortcut, using the values of GROUP as the plotting symbol, make the SAS statements simple. We write:

```
PROC PLOT;
   PLOT ACTIVITY*DRUG=GROUP;
RUN;
```

The resulting graph is shown below:

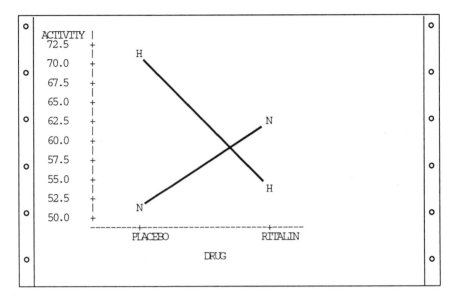

The graph shows that normal children increase their activity when given ritalin while hyperactive children are calmed by ritalin. In the analysis of variance, the comparison of placebo to ritalin values is done by combining the data from normal and hyperactive children. Since these values tend to cancel each other, the average activity with placebo and ritalin is about the same. What we have found here is that it is **not** possible to understand the activity level of children by **just** knowing whether they had ritalin or not. One must also know whether they are hyperactive or not. This is why it is critical to understand the interaction before looking at main effects. If we really want to study the effect of ritalin, we should look **separately** at normal and hyperactive children. For each of these groups we have two levels of the DRUG. We can therefore do a t-test between placebo and ritalin within the normal and hyperactive groups. As we know from Chapter 6, this is accomplished by first sorting the data set by GROUP and then including a BY variable in the t-test request. We have:

```
PROC SORT;
  BY GROUP;
PROC TTEST; BY GROUP;
  CLASS DRUG;
    VAR ACTIVITY;
RUN;
```

The output from these statements is shown below:

```
GROUP=HYPER

TTEST PROCEDURE

VARIABLE: ACTIVITY

DRUG          N            MEAN           STD DEV         STD ERROR

PLACEBO       4        71.25000000      2.98607881       1.49303941
RITALIN       4        52.75000000      4.03112887       2.01556444

VARIANCES       T      DF    PROB  |T|

UNEQUAL      7.3755    5.5     0.0005
EQUAL        7.3755    6.0     0.0003

FOR H0: VARIANCES ARE EQUAL, F'=   1.82 WITH 3 AND 3 DF
        PROB  F'= 0.6343


GROUP=NORM --------------------------------------------------------

VARIABLE: ACTIVITY

DRUG          N            MEAN           STD DEV         STD ERROR

PLACEBO       4        50.50000000      4.20317340       2.10158670
RITALIN       4        62.50000000      4.20317340       2.10158670

VARIANCES       T      DF    PROB  |T|

UNEQUAL     -4.0376    6.0     0.0068
EQUAL       -4.0376    6.0     0.0068

FOR H0: VARIANCES ARE EQUAL, F'=   1.00 WITH 3 AND 3 DF
        PROB  F'= 1.0000
```

Notice that in both groups, the two drug means are significantly different ($p < .05$). However, in the normal group, the ritalin mean is higher than the placebo mean while in the hyperactive group the reverse is true. So, **watch out for those interactions!**

An alternative to the t-tests above is to break down the two-way ANOVA into a one-way ANOVA by creating an independent (CLASS) variable that has a level for each **combination** of the original independent variables. In our case, we will create a variable (let's call it COND) that has a level for each combination of DRUG and GROUP. Thus, we will have NORMAL-PLACEBO, NORMAL-RITALIN, HYPERACTIVE-PLACEBO, and HY-PERACTIVE-RITALIN as levels of our COND variable. A quick and easy way to create this variable is to **concatenate** (join) the two original independent variables (this will be performed directly for character variables.

(In the case of numeric variables, SAS software will convert them to character and perform the concatenation). In the SAS system, concatenation is accomplished with the concatenation operator, "| |."

To create the COND variable, we have

```
COND = GROUP || DRUG;
```

The SAS statements to produce the one-way ANOVA are

```
PROC ANOVA;
   TITLE 'ONE-WAY ANOVA RITALIN STUDY';
   CLASSES COND;
   MODEL ACTIVITY = COND;
   MEANS COND / DUNCAN;
RUN;
```

The results of running this procedure are shown next:

Class Level Information

Class	Levels	Values		
COND	4	HYPER	PLACEBO HYPER	RITALIN
		NORM	PLACEBO NORM	RITALIN

Number of observations in data set = 16

Dependent Variable: ACTIVITY

Source	DF	Sum of Squares	F Value	Pr > F
Model	3	1093.50000000	24.10	0.0001
Error	12	181.50000000		
Corrected Total	15	1275.00000000		

R-Square	C.V.	ACTIVITY Mean
0.857647	6.5638604	59.25000000

Source	DF	Anova SS	F Value	Pr > F
COND	3	1093.50000000	24.10	0.0001

```
Duncan's Multiple Range Test for variable: ACTIVITY

NOTE: This test controls the type I comparisonwise error rate,
      not the experimentwise error rate

Alpha= 0.05  df= 12  MSE= 15.125

Number of Means        2         3         4
Critical Range  5.9802927 6.2645621 6.4545514

Means with the same letter are not significantly different.

Duncan Grouping            Mean     N  COND

                  A       71.250     4  HYPER    PLACEBO

                  B       62.500     4  NORM     RITALIN

                  C       52.750     4  HYPER    RITALIN
                  C
                  C       50.500     4  NORM     PLACEBO
```

Notice that this analysis tells us more than the two t-tests. Besides verifying that PLACEBO is different from RITALIN **within** each GROUP (NORMAL and HYPER), we can also see the other pairwise comparisons.

In the next chapter, dealing with repeated measures designs, we will find cases where it is the interaction term that is of primary interest.

D. N-WAY FACTORIAL DESIGNS

The method we used to perform a two-way analysis of variance can be extended to cover any number of independent variables. An example with three independent variables (GROUP SEX DOSE) is shown below:

```
PROC ANOVA;
    TITLE '3-WAY ANALYSIS OF VARIANCE';
    CLASSES GROUP SEX DOSE;
    MODEL ACTIVITY = GROUP|SEX|DOSE;
    MEANS GROUP|SEX|DOSE;
     RUN;
```

With three independent variables, we have three main effects (GROUP SEX DOSE), three two-way interactions (GROUP*SEX GROUP*DOSE SEX*DOSE), and one three-way interaction (GROUP*SEX*DOSE). One usually hopes that the higher-order interactions are not significant since they complicate the interpretation of the main effects and the lower-order interactions. See Winer for a more complete discussion of this topic.

It clearly becomes difficult to perform factorial design experiments with a large number of independent variables without expert assistance. The number of subjects in the experiment will also need to be large so that there are a reasonable number of subjects per cell.

E. UNBALANCED DESIGNS: PROC GLM

As we mentioned before, designs that have an unequal number of subjects per cell (called unbalanced designs) cannot be run using PROC ANOVA. PROC GLM (general linear model) is used instead. The only exception is for one-way unbalanced designs (designs with one CLASS variable and unequal numbers of subjects per group), which can be run with PROC ANOVA. CLASSES, MEANS, and MODEL statements for PROC GLM are identical to those used with PROC ANOVA. The only difference between the procedures is the mathematical methods used for each and some additional information that is computed when PROC GLM is used.

Here is an example of a two-way analysis of variance that is unbalanced:

A pudding company wanted to test-market a new product. Three levels of sweetness and two flavors were produced. Each subject was given a pudding to taste and was asked to rate the taste on a scale from 1 to 10. The following data were collected:

	SWEETNESS LEVEL		
	1	2	3
VANILLA	9	8	6
	7	7	5
	8	8	7
	7		
CHOCOLATE	9	8	4
	9	7	5
	7	6	6
	7	8	4
	8		4

The SAS INPUT statement was written:

```
INPUT SWEET FLAVOR $ RATING;
```

Since the number of subjects in each cell is unequal, we will use PROC GLM.

```
PROC GLM;
   TITLE 'PUDDING TASTE EVALUATION';
   TITLE3 'TWO-WAY ANOVA - UNBALANCED DESIGN';
   TITLE5 '--------------------------------';
   CLASSES SWEET FLAVOR;
   MODEL RATING = SWEET|FLAVOR;
   MEANS SWEET|FLAVOR;
RUN;
```

Portions of the output are shown below:

```
PUDDING TASTE EVALUATION

TWO-WAY ANOVA - UNBALANCED DESIGN

--------------------------------

SOURCE              DF           TYPE I SS    F VALUE    PR > F

SWEET                2         35.85515873     21.00     0.0001
FLAVOR               1          1.33341530      1.56     0.2274
SWEET*FLAVOR         2          2.77809264      1.63     0.2241

SOURCE              DF          TYPE III SS    F VALUE    PR > F

SWEET                2         29.77706840     17.44     0.0001
FLAVOR               1          1.56666667      1.84     0.1923
SWEET*FLAVOR         2          2.77809264      1.63     0.2241
```

Notice that there are two sets of values for SUM OF SQUARES, F VALUES, and probabilities: one labeled TYPE I, the other labeled TYPE III. When designs do not have equal cell sizes, the TYPE I and TYPE III sums of squares usually will not be equal for all variables. The difference between TYPE I and TYPE III sum of squares is that TYPE I lists the sums of squares for each variable as if they were entered one at a time into the model in the order they are specified in the MODEL statement. Hence they can be thought of as incremental sums of squares. If there is any variance that is common to two or more variables, the variance will be attributed to the variable that is entered first. This may or may not be desirable. The TYPE III sum of squares gives the sum of squares that would be obtained for each variable if it were entered last into the model. That is, the effect of each variable is evaluated after all other factors have been accounted for. In any given situation, whether you want to look at TYPE I or TYPE III sum of squares will vary; however, for most analysis of variance applications, you will want to use TYPE III sum of squares.

Just to keep you on your toes, we have added a new form of the TITLE statement to the program. As you probably can guess, TITLE3 provides a third title line; TITLE5, a fifth. Since TITLE2 and TITLE4 are missing, lines 2 and 4 will be blank. In general, TITLEn will be the nth title line on the SAS output, where n is an integer. Note that TITLE is equivalent to TITLE1.

In our example, the sweetness factor was significant (p=.0001). The probabilities for FLAVOR and the interaction between FLAVOR and SWEETNESS were .1923 and 0.2241, respectively.

PROBLEMS

7-1. The next two questions were inspired by one of the authors (Cody) watching the French Open Tennis tournament while working on problem sets. (McEnroe versus Lendl (1984). Lendl won in 5 sets.)

Three brands of tennis shoes were tested to see how many months of playing would wear out the sole. Eight pairs of brands A, N, and T were randomly assigned to a group of 24 volunteers. The table below shows the results of the study:

		BRAND	
	A	**N**	**T**
	8	4	12
	10	7	8
Wear time	9	5	10
in months	11	5	10
	10	6	11
	10	7	9
	8	6	9
	12	4	12

Are the brands equal in wear quality? Write a SAS program to solve this problem, using ANOVA.

7-2. Tennis balls are tested in a machine to see how many bounces they can withstand before they fail to bounce 30% of their dropping height. Two brands of balls (W and P) are compared. In addition, the effect of shelf life on these brands is tested. Half of the balls of each brand are 6 months old, the other half, fresh. Using a two-way analysis of variance, what conclusions can you reach? The data are shown below:

		BRAND	
		W	P
	NEW	67	75
		72	76
		74	80
		82	72
		81	73
AGE			
	OLD	46	63
		44	62
		45	66
		51	62
		43	60

7-3. A taste test was conducted to rate the preference between brands C and P of a popular soft drink. In addition, the age category (1= less than 20, 2= 20 or older) was recorded. Preference data (on a scale of 1-10) are displayed below:

BRAND

		C	P
		7	9
		6	8
		6	9
	<20	5	9
		6	8
AGE			
		9	6
		8	7
		8	6
	>=20	9	6
		7	5
		8	
		8	

(a) Write a SAS program to analyze these data with a two-way analysis of variance. (Careful: Is the design balanced?)

(b) Draw an interaction graph.

(c) Follow up with a t-test comparing brand C to brand P for each age group separately.

7-4. A manufacturer wants to reanalyze the data in Problem 7-1, omitting all data for brand N. Run the appropriate analysis.

7-5. What's wrong with this program?

```
1      DATA TREE;
2      INPUT TYPE $ LOCATION $ HEIGHT;
3      CARDS;
       PINE NORTH 35
       PINE NORTH 37
       PINE NORTH 41
       PINE NORTH 41
       MAPLE NORTH 44
       MAPLE NORTH 41
       PINE SOUTH 53
       PINE SOUTH 55
       MAPLE SOUTH 28
       MAPLE SOUTH 33
       MAPLE SOUTH 32
       MAPLE SOUTH 22
4      PROC ANOVA;
5         CLASSES TYPE LOCATION;
6         MODEL HEIGHT = TYPE|LOCATION;
7         MEANS TYPE LOCATION TYPE*LOCATION;
```

CHAPTER 8
REPEATED MEASURES DESIGNS

A BRIEF NOTE ABOUT REPEATED MEASURES

This chapter covers the analysis of repeated measures designs. These designs involve a repeated measurement on the unit of analysis (usually subjects) in one or more of the independent variables. For example, an experiment where each subject received each of four drugs or an experiment where each subject was measured each hour for five hours would need a repeated measures design. With the introduction of version 6 of SAS software, a REPEATED statement was added to the analysis of variance procedures (ANOVA and GLM) which greatly simplified the coding of repeated measures designs. As you will see, there are times when you will want to analyze your data using the REPEATED statement and there will be times when you will choose not to. For each of the repeated measures designs in this chapter, we will demonstrate **both** methods of analysis.

A. ONE-FACTOR EXPERIMENTS

Consider the following experiment. We have four drugs (A,B,C,D) that relieve pain. Each subject is given each of the four drugs in random order. The subject's pain tolerance is then measured. Enough time is allowed to pass between successive drug administrations so that we can be sure there is no residual effect from the previous drug. (In clinical terms, this is called a "wash-out" period.)

The null hypothesis is:

MEAN (A) =MEAN (B) =MEAN (C) =MEAN (D)

If the analysis of variance is significant at $p < .05$ we will want to look at pairwise comparisons of the drugs using Duncan's multiple range test or other post hoc tests.

Notice how this experiment differs from a one-way analysis of variance without a repeated measure. With the designs we have discussed so far, we would have each subject receive only one of the four drugs. In this design, each subject is measured under each of the drug conditions. This has several important advantages.

First, each subject acts as his own control. That is, drug effects are calculated by recording deviations between each drug score and the average drug score for each subject. The normal subject-to-subject variation can thus be removed from the error sum of squares. Let's look at a table of data from the pain experiment:

SUBJECT	DRUG A	DRUG B	DRUG C	DRUG D
1	5	9	6	11
2	7	12	8	9
3	7	8	6	10
4	5	10	7	10

To analyze this experiment, we can consider the subject as an independent variable. We therefore have SUBJECT and DRUG as independent variables.

One way of arranging our data and writing our INPUT statement would be like this:

```
INPUT SUBJ DRUG PAIN;
CARDS;
1 1 5
1 2 9
1 3 6
1 4 11
2 1 7
  etc.
```

It is usually more convenient to arrange all the data for each subject on one line like this:

SUBJ	DRUG A	DRUG B	DRUG C	DRUG D
1	5	9	6	11
2	7	12	8	9
etc.				

We can read the data arranged like this but restructure it to look as if we had read it with the first program.

One way of writing the program is as follows:

```
DATA PAIN;
INPUT SUBJ @;
DO DRUG=1 TO 4;
    INPUT PAIN @;
    OUTPUT;
    END;
CARDS;
1 5 9 6 11
2 7 12 8 9
3 11 12 10 14
4 4 9 6 9
RUN;
```

The first INPUT statement reads the subject number. The "@" sign following SUBJ is an instruction to keep reading from the same line of data. (See chapter 10 for a more detailed discussion of the trailing @ sign.) The next line, DO DRUG=1 to 4;, is an iterative loop. The value of DRUG is first set to 1. Next, the input statement, INPUT PAIN @; is executed. Again, if the "@" were omitted, the program would go to the next data line to read a value (which we don't want). The OUTPUT statement causes an observation to be written to the internal SAS data set. Look at our first line of data. We would have as the first observation in the SAS data set SUBJ=1, DRUG=1, and PAIN=5. When the END statement is reached, the program flow returns to the DO statement where DRUG is set to 2. A new PAIN value is then read from the data (still from the first line because of the trailing @) and a new observation is added to the SAS data set. This continues until the value of DRUG=4. The general form of a DO statement is:

```
DO variable = S TO E BY I;
    .  .  .

END;
```

where S is the initial value for "variable," E is the ending value, and I is the increment. If I is omitted, the increment defaults to 1.

The initial value of "variable" will be set to S and incremented by I until the value of E is reached. Once the DO loop has been executed 4 times, we go on to the CARDS statement. This is normally the point at which observations are added to SAS data sets, but because we used an OUTPUT statement to write out our observation, no further action is taken. The program control returns to the statement INPUT PAIN @;. Since the CARDS statement was reached, the program will read the subject number from the next line of data.

The first few observations in the SAS data set created from this program are listed below:

```
1 1 5
1 2 9
1 3 6
1 4 11
2 1 7
2 2 12
    etc.
```

We can make one small modification to the program and by so doing, avoid having to enter the subject numbers on each line of data. The new program looks as follows:

```
DATA PAIN;
SUBJ+1;
DO DRUG=1 TO 4;
    INPUT PAIN @;
    OUTPUT;
    END;
CARDS;
5 9 6 11
7 12 8 9
7 8 6 10
5 10 7 10
```

The statement SUBJ+1; creates a variable called SUBJ which starts at 1 and is incremented by 1 each time the statement is executed.

We are ready to write our PROC statements to analyze the data. With this design there are several ways to write the MODEL statement. One way is like this:

```
PROC ANOVA;
   CLASSES SUBJ DRUG;
   MODEL PAIN = SUBJ DRUG;
   MEANS DRUG / DUNCAN;
RUN;
```

Notice that we are not writing SUBJ | DRUG. We are indicating that SUBJ and DRUG are each main effects and that there is no interaction term between them. Once we have accounted for variations from the grand mean due to subjects and drugs, the remaining deviations will be our source of error.

Below is a portion of the output from the one-way repeated measures experiment:

CLASS LEVEL INFORMATION

CLASS	LEVELS	VALUES
SUBJ	4	1 2 3 4
DRUG	4	1 2 3 4

NUMBER OF OBSERVATIONS IN DATA SET = 16
ANALYSIS OF VARIANCE PROCEDURE

DEPENDENT VARIABLE: PAIN

SOURCE	DF	SUM OF SQUARES	MEAN SQUARE
MODEL	6	132.50000000	22.08333333
ERROR	9	13.25000000	1.47222222
CORRECTED TOTAL	15	145.75000000	
MODEL F =	15.00		PR > F = 0.0003

R-SQUARE	C.V.	STD DEV	PAIN MEAN
0.909091	14.4878	1.21335165	8.37500000

SOURCE	DF	ANOVA SS	F VALUE	PR > F
SUBJ	3	82.25000000	18.62	0.0003
DRUG	3	50.25000000	11.38	0.0020

DUNCAN'S MULTIPLE RANGE TEST FOR VARIABLE PAIN

MEANS WITH THE SAME LETTER ARE NOT SIGNIFICANTLY DIFFERENT.

ALPHA LEVEL=.05   DF=9   MS=1.47222

GROUPING	MEAN	N	DRUG
A	10.250000	4	4
A			
A	10.000000	4	2
B	7.000000	4	3
B			
B	6.250000	4	1

What conclusions can we draw from these results? Looking at the very bottom of the analysis of variance table, we find an F value of 11.38 with an associated probability of .0020. We can therefore reject the null hypothesis that the means are equal. Another way of saying this is that the four drugs are not equally effective in reducing pain. Notice that the SUBJ term in the analysis of variance table also has an F value and a probability associated with it. This merely tells us how much variability there was from subject to subject. It is not really interpretable in the same fashion as the drug factor. We include it as part of the model because we don't want the variability associated with it to go into the ERROR sum of squares.

Now that we know that the drugs are not equally effective, we can look at the results of the Duncan Multiple Range Test. This shows two drug groupings. Assuming that a higher mean indicates higher pain, we can say that drugs 1 and 3 were more effective in reducing pain than drugs 2 and 4. We cannot, at the .05 level, claim any differences between drugs 1 and 3 or between drugs 2 and 4.

Looking at the error SS (sum of squares) and the SS due to subjects, we see that SUBJECT SS (82.25) is large compared to the ERROR SS (13.25). Had this same set of data been the result of assigning 16 subjects to the 4 different drugs (instead of repeated measures), the error SS would have been 95.50 (13.25 + 82.25). The resulting F and p values for the DRUG effect would have been 2.10 and .1531, respectively. (Note that the degrees of freedom for the error term would be 12 instead of 9.)

We see, therefore, that controlling for between-subject variability can greatly reduce the error term in our analysis of variance and allow us to identify small treatment differences with relatively few subjects.

B. USING THE REPEATED STATEMENT OF PROC ANOVA

This same design can be analyzed using the REPEATED option, first introduced with version 6 of SAS software. When the REPEATED statement is used, we need our data set in the form:

```
SUBJ PAIN1 PAIN2 PAIN3 PAIN4
```

Where PAIN1-PAIN4 are the pain levels at each drug treatment. Notice that the data set does not have a DRUG variable. The ANOVA statements to analyze this experiment are:

```
PROC ANOVA;
    MODEL PAIN1-PAIN4 = / NOUNI;
    REPEATED DRUG 4 (1 2 3 4);
    RUN;
```

Notice several details. First, there is no CLASS statement; our data set does not have an independent variable. We specify the four dependent variables to the left of the equal sign in the MODEL statement. Since there is no CLASS variable, we have nothing to place to the right of the equal sign. The option NOUNI (**no univariate**) is a request not to conduct a separate analysis for each of the four PAIN variables. Later when we have both repeated and nonrepeated factors in the design, this option will be especially important. The repeated statement indicates that we want to call the repeated factor DRUG. The "4" following the variable name indicates that DRUG has four levels. This is optional. Had it been omitted, the program would have assumed as many levels as there were dependent variables in the MODEL statement. The number of levels needs to be specified only when we have more than one repeated measure factor. Finally, "(1 2 3 4)" indicates the **labels** we want printed for each level of DRUG. The labels also act as spacings when polynomial contrasts are requested. (See the SAS/STAT manual for more details on this topic.) We will omit the complete output from running this procedure, but will show you some excerpts and leave the details of the output to the next model.

```
Oneway ANOVA using the REPEATED statement

Analysis of Variance Procedure
Repeated Measures Analysis of Variance
Repeated Measures Level Information

Dependent Variable    PAIN1    PAIN2    PAIN3    PAIN4

     Level of DRUG        1        2        3        4


Univariate Tests of Hypotheses for Within Subject Effects

Source: DRUG
                                                      Adj  Pr > F
      DF      Anova SS    Mean Square    F Value   Pr > F    G - G     H -
   3   50.25000000    16.75000000     11.38    0.0020    0.0123    0.0020

Source: Error(DRUG)

      DF        Anova SS       Mean Square
      9      13.25000000       1.47222222
```

The F value and probabilities (F=11.38, p=.002) are identical to those in the previous output. The Adjusted p-values shown to the right are more conservative, the G - G representing the Greenhouse-Geisser correction and the H - F representing the Huynh-Feldt value. (See Edwards for an explanation - reference in chapter 1.)

When we use the REPEATED statement, we **cannot** use a MEANS statement with the repeated factor name. The only way to compute pairwise comparisons in this case is to use the keyword CONTRAST(n) with the REPEATED statement. The form is:

```
REPEATED factor_name CONTRAST(n);
```

Where n is a number from 1 to k, with k being the number of levels of the repeated factor. CONTRAST(1) will compare the first level of the factor with each of the other levels. If the first level were a control value, for example, the CONTRAST(1) statement would compare the control to each of the other drugs. If we want all of the pairwise contrasts, we need to write k-1 repeated statements. In our DRUG example, where there were four levels of DRUG, we would write:

```
PROC ANOVA;
    TITLE 'ONEWAY ANOVA USING THE REPEATED STATEMENT';
    MODEL SCORE1-SCORE4 = / NOUNI;
    REPEATED DRUG 4 CONTRAST(1)/ NOM SUMMARY;
    REPEATED DRUG 4 CONTRAST(2)/ NOM SUMMARY;
    REPEATED DRUG 4 CONTRAST(3)/ NOM SUMMARY;
RUN;
```

These three CONTRAST statements will produce all the two-way comparisons. (CONTRAST(1) gives us 1 vs. 2,3,4; CONTRAST(2) gives use 2 vs. 1,3,4; and CONTRAST(3) gives us 3 vs. 1,2,4.) The contrasts are equivalent to multiple t-tests between the levels and you may want to protect yourself against a type I error with a Bonferroni correction or some other method. There is no provision for making these corrections using existing SAS procedures. The option NOM asks that no multivariate statistics be printed; the option SUMMARY requests analysis of variance tables for each contrast defined by the repeated factor.

C. TWO-FACTOR EXPERIMENTS WITH A REPEATED MEASURE ON ONE FACTOR

One very popular form of a repeated measures design is the following:

	SUBJ	PRE	POST
CONTROL	1		
	2		
	3		
TREATMENT	4		
	5		
	6		

Subjects are randomly assigned to a control or treatment group. Then, each subject is measured before and after treatment. The "treatment" for the control group can either be a placebo or no treatment at all. The goal of an experiment of this sort is to compare the pre/post changes of the control group to the pre/post changes of the treatment group. This design has a definite advantage over a simple pre/post design where one group of subjects is measured before and after a treatment (such as having only a treatment group in our design). Simple pre/post designs suffer from the problem that we cannot be sure if it is our treatment that causes a change (e.g., TIME may have an effect). By adding a pre/post control group, we can compare the pre/post control scores to the pre/post treatment scores and thereby control for any built in, systematic, pre/post changes.

A simple way to analyze our design is to compute a difference score (post minus pre) for each subject. We then have two groups of subjects with one score each (the difference score). Then we use a t-test to look for significant differences between the difference scores of the control and treatment groups. With more than two levels of time, however, we will need to use analysis of variance.

Here are some sample data and a SAS program that calculates difference scores and computes a t-test:

	SUBJ	PRE	POST
	1	80	83
CONTROL	2	85	86
	3	83	88
	4	82	94
TREATMENT	5	87	93
	6	84	98

```
DATA PREPOST;
INPUT SUBJ GROUP $ PRETEST POSTEST;
DIFF = POSTEST-PRETEST;                        (cont.)
```

```
CARDS;                    (Continued from previous page)
1 C 80 83
2 C 85 86
3 C 83 88
4 T 82 94
5 T 87 93
6 T 84 98
RUN;
PROC TTEST;
    TITLE 'T-TEST ON DIFFERENCE SCORES';
    CLASS GROUP;
    VAR DIFF;
RUN;
```

Results of this analysis show the treatment mean difference to be significantly different from the control mean difference (p=.045). See below:

T-TEST ON DIFFERENCE SCORES

Ttest Procedure

Variable: DIFF

GROUP	N	Mean	Std Dev	Std Error
C	3	3.00000000	2.00000000	1.15470054
T	3	10.66666667	4.16333200	2.40370085

Variances	T	DF	Prob>|T|
Unequal	-2.8750	2.9	0.0686
Equal	-2.8750	4.0	0.0452

For H0: Variances are equal, F'=   4.33 with 2 and 2 DF
         Prob > F'= 0.3750

We can alternatively treat this design as a two-way analysis of variance (GROUP X TIME) with TIME as a repeated measure. This method has the advantage of analyzing designs with more than two levels of one or both factors. It also has some other statistical benefits which are beyond our efforts here.

We will first write a program using the **REPEATED** statement of ANOVA. No changes in the data set are necessary. The ANOVA statements are:

```
PROC ANOVA;
   CLASSES GROUP;
   TITLE 'TWO WAY ANOVA WITH A REPEATED MEASURE';
   TITLE2 'ON ONE FACTOR';
   MODEL PRETEST POSTEST = GROUP / NOUNI;
   REPEATED TIME  2 (0 1);
   MEANS GROUP;
```

The REPEATED statement indicates that we want to call the repeated factor TIME, it has 2 levels, and we want to label the levels 0 and 1.

Output from these procedure statements are shown below:

```
TWO-WAY ANOVA WITH A REPEATED MEASURE
ON ONE FACTOR

Analysis of Variance Procedure
Class Level Information

Class    Levels    Values

GROUP       2      C T


Number of observations in data set = 6


TWO-WAY ANOVA WITH A REPEATED MEASURE
ON ONE FACTOR

Analysis of Variance Procedure
Repeated Measures Analysis of Variance
Repeated Measures Level Information

Dependent Variable    PRETEST  POSTEST

     Level of TIME           0          1Manova Test Criteria and Exact F
Statistics for
the Hypothesis of no TIME Effect
H = Anova SS&CP Matrix for: TIME    E = Error SS&CP Matrix

S=1    M=-0.5    N=1.5
```

Statistic	Value	F	Num DF	Den DF	Pr > F
Wilks' Lambda	.13216314	26.266	1	4	0.0069
Pillai's Trace	.86783686	26.266	1	4	0.0069
Hotelling-Lawley Trace	6.5664063	26.266	1	4	0.0069
Roy's Greatest Root	6.5664063	26.266	1	4	0.0069

Manova Test Criteria and Exact F Statistics for
the Hypothesis of no TIME*GROUP Effect
H = Anova SS&CP Matrix for: TIME*GROUP   E = Error SS&CP Matrix

S=1   M=-0.5   N=1.5

Statistic	Value	F	Num DF	Den DF	Pr > F
Wilks' Lambda	.32611465	8.2656	1	4	0.0452
Pillai's Trace	.67388535	8.2656	1	4	0.0452
Hotelling-Lawley Trace	2.0664063	8.2656	1	4	0.0452
Roy's Greatest Root	2.0664063	8.2656	1	4	0.0452

TWO-WAY ANOVA WITH A REPEATED MEASURE
ON ONE FACTOR

Analysis of Variance Procedure
Repeated Measures Analysis of Variance
Tests of Hypotheses for Between Subjects Effects

Source	DF	Anova SS	F Value	Pr > F
GROUP	1	90.75000000	**11.84**	**0.0263**
Error	4	30.66666667		

TWO-WAY ANOVA WITH A REPEATED MEASURE
ON ONE FACTOR

Analysis of Variance Procedure
Repeated Measures Analysis of Variance
Univariate Tests of Hypotheses for Within Subject Effects

Source: TIME

					Adj Pr > F	
DF	ANOVA SS	Mean Square	F Value	Pr > F	G - G	H - F
1	140.083333	140.083333	26.27	0.0069	.	.

Source: TIME*GROUP

					Adj Pr > F	
DF	ANOVA SS	Mean Square	F Value	Pr > F	G - G	H - F
1	44.083333	44.083333	8.27	0.0452	.	.

Source: ERROR(TIME)

DF	ANOVA SS	Mean Square
4	21.333333	5.333333

Level of GROUP	N	----------PRETEST---------		----------POSTEST---------	
		Mean	SD	Mean	SD
C	3	82.6666667	2.51661148	85.6666667	2.51661148
T	3	84.3333333	2.51661148	95.0000000	2.64575131

We will discuss the output from PROC ANOVA after we show an alternative method of analyzing this experiment. However, a portion of the output above is unique and will be discussed here. Notice the rows labeled Wilks' Lambda, Pillai's Trace, Hotelling-Lawley Trace, and Roy's Greatest Root. These are multivariate statistics which are of special interest when more than one dependent variable is indicated. Unlike univariate statistics, when you use multivariate procedures, there is no single test analogous to the F-test. Instead, there are about half a dozen. A question arises as to which one to use. Multivariate statisticians spend many pleasant hours investigating this question. The answer to the question is ambiguous: it depends. Bock (1975—see Chapter 1 for references) presents a nice discussion of the options. Our advice is: when there are only very small differences among the p- values, it doesn't really matter which one you use. When there are differences among the p-values, find a consultant.

We will now analyze the same experiment as a two-factor analysis of variance **without** using the **REPEATED** statement of PROC ANOVA. We may want to do this so that we can use the "built-in" multiple comparison tests. To do this, we must first create a new variable—say TIME—which will have two possible values: PRE or POST. Each subject will then have two observations, one with TIME = PRE and one with TIME = POST.

As with our one-way, repeated measures design, the method of creating several observations from one is with the OUTPUT statement.

We can add the following SAS statements to the end of the previous program:

```
1      DATA TWOWAY;
2      SET PREPOST;
3      TIME = 'PRE ';
4      SCORE = PRETEST;
5      OUTPUT;
6      TIME = 'POST';
7      SCORE = POSTEST;
8      OUTPUT;
9      DROP PRETEST POSTEST DIFF;
```

This section of the program creates a SAS data set called "TWOWAY" which has variables SUBJ GROUP TIME and SCORE. The first few observations in this data set are

SUBJ	GROUP	TIME	SCORE
1	C	PRE	80
1	C	POST	83
2	C	PRE	85
2	C	POST	86

Let's follow this portion of the SAS program step by step to see exactly how the new data set is created.

Line 1 prepares a data set called TWOWAY. Line 2 causes observations to be read from the original data set, PREPOST. The first observation is

```
SUBJ=1 GROUP=C PRETEST=80 POSTEST=83 DIFF=3.
```

Line 3 creates a new variable called TIME and sets the value of TIME to "PRE ." It should be noticed that there is a space after the 'E' in PRE. The reason is that the length of the variable TIME is defined by the first value that is assigned to it. Had we coded TIME = 'PRE', the length would be equal to three and the statement TIME = 'POST' would have assigned the value 'POS' to TIME instead of 'POST'.

Line 4 creates a new variable, SCORE, which is equal to the PRETEST value. When line 5 is executed, the first observation of the data set called TWOWAY becomes the following:

```
SUBJ=1 GROUP=C PRETEST=80 POSTEST=83 DIFF=3 TIME=PRE
SCORE=80.
```

However, since we included a DROP statement in line 9, the first observation in data set TWOWAY is actually

```
SUBJ=1 GROUP=C TIME=PRE SCORE=80.
```

Next, line 6 sets TIME='POST' and line 7 sets the variable SCORE to the POSTEST value. A new observation is added to the data set TWOWAY in line 8. This second observation has SUBJ=1 GROUP=C TIME=POST SCORE=83.

Finally, as we mentioned, line 9 is an instruction to drop the variables PRETEST, POSTEST, and DIFF from the new data set. Note: The **DROP** statement can appear **anywhere** in the data step and it controls which variables get written to the SAS data set. **Since the next line of the program is a SAS PROCEDURE,** the program logic returns to line 2 where a new observation is read from the data set PREPOST.

We are now ready to write our ANOVA statements. Unlike any of our previous examples, we will have to specify all the terms, including the sources of error, in the MODEL statement. This is necessary because our main effects and interaction terms are **not** tested by the same error term. Therefore, we need to specify each of these terms in the MODEL statement so they can be used later in tests of our hypotheses. In this design, we have one group of subjects that are assigned to a control group and another group assigned to a treatment group. Within each group, each subject is measured at TIME=PRE and TIME=POST. In this design, the subjects are said to be **nested** within the GROUP. In SAS programs, the term subjects nested within group is written

```
SUBJ(GROUP)
```

Since the model statement will define **ALL** sources of variation about the grand mean, the **ERROR SUM OF SQUARES** printed in the ANOVA table will be **zero.** To specify which error term is to be used to test each hypothesis in our design, we will use **TEST** statements following the MODEL specification. A TEST statement consists of a hypothesis to be tested (H=) and the appropriate error term (E=). The entire ANOVA procedure looks as follows:

```
PROC ANOVA;
    TITLE '2 WAY ANOVA WITH TIME AS A REPEATED
MEASURE';
    CLASSES SUBJ GROUP TIME;
    MODEL SCORE = GROUP SUBJ(GROUP) TIME
                  GROUP*TIME TIME*SUBJ(GROUP);
    MEANS GROUP|TIME;
    TEST H=GROUP                 E=SUBJ(GROUP);
    TEST H=TIME GROUP*TIME       E=TIME*SUBJ(GROUP);
RUN;
```

Notice that the error term for GROUP is SUBJ(GROUP) (subject nested within group) and the error term for TIME and the GROUP*TIME interaction is TIME*SUBJ(GROUP).

Below are portions of the PROC ANOVA output:

```
CLASS LEVEL INFORMATION

CLASS      LEVELS    VALUES

SUBJ          6       1 2 3 4 5 6

GROUP         2       C T

TIME          2       POST PRE

DEPENDENT VARIABLE: SCORE

SOURCE                   DF      SUM OF SQUARES        MEAN SQUARE

MODEL                    11       326.91666667        29.71969697

ERROR                     0         0.00000000         0.00000000

CORRECTED TOTAL          11       326.91666667


MODEL F =        99999.99                    PR > F = 0.0000


SOURCE                   DF       ANOVA SS    F VALUE    PR > F

GROUP                     1      90.75000000     .          .
SUBJ (GROUP)              4      30.66666667     .          .
TIME                      1     140.08333333     .          .
GROUP*TIME                1      44.08333333     .          .
SUBJ*TIME (GROUP)         4      21.33333333     .          .


TESTS OF HYPOTHESES USING THE ANOVA MS FOR SUBJ (GROUP)
AS AN ERROR TERM

SOURCE                   DF       ANOVA SS    F VALUE    PR > F

GROUP                     1      90.75000000    11.84     0.0263


TESTS OF HYPOTHESES USING THE ANOVA MS FOR SUBJ*TIME (GROUP)
AS AN ERROR TERM

SOURCE                   DF       ANOVA SS    F VALUE    PR > F

TIME                      1     140.08333333    26.27     0.0069
GROUP*TIME                1      44.08333333     8.27     0.0452
```

Since all sources of variation were included in the MODEL statement, the error sum of squares is zero and the F value is undefined (it prints as 99999.99). The requested tests are shown at the bottom of the table. Group differences had an F=11.84 and p=.0263. TIME and GROUP*TIME had F values of 26.27 and 8.27 and probabilities of .0069 and .0452, respectively.

In this experimental design, it is the interaction of GROUP and TIME that is of primary importance. This interaction term tells us if **the pre/post changes were the same for control and treatment subjects.** An interaction graph will make this clear. The output from the MEANS request is shown below:

```
MEANS

GROUP        N          SCORE

C            6       84.1666667
T            6       89.6666667


TIME         N          SCORE

POST         6       90.3333333
PRE          6       83.5000000


GROUP   TIME       N           SCORE

C       POST       3       85.6666667
C       PRE        3       82.6666667
T       POST       3       95.0000000
T       PRE        3       84.3333333
```

We can use the last set of means (interaction of GROUP and TIME) to plot the interaction graph. We pick one of the independent variables (we will use TIME) to go on the x-axis and then plot means for each of the levels of the other independent variable (GROUP). The resulting graph is shown below:

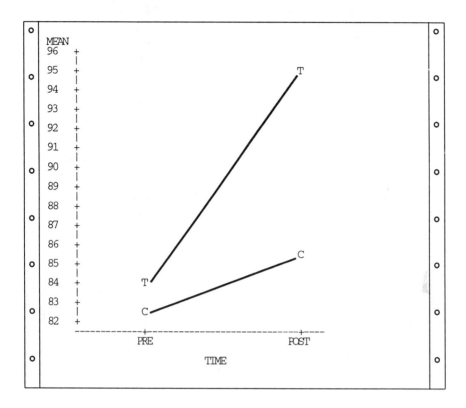

```
  o                                                                        o
        MEAN
        96   +
  o     95   +                                           T
             |
        94   +
             |
        93   +
  o          |
        92   +
             |
        91   +
             |
  o     90   +
             |
        89   +
             |
        88   +
  o          |
        87   +
             |
        86   +
             |                                      C
  o     85   +
             |
        84   +                T.
             |
        83   +
  o          |                C
        82   +
             ------------+------------------------------+----
                        PRE                           POST
  o                              TIME                                      o
```

A significant interaction term shows us that the two pre/post lines are not parallel. This tells us that the change from pre to post was different depending on which GROUP a subject was in. This is precisely what we wanted to know. The treatment group and control group were quite similar in terms of pain relief **before** the drug was administered (means=84.33 and 82.67, respectively). After the drug was given (the POST measure), the treatment group showed dramatic gains and the control group only modest gains. The F statistic for GROUP X TIME (8.27) and its p-value (.045) tell us that this difference in improvement is greater than could be expected by chance alone. The F statistic for GROUP (F=11.84, p=.0263) tells us that if we summed over the pre and post tests, the groups were different. This isn't of use to us since it combines the pre measure (where we anticipated scores being the same) with the post measure (where we anticipated a difference). The same logic is true for TIME. Here we are summing over the control and treatment groups. Finally, note that the p-value for GROUP X TIME is **the same** as for the t-test of the difference scores. This is because we are essentially making the same test in both analyses. Next, we will move to a somewhat more complex setting.

D. TWO-FACTOR EXPERIMENTS WITH REPEATED MEASURES ON BOTH FACTORS

This design is similar to the previous design except that each subject is measured under all levels of both factors. An example follows.

A group of subjects is tested in the morning and afternoon of two different days. On one of the days, the subjects receive a strong sleeping aid the night before the experiment is to be conducted, on the other, a placebo. The subjects' reaction time to a stimulus is measured. A diagram of the experiment is shown below:

		TREAT		
	CONTROL		DRUG	
TIME				
	SUBJ	REACT	SUBJ	REACT
	1	65	1	70
A.M.	2	72	2	78
	3	90	3	97
	1	55	1	60
P.M.	2	64	2	68
	3	80	3	85

We would like to see if the drug had any effect on the reaction time and if the effect was the same for the whole day. We can use the AM/PM measurements on the control day as a comparison for the AM/PM changes on the drug day.

Since each subject is measured under all levels of treatment (PLACEBO or DRUG) and TIME (AM/PM), we can treat this experiment as a SUBJ by TREATMENT by TIME factorial design. However, we must specify the error terms to test our hypotheses.

To create our SAS data set, we could use the following statements:

```
DATA SLEEP;
INPUT SUBJ TREAT $ TIME $ REACT;
CARDS;
1 CONT AM 65
1 CONT PM 55
1 DRUG AM 70
1 DRUG PM 60
2 CONT AM 72
   etc.
```

The ANOVA statements can be written:

```
PROC ANOVA;
   CLASSES SUBJ TREAT TIME;
   MODEL REACT = SUBJ|TREAT|TIME;
   MEANS TREAT|TIME;
   TEST H=TREAT        E=SUBJ*TREAT;
   TEST H=TIME         E=SUBJ*TIME;
   TEST H=TREAT*TIME   E=SUBJ*TREAT*TIME;
```

Before we investigate the output from the above program, we would like to show an alternate way of programming this problem. This method differs from the one above only in the way that the data are read; the PROC statements are exactly the same. The purpose of the alternate programming method is to simplify data entry. Please feel free to skip this discussion if you wish; it is useful only if you will be using SAS software frequently with moderate to large amounts of data. In that case you will save considerable time. Here is the program:

ALTERNATIVE PROGRAM FOR SLEEP STUDY

```
1       DATA;
2       SUBJ+1;
3       DO TIME=1 TO 2;
4           DO TREAT=1 TO 2;
5           INPUT REACT @;
6           OUTPUT;
7           END;
8       END;
9       CARDS;
10      65 70 55 60
11      72 78 64 68
12      90 97 80 85
13       PROC ANOVA;
      etc.
```

This program allows us to place all the data for one subject on a single line. We begin creating our data set with the DATA statement on line 1. Since we are not explicitly entering a subject number, line 2 will provide us with a SUBJ variable that starts with 1 and is incremented by 1 for each new subject.

The reaction times for each subject are arranged as follows:

CONTROL AM • DRUG AM • CONTROL PM • DRUG PM

We want to create 4 observations for each subject (one for each combination of treatment and time). Line 3 first sets the variable TIME equal to 1. Then the inner "DO" loop (lines 4 through 7) first sets TREAT equal to 1. The first response time (65) is read and an observation is placed into the data set with the OUTPUT statement (line 6). The first observation is therefore

```
SUBJ=1 TIME=1 TREAT=1 REACT=65
```

The inner loop now sets TREAT=2, reads the next reaction time (on the same line because of the trailing '@' sign in the INPUT statement), and outputs the next observation:

```
SUBJ=1 TIME=1 TREAT=2 REACT=70
```

Since the inner loop has reached its limit (2), the program logic returns to the outer loop starting at line 3, where the value of TIME is set to 2. The inner loop then outputs two more observations (TREAT=1 and 2). At this point, we return to line 2 where SUBJ is incremented by 1 and four more observations will be added to the data set.

A **FORMAT** statement to assign formats to the variables TREAT and TIME would make output from the statistical procedures easier to read. The complete program, modified to include formats, is shown next:

```
PROC FORMAT;
   VALUE FTREAT 1=CONTROL 2=DRUG;
   VALUE FTIME 1=AM 2=PM;
DATA;
SUBJ+1;
DO TIME=1 TO 2;
   DO TREAT=1 TO 2;
   INPUT REACT @;
   OUTPUT;
   END;
END;
FORMAT TREAT FTREAT. TIME FTIME.;
CARDS;
65 70 55 60
72 78 64 68
90 97 80 85

PROC ANOVA;
   etc.
```

END OF ALTERNATIVE PROGRAM EXPLANATION

Which method you choose to create the SAS data set will not affect the PROC ANOVA statements. In any design where **ALL** factors are repeated, such as this one, we can treat the SUBJ variable as being crossed by all other factors (as opposed to nested). The MODEL statement is therefore the same as our factorial design. However, by including the SUBJ term in our model, the error term will be zero (as in our previous example). Thus, our ANOVA table will **not** show F values or probabilities. These will be obtained by specifying **TEST** statements following the MODEL statement, as previously described.

The error terms to test each hypothesis are simple to remember: for factor X, the error term will be SUBJ*X. For example, the error term to test TREAT is SUBJ*TREAT; the error term to test the interaction TREAT*TIME is SUBJ*TREAT*TIME. To specify the correct error term for each main effect and interaction, the three TEST statements following the MODEL statement were added, each specifying a hypothesis to be tested and the error term to be used in calculating the F ratio.

A portion of the output from PROC ANOVA is shown below:

```
ANALYSIS OF VARIANCE PROCEDURE
DEPENDENT VARIABLE: REACT
```

SOURCE	DF	SUM OF SQUARES	MEAN SQUARE
MODEL	11	1750.66666667	159.15151515
ERROR	0	0.00000000	0.00000000
CORRECTED TOTAL	11	1750.66666667	

SOURCE	DF	ANOVA SS	F VALUE	PR > F
SUBJ	2	1360.66666667	.	.
TREAT	1	85.33333333	.	.
SUBJ*TREAT	2	0.66666667	.	.
TIME	1	300.00000000	.	.
SUBJ*TIME	2	2.00000000	.	.
TREAT*TIME	1	1.33333333	.	.
SUBJ*TREAT*TIME	2	0.66666667	.	.

```
TESTS OF HYPOTHESES USING THE ANOVA MS FOR SUBJ*TREAT
AS AN ERROR TERM
```

SOURCE	DF	ANOVA SS	F VALUE	PR > F

```
TESTS OF HYPOTHESES USING THE ANOVA MS FOR SUBJ*TIME
AS AN ERROR TERM

SOURCE                      DF              ANOVA SS    F VALUE    PR > F

TIME                        1           300.00000000    300.00     0.0033

TESTS OF HYPOTHESES USING THE ANOVA MS FOR SUBJ*TREAT*TIME
AS AN ERROR TERM

SOURCE                      DF              ANOVA SS   F VALUE    PR > F

TREAT*TIME                  1             1.33333333     4.00     0.1835
```

What conclusions can we draw? (1) The drug increases reaction time ($F=256.00$, $p=.0039$); (2) reaction time is longer in the morning compared to the afternoon ($F=300.00$, $p=.0033$); and (3) we cannot conclude that the effect of the drug on reaction time is related to the time of day since the interaction of TREAT and TIME is not significant ($F=4.00$, $p=0.1835$). Note that this study was **not** a pre/post study as in the previous example. Even so, had the TREAT X TIME interaction been significant, we would have been more cautious in looking at the TREAT and TIME effects.

If this were a real experiment, we would have to control for the learning effect that might take place. For example, if we measure each subject in the same order, we might find a decrease in reaction time from CONTROL AM to DRUG PM because the subject became more familiar with the apparatus. To avoid this, we would either have to acquaint the subject with the equipment before the experiment begins to assure ourselves that the learning has stabilized, or to measure each subject using TREATMENT and TIME in random order.

This design may also be analyzed using the REPEATED statement of PROC ANOVA. If we read in the four reaction times for each subject in the order AM Control, AM Drug, PM Control, PM Drug, and name our variables REACT1-REACT4, the ANOVA statements are:

```
PROC ANOVA;
    MODEL REACT1-REACT4 = / NOUNI;
    REPEATED TIME 2 , TREAT 2  / NOM;
RUN;
```

When there is more than one repeated factor, we need to specify the number of levels of each factor after the factor name. The factor we name first changes the slowest. That is, the first two reaction times are for TIME=AM with REACT1 associated with TREAT=control and REACT2 associated with TREAT=drug. We have now exhausted all levels of TREAT, and set TIME=PM; REACT3 and REACT4 are both PM measurements.

E. THREE-FACTOR EXPERIMENTS WITH A REPEATED MEASURE ON THE LAST FACTOR

For this example, we will consider a marketing experiment. Male and female subjects are offered one of three different brands of coffee. Each brand is tasted twice; once immediately after breakfast, the other time after dinner (the order of presentation is randomized for each subject). The preference of each brand is measured on a scale from 1 to 10 (1=lowest, 10=highest). The experimental design is shown below:

BRAND (of coffee)

| | | A | | B | | C | |
		BRKFST	DINNER	BRKFST	DINNER	BRKFST	DINNER
S							
E							
X	subj			subj		subj		
	1	7	8	7	4	6	13	8	9
MALE	2	6	7	8	3	5	14	6	9
	3	6	8	9	3	5	15	5	8
	4	5	7	10	3	4	16	6	9
FEM	5	4	7	11	4	4	17	6	9
	6	4	6	12	2	3	18	7	8

In this experiment, the factors BRAND and SEX are crossed factors while MEAL is a repeated measure factor (each subject tastes coffee after breakfast and dinner). Since a single subject tastes only **one** brand of coffee and is clearly only **one** sex, the subject term is said to be nested within BRAND and SEX (written SUBJ(BRAND SEX)). We could arrange our data several ways. First, we will arrange data so that we can take advantage of the **REPEATED** statement of ANOVA. To do this, we will place all data for each subject on one line. Thus, our program and data will look as follows:

```
DATA;
INPUT SUBJ BRAND $ SEX $ SCORE_B SCORE_D;
CARDS;
1 A M 7 8
2 A M 6 7
3 A M 6 8
4 A F 5 7
5 A F 4 7
6 A F 4 6
7 B M 4 6
   etc.
PROC ANOVA;
   TITLE 'COFFEE STUDY';
   CLASSES BRAND SEX;
   MODEL SCORE_B SCORE_D = BRAND|SEX / NOUNI;
   REPEATED MEAL;
   MEANS BRAND|SEX;
```

Notice that BRAND and SEX are crossed while MEAL is the repeated measures factor. As before, the option NOUNI on the MODEL statement indicates that we do **not** want **UNI**variate statistics for SCORE_B and SCORE_D.

Selected portions of the output from the above program are shown below:

COFFEE STUDY

Analysis of Variance Procedure
Class Level Information

Class	Levels	Values
BRAND	3	A B C
SEX	2	F M

Number of observations in data set = 18

Repeated Measures Analysis of Variance
Repeated Measures Level Information

```
Dependent Variable    SCORE_B  SCORE_D

     Level of MEAL        1        2

Tests of Hypotheses for Between Subjects Effects

Source          DF     Anova SS   Mean Square    F Value     Pr > F

BRAND            2    83.388889    41.694444      51.76      0.0001
SEX              1     6.250000     6.250000       7.76      0.0165
BRAND*SEX        2     3.500000     1.750000       2.17      0.1566

Error           12     9.666667     0.805556

Univariate Tests of Hypotheses for Within Subject Effects

Source: MEAL

     DF        ANOVA SS       Mean Square   F Value   Pr > F
     1       30.25000000     30.25000000     99.00    0.0001

Source: MEAL*BRAND

     DF        ANOVA SS       Mean Square   F Value   Pr > F
     2        1.50000000      0.75000000      2.45    0.1278

Source: MEAL*SEX

     DF        ANOVA SS       Mean Square   F Value   Pr > F
     1        0.02777778      0.02777778      0.09    0.7682

Source: MEAL*BRAND*SEX

     DF        ANOVA SS       Mean Square   F Value   Pr > F
     2        2.05555556      1.02777778      3.36    0.0692

Source: ERROR(MEAL)

     DF        ANOVA SS       Mean Square
     12       3.66666667      0.30555556
```

Level of BRAND	N	--------SCORE_B--------- Mean	SD	--------SCORE_D-------- Mean	SD
A	6	5.33333333	1.21106014	7.16666667	0.75277265
B	6	3.16666667	0.75277265	4.50000000	1.04880885
C	6	6.33333333	1.03279556	8.66666667	0.51639778

Level of SEX	N	--------SCORE_B--------- Mean	SD	--------SCORE_D-------- Mean	SD
F	9	4.55555556	1.58989867	6.33333333	2.23606798
M	9	5.33333333	1.73205081	7.22222222	1.56347192

Level of BRAND	Level of SEX	N	------SCORE_B------ Mean	SD	------SCORE_D------ Mean	SD
A	F	3	4.333333	0.577350	6.666666	0.577350
A	M	3	6.333333	0.577350	7.666666	0.577350
B	F	3	3.000000	1.000000	3.666666	0.577350
B	M	3	3.333333	0.577350	5.333333	0.577350
C	F	3	6.333333	0.577350	8.666666	0.577350
C	M	3	6.333333	1.527525	8.666666	0.577350

We will explain the results after the alternative program below.

An alternative program can be written that does not use the REPEATED statement of PROC ANOVA. You might find this useful if the data were arranged with two observations per subject and a MEAL variable already in the data set. So, if the data were arranged like this:

SUBJ	BRAND	SEX	MEAL	SCORE
1	A	M	BRKFST	7
1	A	M	DINNER	8
2	A	M	BRKFST	6

etc.,

your INPUT statement would look like this:

```
INPUT  SUBJ BRAND $ SEX $ MEAL $ SCORE;
```

The ANOVA statements are written:

```
PROC ANOVA;
   CLASSES SUBJ BRAND SEX MEAL;
   MODEL SCORE = BRAND SEX BRAND*SEX SUBJ(BRAND SEX)
                 MEAL BRAND*MEAL SEX*MEAL
BRAND*SEX*MEAL
                 MEAL*SUBJ(BRAND SEX);
   MEANS BRAND|SEX / DUNCAN E=SUBJ(BRAND SEX);
   MEANS MEAL BRAND*MEAL SEX*MEAL BRAND*SEX*MEAL;
```

This is followed by TEST statements:

```
TEST H=BRAND SEX BRAND*SEX
     E=SUBJ(BRAND SEX);
TEST H=MEAL BRAND*MEAL SEX*MEAL BRAND*SEX*MEAL
     E=MEAL*SUBJ(BRAND SEX);
```

The first test statement will test **each** of the terms (BRAND SEX and BRAND*SEX) with the error term SUBJ(BRAND SEX). The effects MEAL,

BRAND*MEAL, SEX*MEAL, and BRAND*SEX*MEAL will all be tested with the error term MEAL*SUBJ(BRAND SEX). We have also made a change in the way the MEANS statements were written. Included after the DUNCAN option is an "E=" specification. This is done because the DUNCAN procedure will use the residual mean square as the error term unless otherwise instructed. Since we have completely defined every source of variation in our model, the residual mean square is zero. The "E=error term" option uses the same error term as the "H=" option of the corresponding TEST statement. Also, since different error terms are used to test different hypotheses, a separate MEANS statement is required each time a different error term is used. Note then we did not need to perform a DUNCAN test for MEAL since this variable has only two levels.

A portion of the results of running this alternative program are shown below:

```
Analysis of Variance Procedure Class Level Information

Class    Levels    Values

SUBJ       18       1 2 3 4 5 6 7 8 9 10 11 12 13 14 15 16 17 18

BRAND      3        A B C

SEX        2        F M

MEAL       2        BRKFST DINNER


Number of observations in data set = 36

Source              DF    Anova SS    Mean Square    F Value   Pr > F

BRAND                2    83.388889    41.694444        .        .
SEX                  1     6.250000     6.250000        .        .
BRAND*SEX            2     3.500000     1.750000        .        .
SUBJ(BRAND*SEX)     12     9.666667     0.805556        .        .
MEAL                 1    30.250000    30.250000        .        .
BRAND*MEAL           2     1.500000     0.750000        .        .
SEX*MEAL             1     0.027778     0.027778        .        .
BRAND*SEX*MEAL       2     2.055556     1.027778        .        .
SUBJ*MEAL(BRAND*SEX) 12    3.666667     0.305556        .        .

Duncan's Multiple Range Test for variable: SCORE

NOTE: This test controls the type I comparisonwise error rate,
      not the experimentwise error rate

Alpha= 0.05  df= 12  MSE= .8055556

Number of Means         2         3
Critical Range   .79682302 .83469949

Means with the same letter are not significantly different.
```

```
Duncan Grouping                    Mean      N  BRAND

                       A          7.500     12  C

                       B          6.250     12  A

                       C          3.833     12  B


Level of  Level of      -------------SCORE------------
BRAND     SEX       N        Mean                    SD

A         F         6     5.50000000            1.37840488
A         M         6     7.00000000            0.89442719
B         F         6     3.33333333            0.81649658
B         M         6     4.33333333            1.21106014
C         F         6     7.50000000            1.37840488
C         M         6     7.50000000            1.64316767

Level of           -------------SCORE------------
MEAL      N         Mean                    SD

BRKFST    18      4.94444444            1.66175748
DINNER    18      6.77777778            1.92676369

Level of           -------------SCORE------------
BRAND     N         Mean                    SD

A         12      6.25000000            1.35680105
B         12      3.83333333            1.11464086
C         12      7.50000000            1.44599761

Level of  Level of      -------------SCORE------------
BRAND     MEAL       N        Mean                    SD

A         BRKFST     6     5.33333333            1.21106014
A         DINNER     6     7.16666667            0.75277265
B         BRKFST     6     3.16666667            0.75277265
B         DINNER     6     4.50000000            1.04880885
C         BRKFST     6     6.33333333            1.03279556
C         DINNER     6     8.66666667            0.51639778
```

Tests of Hypotheses using the Anova MS for SUBJ(BRAND*SEX)
       as an error term

Source	DF	Anova SS	Mean Square	F Value	Pr > F
BRAND	2	83.38888889	41.69444444	51.76	0.0001
SEX	1	6.25000000	6.25000000	7.76	0.0165
BRAND*SEX	2	3.50000000	1.75000000	2.17	0.1566

Tests of Hypotheses using the Anova MS for
SUBJ*MEAL(BRAND*SEX) as an error term

Source	DF	Anova SS	Mean Square	F Value	Pr > F
MEAL	1	30.25000000	30.25000000	99.00	0.0001
BRAND*MEAL	2	1.50000000	0.75000000	2.45	0.1278
SEX*MEAL	1	0.02777778	0.02777778	0.09	0.7682
BRAND*SEX*MEAL	2	2.05555556	1.02777778	3.36	0.0692

What conclusions can we draw from these results? First, we notice that
the variables BRAND, MEAL, and SEX are all significant effects (BRAND

and MEAL at p=.0001, SEX at p=.016). We also see, from the Duncan test, that brand C is the preferred brand, followed by A and B. The fact that MEAL (breakfast or dinner) is significant and that BRAND*MEAL is not, tells us that all three brands of coffee are preferred after dinner.

F. THREE-FACTOR EXPERIMENTS WITH REPEATED MEASURES ON TWO FACTORS

As an example of a three-factor experiment with two repeated measures factors, we have designed a hypothetical study involving reading comprehension and a concept called "slippage." It is well known that many students will do less well on a reading comprehension test in the early fall compared to the previous spring because of "slippage" during the summer vacation. As children grow older, the slippage should decrease. Also, slippage tends to be smaller with high-SES (socioeconomic status—roughly speaking, "wealthier") children compared to low-SES children, since high-SES children typically do more reading over the summer.

To test these ideas, the following experiment was devised.

A group of high- and low-SES children was selected for the experiment. Their reading comprehension was tested each spring and fall for three consecutive years. A diagram of the design is shown below:

YEARS

		1		2		3	
		SPRING	FALL	SPRING	FALL	SPRING	FALL
HIGH	subj						
SES	1	61	50	60	55	59	62
	2	64	55	62	57	63	63
	3	59	49	58	52	60	58
	4	63	59	65	64	67	70
	5	62	51	61	56	60	63
LOW	6	57	42	56	46	54	50
SES	7	61	47	58	48	59	55
	8	55	40	55	46	57	52
	9	59	44	61	50	63	60
	10	58	44	56	49	55	49

Notice that each subject is measured each spring and fall of each year so that the variables SEASON and YEAR are both repeated measures factors.

In this design each subject belongs to either the high-SES or the low-SES group. Therefore, subjects are **nested** within SES.

We will show three ways of writing a SAS program to analyze this experiment. First, using the REPEATED statement of PROC ANOVA:

```
DATA;
INPUT SUBJ SES $ READ1-READ6;
LABEL READ1 = 'SPRING YR 1'
      READ2 = 'FALL YR 1'
      READ3 = 'SPRING YR 2'
      READ4 = 'FALL YR 2'
      READ5 = 'SPRING YR 3'
      READ6 = 'FALL YR 3';
CARDS;
1 HIGH 61 50 60 55 59 62
2 HIGH 64 55 62 57 63 63
3 HIGH 59 49 58 52 60 58
4 HIGH 63 59 65 64 67 70
5 HIGH 62 51 61 56 60 63
6 LOW  57 42 56 46 54 50
7 LOW  61 47 58 48 59 55
8 LOW  55 40 55 46 57 52
9 LOW  59 44 61 50 63 60
10 LOW 58 44 56 49 55 49
PROC ANOVA;
   CLASSES SES;
   MODEL READ1-READ6 = SES / NOUNI;
   REPEATED YEAR 3, SEASON 2;
   MEANS SES;
```

Since the REPEATED statement is confusing when we have more than one repeated factor, we will, again show you how to determine the order of the factor names. The data are arranged in the order:

YEAR 1		YEAR 2		YEAR 3	
SPRING	FALL	SPRING	FALL	SPRING	FALL
1	2	3	4	5	6

There are **three** levels of YEAR and **two** levels of SEASON. The **factors** following the keyword REPEATED are placed in order from the one that varies the **slowest** to the one that varies the **fastest**. For example, the first number (READ1) is from YEAR 1 in the SPRING. The next number (READ2) is still YEAR 1 but in the FALL. Thus, we say that SEASON is varying faster than YEAR. We must also be sure to indicate the number of levels of each factor following the factor name on the REPEATED statement. The line:

```
REPEATED YEAR 3, SEASON 2;
```

tells the SAS software to choose the first level of YEAR (1), then loop through two levels of SEASON (SPRING FALL), then return to the next level of YEAR (2), followed by two levels of SEASON, etc. The product of the two levels must equal the number of variables in the dependent variable list of the MODEL statement. To check, 3*2=6 and we have READ1 to READ6 on the MODEL statement.

Results of running this program are shown next:

```
Analysis of Variance Procedure
Class Level Information

Class      Levels    Values

SES           2      HIGH LOW

Number of observations in data set = 10

Repeated Measures Analysis of Variance
Repeated Measures Level Information

Dependent Variable    READ1   READ2   READ3   READ4   READ5   READ6

     Level of YEAR       1       1       2       2       3       3
     Level of SEASON     1       2       1       2       1       2

Tests of Hypotheses for Between Subjects Effects

Source         DF    Anova SS  Mean Square    F Value     Pr > F

SES             1    680.0667    680.0667      13.54       0.0062

Error           8    401.6667     50.2083
Univariate Tests of Hypotheses for Within Subject Effects

Source: YEAR
                                                    Adj  Pr > F
DF      ANOVA SS      Mean Square   F Value  Pr > F  G - G   H - F
 2    252.03333333   126.01666667    26.91   0.0001  0.0002  0.0001
```

Source: YEAR*SES

DF	ANOVA SS	Mean Square	F Value	Pr > F	Adj G - G	Pr > F H - F
2	1.03333333	0.51666667	0.11	0.8962	0.8186	0.8700

Source: ERROR(YEAR)

DF	ANOVA SS	Mean Square
16	74.93333333	4.68333333

Greenhouse-Geisser Epsilon = 0.6757
Huynh-Feldt Epsilon = 0.8658

Source: SEASON

DF	ANOVA SS	Mean Square	F Value	Pr > F
1	680.06666667	680.06666667	224.82	0.0001

Source: SEASON*SES

DF	ANOVA SS	Mean Square	F Value	Pr > F
1	112.06666667	112.06666667	37.05	0.0003

Source: ERROR(SEASON)

DF	ANOVA SS	Mean Square
8	24.20000000	3.02500000

Source: YEAR*SEASON

DF	ANOVA SS	Mean Square	F Value	Pr > F
2	265.43333333	132.71666667	112.95	0.0001

Source: YEAR*SEASON*SES

DF	ANOVA SS	Mean Square	F Value	Pr > F
2	0.43333333	0.21666667	0.18	0.8333

Source: ERROR(YEAR*SEASON)

DF	ANOVA SS	Mean Square
16	18.80000000	1.17500000

Greenhouse-Geisser Epsilon = 0.7073
Huynh-Feldt Epsilon = 0.9221

Level of SES	N	-----------READ1--------- Mean	SD	-----------READ2---------- Mean	SD
HIGH	5	61.8000000	1.92353841	52.8000000	4.14728827
LOW	5	58.0000000	2.23606798	43.4000000	2.60768096

Level of SES	N	-----------READ3--------- Mean	SD	-----------READ4--------- Mean	SD
HIGH	5	61.2000000	2.58843582	56.8000000	4.43846820
LOW	5	57.2000000	2.38746728	47.8000000	1.78885438

Level of SES	N	-----------READ5--------- Mean	SD	-----------READ6--------- Mean	SD
HIGH	5	61.8000000	3.27108545	63.2000000	4.32434966
LOW	5	57.6000000	3.57770876	53.2000000	4.43846820

We will discuss the statistical results later, after two alternate programs have been presented. However, the program above which uses the REPEATED statement, produces two statistics, Greenhouse-Geisser-Epsilon and the Huynh-Feldt-Epsilon which we will explain here. There are some assumptions in repeated measures designs which are rather complicated. You may see these mentioned as symmetry tests or even sphericity tests. Somewhat simplified, what is being tested is the assumption that the variances and correlations are the same among the various dependent variables (See Edwards, 1985 mentioned in Chapter 1). It is more or less an extension of the assumption of equal variances in t-tests or ANOVA. SAS software provides tests for these assumptions listed as the Greenhouse-Geisser and the Huynh-Feldt tests. If they are nonsignificant, you may proceed with the analysis. If they are significant, under certain circumstances, you can still do the analysis, but you'll need some consultation with a statistician.

We will now present the other two programs that analyze this experiment without use of the REPEATED statement. Here is a second method.

We have arranged our data so that each line represents one cell of our design. In practice, this would be tedious, but it will help you understand the last program for this problem in which all data for a subject are read on one line and the data set is transformed to look like this one.

```
DATA;
INPUT SUBJ SES $ YEAR SEASON $ READ;
CARDS;
1 HIGH 1 SPRING 61
1 HIGH 1 FALL 50
1 HIGH 2 SPRING 60
1 HIGH 2 FALL 55
1 HIGH 3 SPRING 59
1 HIGH 3 FALL 62
2 HIGH 1 SPRING 64
     etc.
```

This final approach places all the data for each subject on one line and does **not** use the REPEATED statement. This was the approach that had to be used before SAS software supported the REPEATED statement of

ANOVA and GLM. We have left it in since the programming techniques are useful and are needed in cases where **all** the factors are repeated. As we have mentioned before, since there is an alternative easier method (above), you may skip the more elaborate program below and not sacrifice anything in the way of statistical understanding.

ALTERNATIVE PROGRAM FOR READING EXPERIMENT

```
1      PROC FORMAT;
2          VALUE FSEASON 1=SPRING 2=FALL;
3          VALUE FSES 1=HIGH 2=LOW;
4      DATA;
5      DO SES=1 TO 2;
6          DO I=1 TO 5;
7              SUBJ+1;
8              DO YEAR=1 TO 3;
9                  DO SEASON=1 TO 2;
10                     INPUT READ @;
11                     OUTPUT;
12                     END;
13                 END;
14              END;
15          END;
16     FORMAT SEASON FSEASON. SES FSES.;
17     DROP I;
18     CARDS;
       61 50 60 55 59 62
       64 55 62 57 63 63
                etc.
```

NOTE: The indentation is **not** necessary. It is used as a visual aid to keep the DO loops straight.

This program is **not** as complicated as it may seem at first glance. Lines 1 through 4 create two formats to be used later. Our data will be arranged in the same order as they appear in the diagram of the experimental design. All high-SES students will be read followed by the low-SES students. Each student will have a spring/fall set of reading comprehension scores for each of the three years. Since we have 5 subjects in each SES group, the loop in line 6 will go from 1 to 5. The next loop in line 8 initially sets the variable YEAR to 1 and the next loop in line 9 starts at SEASON=1. Finally, in line 10, a data value is read. The "@" causes the next input statement to read data from the same line of data. When line 11, OUTPUT, is executed, a line is written in the SAS data set consisting of the variables:

```
SES SUBJ YEAR SEASON READ
```

Note that the variable I is not included because of the DROP statement in line 17. It is not necessary to drop I; we simply don't need it. We could leave it in the data set and just not use it. You should also be aware that DO loops can have character arguments. Thus, we could have written "DO SES='HIGH', 'LOW';" and "DO SEASON='SPRING', 'FALL';." Be careful, because if the length of the first value in the DO loop is shorter than the other levels, the program will truncate the length of the character variable to the first length it encounters. To avoid this problem, either pad the first value with blanks to be equal to the length of the longest value or use a LENGTH statement to define the length of the character variable. For example: "DO GRP = 'ONE ','TWO','THREE';"

END OF ALTERNATIVE PROGRAM

Now, regardless of the SAS data statements you used, the ANOVA statements will be the following:

```
PROC ANOVA;
    TITLE 'READING COMPREHENSION STUDY';
    CLASSES SUBJ SES YEAR SEASON;
    MODEL READ = SES SUBJ(SES)
                YEAR SES*YEAR YEAR*SUBJ(SES)
                SEASON SES*SEASON SEASON*SUBJ(SES)
                YEAR*SEASON SES*YEAR*SEASON
                YEAR*SEASON*SUBJ(SES);
    MEANS YEAR / DUNCAN E=YEAR*SUBJ(SES);
    MEANS SES SEASON SES*YEAR SES*SEASON YEAR*SEASON
          SES*YEAR*SEASON;
    TEST H=SES                    E=SUBJ(SES);
    TEST H=YEAR SES*YEAR          E=YEAR*SUBJ(SES);
    TEST H=SEASON SES*SEASON      E=SEASON*SUBJ(SES);
    TEST H=YEAR*SEASON SES*YEAR*SEASON
                                  E=YEAR*SEASON*SUBJ(SES);
```

As before, we specify hypotheses and error terms with TEST statements following our MODEL and we include the appropriate error terms with the Duncan requests.

Have our original ideas about "slippage" been confirmed by the data?

First, let us examine each of the main effects and their interactions:

SOURCE	F VALUE	PR > F
SES	13.54	.0062
YEAR	26.91	.0001
SEASON	224.82	.0001
SES*YEAR	.11	.8962
SES*SEASON	37.05	.0003
YEAR*SEASON	112.95	.0001
SES*YEAR*SEASON	0.18	.8333

Next are the means for each of the main effects and two-way interactions:

```
Level of          ------------READ-------------
SES        N        Mean              SD

1          30     59.6000000       4.92425384
2          30     52.8666667       6.23523543

Level of          ------------READ-------------
SEASON     N        Mean              SD

1          30     59.6000000       3.22276386
2          30     52.8666667       7.26224689

Level of  Level of          -------------READ-------------
SES       YEAR     N        Mean              SD

1         1        10     57.3000000       5.63816361
1         2        10     59.0000000       4.13655788
1         3        10     62.5000000       3.68932394
2         1        10     50.7000000       8.02842174
2         2        10     52.5000000       5.33853913
2         3        10     55.4000000       4.45221543

Level of  Level of          -------------READ-------------
SES       SEASON   N        Mean              SD

1         1        15     61.6000000       2.47270817
1         2        15     57.6000000       5.96178305
2         1        15     57.6000000       2.61315354
2         2        15     48.1333333       5.06904706
```

Level of YEAR	Level of SEASON	N	----------------READ---------------- Mean	SD
1	1	10	59.9000000	2.80673792
1	2	10	48.1000000	5.93389510
2	1	10	59.2000000	3.15524255
2	2	10	52.3000000	5.71644800
3	1	10	59.7000000	3.91719855
3	2	10	58.2000000	6.69659947

What conclusions can we draw from these results?

1. High-SES students have higher reading comprehension scores than low-SES students ($F=13.54$, $p=.0062$).
2. Reading comprehension increases with each year ($F=26.91$, $p=.0001$). However, this increase is due partly to the smaller "slippage" in the later years (see 5 below).
3. Students had higher reading comprehension scores in the spring compared to the following fall ($F=224.82$, $p=.0001$).
4. The "slippage" was greater for the low-SES students (there was a significant SES*SEASON interaction — $F=37.05$, $p=.0003$).
5. "Slippage" decreases as the students get older (YEAR*SEASON is significant — $F=112.95$, $p=.0001$).

Repeated measures designs can be a powerful ally of the applied researcher. They can also be a little bit tricky. For example, in our coffee study, even though we randomized the order of first drinking the coffee with dinner or breakfast, there may be an effect we're overlooking. It may be that one (or all) of the brands take a little "getting used to." This could result in subjects preferring their second drinking of the coffee (whether breakfast **or** dinner). We are ignoring this in our study and maybe we shouldn't be. Had we **not** randomized which drinking came first, we would have **confounded** drinking order with MEAL. The best way to make sure that you are getting what you want out of a repeated measures design is to consult a text which deals solely with the design and statistical issues involved. (Winer does an excellent job of this.)

PROBLEMS

8-1. A marketing survey is conducted to determine sport shirt preference. A questionnaire is administered to a panel of 4 judges.

Each judge rates three shirts of each of three brands (X, Y, and Z).
The data entry form is shown below:

MARKETING SURVEY FORM

1. Judge ID	|__|1
2. Brand (1=X, 2=Y, 3=Z)	|__|2
3. Color rating 9=Best, 1=Worst	|__|3
4. Workmanship rating	|__|4
5. Overall preference	|__|5

An index is computed as follows:

```
INDEX = (3*OVERALL PREFERENCE + 2*WORKMANSHIP +
         COLOR RATING) / 6.0
```

The collected data follow:

```
11836
21747
31767
41846
12635
22534
32546
42436
13988
23877
33978
43887
11758
21755
31847
41756
12464
22545
32455
42554
13786
```

```
23889
33976
43879
```

Compare the color rating, workmanship, overall preference, and index among the three brands, using analysis of variance.

8-2. A taste test is conducted to see which city has the best-tasting tap water. A panel of 4 judges tastes each of the samples from the four cities represented. The rating scale is a Likert scale with 1=worst to 9=best. Sample data and the coding scheme are shown below:

COLUMN	DESCRIPTION
1-3	Judge identification number
4	City code:
	1=New York 2=New Orleans
	3=Chicago 4=Denver
5	Taste rating 1=worst 9=best

Data:

```
00118
00126
00138
00145
00215
00226
00235
00244
00317
00324
00336
00344
00417
00425
00437
00443
```

Write a SAS program to describe these data and to perform an analysis of variance.

*8-3. The same data as in Problem 8-2 are to be analyzed. However, they are arranged so that the four ratings from each judge are on one line. Thus, columns 1-3 are for the judge ID, column 4 is the rating for New York, column 5 for New Orleans, column 6 for Chicago, and column 7 for Denver. Our reformed data are shown below:

```
0018685
0025654
0037464
0047573
```

Write the DATA statements to analyze this arrangement of the data. Remember, you will need to create a variable for CITY and to have one observation per city.

*8-4. A study is conducted to test the area of nerve fibers in NORMAL and DIABETIC rats. A sample from the DISTAL and PROXIMAL ends of each nerve fiber is measured for each rat. Therefore, we have GROUP (Normal versus Diabetic) and LOCATION (Distal versus proximal) as independent variables, with location as a repeated measure (each rat nerve is measured at each end of the nerve fiber). The data are shown below:

	RATNO	DISTAL	PROXIMAL
	1	34	38
NORMAL	2	28	38
	3	38	48
	4	32	38
	5	44	42
DIABETIC	6	52	48
	7	46	46
	8	54	50

Write a SAS program to enter these data and run a two-way analysis of variance, treating the location as a repeated measure. Use the REPEATED option for the LOCATION variable. Is there any difficulty in interpreting the main effects? Why?

8-5. What's wrong with this program?

```
1       DATA FINDIT;
2       DO GROUP='CONTROL','DRUG';
3          DO TIME='BEFORE','AFTER';
4             DO SUBJ=1 TO 3;
5                INPUT SCORE @;
6                END;
7             END;
8          END;
9       CARDS;
        10 13 15 20     (data for subject 1)
        12 14 16 18     (data for subject 2)
        15 18 22 28     (data for subject 3)
10      PROC ANOVA;
11         TITLE 'ANALYSIS OF VARIANCE';
12         CLASSES SUBJ GROUP TIME;
13         MODEL SCORE = GROUP SUBJ(GROUP)
14            TIME GROUP*TIME TIME*SUBJ(GROUP);
15         TEST H=GROUP E=SUBJ(GROUP);
16         TEST H=TIME GROUP*TIME E=TIME*SUBJ(GROUP);
17         MEANS GROUP|TIME;
```

NOTE: The comments in parentheses next to the data lines are not part of the program.

CHAPTER 9
MULTIPLE REGRESSION ANALYSIS

A. INTRODUCTION

Multiple regression analysis is a method for relating two or more independent variables to a dependent variable. In **most** applications, all of the variables are continuous variables (as opposed to categorical variables such as "sex" or "type of medication," where analysis of variance is the technique of choice). There are two rather distinct uses of multiple regression, and they will be addressed separately. The first use is in studies where the levels of the independent variables have been experimentally controlled (such as amount of medication and number of days between dosages). This use will be referred to as "**designed regression.**" The second use involves settings where a sample of subjects have been observed on a number of naturally occurring variables (age, income, level of anxiety, etc.) which are then related to some outcome of interest. This use of regression will be referred to as "**nonexperimental regression.**"

It is fairly easy to misuse regression. We will try to note some popular pitfalls, but we cannot list them all. A rule of thumb is to use your common sense. If the results of an analysis don't make any sense, get help. Ultimately, statistics is a tool employed to help us understand life. Although understanding life can be tricky, it is not usually perverse. Before accepting conclusions which seem silly based on statistical analyses, consult with a veteran data analyst. Most truly revolutionary results from data analyses are based on data entry errors.

In the second edition of this book, separate SAS procedures were used for such tasks as simple multiple regression, stepwise regression, and r-square. With version 6, all the regression procedures have been combined under PROC REG.

B. DESIGNED REGRESSION

Imagine a researcher interested in the effects of scheduled exercise and the use of a stimulant on weight loss. She constructs an experiment on 24 college sophomores in which 4 levels of stimulant and 3 levels of exercise are used. There are 24 subjects in the experiment and each is randomly assigned to a level of exercise and stimulant such that two students are in each of the 12 (3X4) possible combinations of exercise and stimulant. After 3 weeks of participation, a measure of weight loss (post-pre weight) is obtained on each subject. The data for the experiment might look as shown below:

DATA FOR WEIGHT LOSS EXPERIMENT

SUBJECT	STIMULANT (mg/day)	EXERCISE (hrs/week)	WEIGHT LOSS (pounds)
1	100	0	-4
2	100	0	0
3	100	5	-7
4	100	5	-6
5	100	10	-2
6	100	10	-14
7	200	0	-5
8	200	0	-2
9	200	5	-5
10	200	5	-8
11	200	10	-9
12	200	10	-9
13	300	0	1
14	300	0	0
15	300	5	-3
16	300	5	-3
17	300	10	-8
18	300	10	-12
19	400	0	-5
20	400	0	-4
21	400	5	-4
22	400	5	-6
23	400	10	-9
24	400	10	-7

These data could be analyzed either as a 3X4 analysis of variance or as a two-variable multiple regression. The regression approach assumes that the effects of exercise and medication increase linearly (i.e., in a straight line); the ANOVA model makes no such assumption. If we use the multiple regression approach, the following program will provide the desired results:

```
1  DATA REGRESSN;
2  INPUT ID DOSAGE EXERCISE LOSS;
3  CARDS;
   1 100 0 -4
   2 100 0 0
   3 100 5 -7
  etc.
4  PROC REG;
5     MODEL LOSS = DOSAGE EXERCISE / P R;
6  RUN;
```

Lines 1-3 define the data set. Line 4, PROC REG, is the SAS procedure which performs multiple regression. Line 5 specifies the MODEL to be estimated. This model simply calls for the dependent variable LOSS to be regressed upon the independent variables DOSAGE and EXERCISE. The options "P" and "R" indicate that we want predicted values and residuals to be computed. The output from this program is presented below:

Model: MODEL1
Dependent Variable: LOSS

Analysis of Variance

Source	DF	Sum of Squares	Mean Square	F Value	Prob>F
Model	2	162.97083	81.48542	11.185	0.0005
Error	21	152.98750	7.28512		
C Total	23	315.95833			

Root MSE	2.69910	R-square	0.5158
Dep Mean	-5.45833	Adj R-sq	0.4697
C.V.	-49.44909		

Parameter Estimates

Variable	DF	Parameter Estimate	Standard Error	T for H0: Parameter=0	Prob > |T|
INTERCEP	1	-2.562500	1.50884052	-1.698	0.1042
DOSAGE	1	0.001167	0.00492785	0.237	0.8151
EXERCISE	1	-0.637500	0.13495480	-4.724	0.0001

Obs	Dep Var LOSS	Predict Value	Residual	Student Residual	-2-1-0 1 2	Cook's D
1	-4.0000	-2.4458	-1.5542	-0.636	| *| |	0.029
2	0	-2.4458	2.4458	1.000	| |** |	0.073
3	-7.0000	-5.6333	-1.3667	-0.539	| *| |	0.013
4	-6.0000	-5.6333	-0.3667	-0.145	| | |	0.001
5	-2.0000	-8.8208	6.8208	2.789	| |***** |	0.566
6	-14.0000	-8.8208	-5.1792	-2.118	|****| |	0.326
7	-5.0000	-2.3292	-2.6708	-1.050	| **| |	0.047
8	-2.0000	-2.3292	0.3292	0.129	| | |	0.001
9	-5.0000	-5.5167	0.5167	0.196	| | |	0.001
10	-8.0000	-5.5167	-2.4833	-0.944	| *| |	0.016
11	-9.0000	-8.7042	-0.2958	-0.116	| | |	0.001
12	-9.0000	-8.7042	-0.2958	-0.116	| | |	0.001
13	1.0000	-2.2125	3.2125	1.263	| |** |	0.067
14	0	-2.2125	2.2125	0.870	| |* |	0.032
15	-3.0000	-5.4000	2.4000	0.912	| |* |	0.015
16	-3.0000	-5.4000	2.4000	0.912	| |* |	0.015
17	-8.0000	-8.5875	0.5875	0.231	| | |	0.002
18	-12.0000	-8.5875	-3.4125	-1.342	| **| |	0.076
19	-5.0000	-2.0958	-2.9042	-1.188	| **| |	0.103
20	-4.0000	-2.0958	-1.9042	-0.779	| *| |	0.044
21	-4.0000	-5.2833	1.2833	0.506	| |* |	0.011
22	-6.0000	-5.2833	-0.7167	-0.283	| | |	0.004
23	-9.0000	-8.4708	-0.5292	-0.216	| | |	0.003
24	-7.0000	-8.4708	1.4708	0.601	| |* |	0.026

Sum of Residuals   -5.32907E-15
Sum of Squared Residuals   152.9875
Predicted Resid SS (Press)   212.0359

NOTE: Portions of the output have been edited for simplicity.

The output begins with an analysis of variance table which looks much as it would from a standard ANOVA. We can see that there are 2 degrees of freedom in this model, one for EXERCISE and one for DOSAGE. There is only one degree of freedom for each since the regression estimates a single straight line for each variable rather than estimating a number of cell means. The sum of squares for the model (162.971) tells us how much of the variation in weight loss is attributable to EXERCISE and DOSAGE. The mean square for the model (81.485) is the sum of squares (162.971) divided by the degrees of freedom for the model (2). This mean square is then divided by the mean square error (7.285) to produce the F statistic for the regression (11.185). The p-value for this is reported as .0005. "C TOTAL" means "corrected total" and indicates the total degrees of freedom (23) and sum of squares (315.958) in the dependent variable. The corrected total degrees of freedom is always one less than the total sample size since one degree of freedom is used to estimate the grand mean. The ROOT MSE (2.699) stands for the square root of the mean square error and represents, in standard deviation units, the variation in the system not attributable to

EXERCISE or DOSAGE. DEP Mean (-5.458) is simply the mean of the dependent variable (LOSS). The R-SQUARE (.5158) is the square of the multiple correlation of EXERCISE and DOSAGE with LOSS. It is the proportion of variance in LOSS explained by (attributable to) the independent variables. ADJ R-SQ (.4697) is the adjusted R-square. The adjusted R-square takes into account how many variables were used in the equation and slightly lowers the estimate of explained variance. C.V. (-49.449) stands for coefficient of variation and is calculated by dividing the ROOT MSE by the mean and multiplying by 100. The C.V. is sometimes useful when the mean and standard deviation are related (such as in income data). The bottom part of the output shows us, observation by observation, the actual LOSS, the predicted value and the difference between the two (residual). In addition, the column labeled "Student Residuals," expresses the residual as a t-score and Cook's D is a distance measure that helps us determine how strongly a particular data point affects the overall regression. Large absolute values of D (2 or more) indicate problems with your model or data points that require some careful scrutiny.

Having explained the terms in the analysis of variance table for the regression, let's summarize what meaning we can infer. Basically, the table indicates that the independent variables **were** related to the dependent variable (since the F was significant at p=.0005). Furthermore, we find that about 50% of the variation in weight loss is explained by the two experimental treatments. Many researchers are more interested in the R-square statistic than in the p-value since the R-square represents an estimate of how strongly related the variables were. The bottom half of the printout contains the estimates of the parameters of the regression equation. Three parameters are estimated: (1) the intercept, or constant term, (2) the coefficient for DOSAGE, and (3) the coefficient for EXERCISE. Each parameter estimate was based on 1 degree of freedom (always the case in regressions). For each parameter estimate, a standard error was estimated along with a t-statistic and a p-value for the t-statistic. The t-statistic is simply the parameter estimate divided by its standard error. It is based on the number of degrees of freedom for the error term (21 in this example).

This half of the printout tells us that it was really EXERCISE that caused the weight loss. The regression coefficient for DOSAGE is not statistically significantly different from zero (p=.8151). The fact that the intercept was not significantly different from zero is irrelevant here. The intercept merely tells us where the regression line (or plane in this case) crosses the y-axis and does not explain any variation.

At this point, many researchers would run a new regression with DOSAGE eliminated, to refine the estimate of EXERCISE. Since this was a designed experiment, we would recommend leaving the regression as is for purposes of reporting. Dropping DOSAGE won't affect the estimated impact of EXERCISE since DOSAGE and EXERCISE are uncorrelated (by design). **When the independent variables in a regression are uncorrelated, the estimates of the regression coefficients are unchanged by adding or dropping independent variables.** When the independent variables are correlated, dropping and adding variables may strongly affect the regression estimates.

C. NONEXPERIMENTAL REGRESSION

Many, if not most, regression analyses are conducted on data sets where the independent variables show some degree of correlation. These data sets, resulting from nonexperimental research, are common in all fields. Studies of factors affecting heart disease or the incidence of cancer, studies relating student characteristics to student achievement, and studies predicting economic trends all utilize nonexperimental data. The potential for a researcher to be misled by a nonexperimental data set is high; for a novice researcher, it is near certainty. We strongly urge consultation with a good text in this area (Pedhazur, **Multiple Regression in Behavioral Research** is excellent) or with a statistical consultant. Having presented this caveat, let's venture into regression analysis for nonexperimental data sets.

The Nature of the Data

There are usually many surface similarities between experimental and nonexperimental data sets. First, there are one or more outcome or dependent variables. Second, there are several independent variables (sometimes quite a few). The basic difference here is that the independent variables are correlated with one another. This is because in nonexperimental studies one defines a population of interest (people who have had heart attacks, sixth grade students, etc.), draws a sample, and measures the variables of interest. The goal of the study is usually to explain variation in the dependent variable by one or more of the independent variables. So far, it sounds simple.

The problem is that the correlation among the independent variables causes the regression estimates to change depending on which independent variables are being used. That is, the impact of B on A depends on whether C is in the equation or not. With C omitted, B can look very influential. With C included, the impact of B can disappear completely! The reason for this is as follows: A regression coefficient tells us the **unique** contribution of an independent variable to a dependent variable. That is, the coefficient for B tells us what B contributes all by itself with no overlap with any other variable. If B is the only variable in the equation, this is no problem. But if we add C, and if B and C are correlated, then the **unique** contribution of B on A will be changed. Let's see how this works in an example.

The subjects are a random sample of 6th grade students from Metropolitan City School District. The following measures have been taken on the subjects:

1. ACH6 - Reading achievement at the end of sixth grade.
2. ACH5 - Reading achievement at the end of fifth grade.
3. APT - A measure of verbal aptitude taken in the fifth grade.
4. ATT - A measure of attitude toward school taken in fifth grade.
5. INCOME - A measure of parental income (in thousands of dollars per year).

Our data set is listed below. (Note: These are **not** real data.)

ID	ACH6	ACH5	APT	ATT	INCOME
1	7.5	6.6	104	60	67
2	6.9	6.0	116	58	29
3	7.2	6.0	130	63	36
4	6.8	5.9	110	74	84
5	6.7	6.1	114	55	33
6	6.6	6.3	108	52	21
7	7.1	5.2	103	48	19
8	6.5	4.4	92	42	30
9	7.2	4.9	136	57	32
10	6.2	5.1	105	49	23
11	6.5	4.6	98	54	57
12	5.8	4.3	91	56	29
13	6.7	4.8	100	49	30
14	5.5	4.2	98	43	36
15	5.3	4.3	101	52	31
16	4.7	4.4	84	41	33
17	4.9	3.9	96	50	20

ID	ACH6	ACH5	APT	ATT	INCOME
18	4.8	4.1	99	52	34
19	4.7	3.8	106	47	30
20	4.6	3.6	89	58	27

The purpose of the study is to understand what underlies the reading achievement of the students in the district. The following program was written to analyze the data:

```
DATA NONEXP;
INPUT ACH6 ACH5 APT ATT INCOME;
CARDS;
7.5 6.6 104 60 67
6.9 6.0 116 58 29
     etc.
PROC REG;
   MODEL ACH6 = ACH5 APT ATT INCOME/SELECTION=FORWARD;
   MODEL ACH6 = ACH5 APT ATT INCOME/SELECTION=MAXR;
RUN;
```

By using the SELECTION=FORWARD option of PROC REG, we have specified that a forward, stepwise regression is to be run with ACH6 as the dependent variable and ACH5, APT, ATT, and INCOME as independent variables. We also want to run the model using the MAXR technique. Before examining the output, we should discuss briefly stepwise regression and nonexperimental data.

D. STEPWISE REGRESSIONS

As mentioned earlier, with nonexperimental data sets, the independent variables are not truly "independent" in that they are usually correlated with one another. If these correlations are moderate to high (say 0.50 and above), then the regression coefficients are greatly affected by that particular subset of independent variables in the regression equation. If there are a number of independent variables to consider, coming up with the best subset can be difficult. Stepwise regression (there are a family of different stepwise approaches) was developed to assist researchers in arriving at this optimal subset. Unfortunately, stepwise regression is frequently misused. The problem is that the solution from a purely statistical point of view is often not the best from a substantive perspective. That is, a lot of variance is explained but the regression doesn't make much sense. We'll discuss this more when we examine the printout. Stepwise regression examines a number of different regression equations. Basically, the goal of stepwise techniques is to take a set of independent variables and put them into a regression one at a time in a specified manner until all variables have been added or until a specified criterion has been met. The criterion is usually one of statistical significance such as: there are no more regressors that would be significant if entered or improvement in variance explained (the additional R^2 to be gained by entering the next best regressor is too small to bother with).

SAS software allows for a number of selection techniques. Among them are:

1. FORWARD—This starts with the best single regressor, then finds the best one to add to what exists, the next best, etc.
2. BACKWARD—This starts will all variables in the equation, then it drops the worst one, then the next, etc.
3. STEPWISE—This is similar to FORWARD except that there is an additional step in which all variables in each equation are checked again to see if they remain significant after the new variable has been entered.
4. MAXR—This is a rather complicated procedure, but basically it tries to find the one-variable regression with the highest R^2, then the two-variable regression with the highest R^2, etc.
5. MINR—This is very similar to the MAXR, except that the selection system is slightly different.

Now, let's examine the printout from the program on the previous page:

Forward Selection Method

Forward Selection Procedure for Dependent Variable ACH6

Step 1 Variable ACH5 Entered   R-square = 0.66909805 C(p) = 1.87549647

	DF	Sum of Squares	Mean Square	F	Prob>F
Regression	1	12.17624633	12.17624633	36.40	0.0001
Error	18	6.02175367	0.33454187		
Total	19	18.19800000			

Variable	Parameter Estimate	Standard Error	Type II Sum of Squares	F	Prob>F
INTERCEP	1.83725236	0.71994457	2.17866266	6.51	0.0200
ACH5	0.86756297	0.14380353	12.17624633	36.40	0.0001

Bounds on condition number: 1,   1

Step 2 Variable APT Entered   R-square = 0.70817380 C(p) = 1.76460424

	DF	Sum of Squares	Mean Square	F	Prob>F
Regression	2	12.88734675	6.44367337	20.63	0.0001
Error	17	5.31065325	0.31239137		
Total	19	18.19800000			

Variable	Parameter Estimate	Standard Error	Type II Sum of Squares	F	Prob>F
INTERCEP	0.64269963	1.05397972	0.11615840	0.37	0.5501
ACH5	0.72475202	0.16813652	5.80435251	18.58	0.0005
APT	0.01824901	0.01209548	0.71110042	2.28	0.1497

Bounds on condition number: 1.463985,   5.855938

No other variable met the 0.5000 significance level for entry into the model.

Summary of Forward Selection Procedure for Dependent Variable ACH6

Step	Variable Entered	Number In	Partial R**2	Model R**2	C(p)	F	Prob>F
1	ACH5	1	0.6691	0.6691	1.8755	36.3968	0.0001
2	APT	2	0.0391	0.7082	1.7646	2.2763	0.1497

MAXR method

Maximum R-square Improvement for Dependent Variable ACH6

Step 1 Variable ACH5 Entered   R-square = 0.66909805 C(p) = 1.87549647

	DF	Sum of Squares	Mean Square	F	Prob>F
Regression	1	12.17624633	12.17624633	36.40	0.0001
Error	18	6.02175367	0.33454187		
Total	19	18.19800000			

Variable	Parameter Estimate	Standard Error	Type II Sum of Squares	F	Prob>F
INTERCEP	1.83725236	0.71994457	2.17866266	6.51	0.0200
ACH5	0.86756297	0.14380353	12.17624633	36.40	0.0001

Bounds on condition number: 1,   1

The above model is the best 1-variable model found.

Step 2   Variable APT Entered   R-square = 0.70817380 C(p) = 1.76460424

	DF	Sum of Squares	Mean Square	F	Prob>F
Regression	2	12.88734675	6.44367337	20.63	0.0001
Error	17	5.31065325	0.31239137		
Total	19	18.19800000			

Variable	Parameter Estimate	Standard Error	Type II Sum of Squares	F	Prob>F
INTERCEP	0.64269963	1.05397972	0.11615840	0.37	0.5501
ACH5	0.72475202	0.16813652	5.80435251	18.58	0.0005
APT	0.01824901	0.01209548	0.71110042	2.28	0.1497

Bounds on condition number: 1.463985,   5.855938

The above model is the best 2-variable model found.

Step 3 Variable ATT Entered   R-square = 0.71086255 C(p) = 3.61935632

	DF	Sum of Squares	Mean Square	F	Prob>F
Regression	3	12.93627670	4.31209223	13.11	0.0001
Error	16	5.26172330	0.32885771		
Total	19	18.19800000			

Variable	Parameter Estimate	Standard Error	Type II Sum of Squares	F	Prob>F
INTERCEP	0.80013762	1.15586303	0.15758855	0.48	0.4987
ACH5	0.74739939	0.18222852	5.53198290	16.82	0.0008
APT	0.01972808	0.01298905	0.75861687	2.31	0.1483
ATT	-0.00797735	0.02068119	0.04892995	0.15	0.7048

Bounds on condition number: 1.633564,   14.15998

The above model is the best 3-variable model found.

Step 4 Variable INCOME Entered R-square = 0.72232775 C(p) = 5.00000000

	DF	Sum of Squares	Mean Square	F	Prob>F
Regression	4	13.14492048	3.28623012	9.76	0.0004
Error	15	5.05307952	0.33687197		
Total	19	18.19800000			

Variable	Parameter Estimate	Standard Error	Type II Sum of Squares	F	Prob>F
INTERCEP	0.91164562	1.17841159	0.20161506	0.60	0.4512
ACH5	0.71373964	0.18932981	4.78747493	14.21	0.0019
APT	0.02393740	0.01419278	0.95826178	2.84	0.1124
ATT	-0.02115577	0.02680560	0.20983199	0.62	0.4423
INCOME	0.00898581	0.01141792	0.20864378	0.62	0.4435

Bounds on condition number: 2.431593,   31.79315

The above model is the best 4-variable model found.

No further improvement in R-square is possible.

Since a forward selection was requested first, that is what was run first. In step 1, the technique picked ACH5 as the first regressor since it had the highest correlation with the dependent variable ACH6. The RSQUARE (variance explained) is 0.669, which is quite high. "Cp" is a statistic used in determining how many variables to use in the regression. You will need to consult one of the references in chapter 1 or see your friendly statistician for help in interpreting Mallow's Cp statistic. The remaining statistics are the same as for the PROC REG program run earlier. In step 2, the technique determined that adding APT would lead to the largest increase in R^2. We notice however, that RSQUARE has only moved from 0.669 to 0.708, a slight increase. Furthermore, the regression coefficient for APT is nonsignificant (p=.1497). This indicates that APT doesn't tell us much more than we already knew from ACH5. Most researchers would drop it from the model and use the one-variable (ACH5) model. After step 2 has been run, the forward technique indicates that no other variable would come close to being significant. In fact, no other variable would have a p-value less than .50 (we usually require less than .05, although in regression analysis, it is not uncommon to set the inclusion level at .10).

The MAXR approach finds the best one-variable model, then the best two-variable model, etc. until the full model (all variables included) is estimated. As can be seen, with these data, both these techniques lead to the same conclusions: ACH5 is far and away the best predictor; it is a strong predictor, and no other variables would be included with the possible exception of APT.

There is a problem here, however. Any 6th grade teacher could tell you that the best predictor of 6th grade performance is 5th grade performance. But it doesn't really tell us very much else. It might be more helpful to look at APT, ATT, and INCOME without ACH5 in the regression. Also, it could be useful to make ACH5 the dependent variable and have APT, ATT, and INCOME be regressors. Of course, this is suggesting quite a bit in the way of regressions. There is another regression technique which greatly facilitates looking at a large number of possibilities quickly. This is the RSQUARE option of PROC REG. The RSQUARE option will give us the multiple r-square value for every one, two, three, ... n way combinations of the variables in the independent variable list. The following lines will generate all of the regressions mentioned so far as well as the model with ACH5 as the dependent variable:

```
PROC REG;
   MODEL ACH6 = INCOME ATT APT ACH5 /
                 SELECION =RSQUARE;
   MODEL ACH5 = INCOME ATT APT / SELECTION=RSQUARE;
RUN;
```

The output from PROC REG with RSQUARE as the selection option is shown next:

```
N=     20    REGRESSION MODELS FOR DEPENDENT VARIABLE ACH6

NUMBER IN    R-SQUARE     VARIABLES IN MODEL
  MODEL

    1        0.10173375   INCOME
    1        0.18113085   ATT
    1        0.38921828   APT
    1        0.66909805   ACH5
    ----------------------------------------
    2        0.18564520   ATT INCOME
    2        0.40687404   APT ATT
    2        0.45629702   APT INCOME
    2        0.66917572   ACH5 ATT
    2        0.66964641   ACH5 INCOME
    2        0.70817380   ACH5 APT
    ----------------------------------------
    3        0.45925077   APT ATT INCOME
    3        0.66967022   ACH5 ATT INCOME
    3        0.71079726   ACH5 APT INCOME
    3        0.71086255   ACH5 APT ATT
    ----------------------------------------
    4        0.72232775   ACH5 APT ATT INCOME
    ----------------------------------------

N=     20    REGRESSION MODELS FOR DEPENDENT VARIABLE ACH5

NUMBER IN    R-SQUARE     VARIABLES IN MODEL
  MODEL

    1        0.13195687   INCOME
    1        0.26115761   ATT
    1        0.31693268   APT
    ----------------------------------------
    2        0.26422291   ATT INCOME
    2        0.38784142   APT ATT
    2        0.41273318   APT INCOME
    ----------------------------------------
    3        0.41908115   APT ATT INCOME
    ----------------------------------------
```

The top part contains all of the RSQUARE's for every possible 1-, 2-, 3-, and 4-variable regression with ACH6 as the outcome variable. It is possible to glean a lot of information quickly from this table.

Let us say that you have just decided that you don't want ACH5 as a regressor. You can quickly see from the one-variable regressions that APT is the next best regressor (R^2=.389). The next question is, "What is the best two-variable regression?" and "Is the improvement large enough to be worthwhile?" Let's look at the two-variable regressions which have APT in them:

R^2 for APT + ATT = .407
APT + INCOME = .456

(Remember, we're eliminating ACH5 for now.)

APT and INCOME is best, and the gain is .067 (which is equal to 0.456 - 0.389). Is a 6.7% increase in variance explained worth including? Probably it is, although it may not be statistically significant with our small sample size. In explaining the regressions using ACH5 as an outcome variable, we can see that APT and INCOME look like the best bet there also. In interpreting these data, we might conclude that aptitude combined with parental wealth are strong explanatory variables in reading achievement. It is important to remember that statistical analyses must make substantive sense. The question arises here as to how these two variables work to influence reading scores. Some researchers would agree that APT is a psychological variable and INCOME is a sociological variable and the two shouldn't be mixed in a single regression. It's a bit beyond the scope of this book to speculate on this, but when running nonexperimental regressions, it is best to be guided by these two principles:

1. Parsimony—less is more in terms of regressors. Another regressor will always explain a little bit more, but it often confuses our understanding of life.
2. Common Sense—the regressors must bear a logical relationship to the dependent variable in addition to a statistical one. (ACH6 would be a great predictor of ACH5, but it is a temporal impossibility.)

Finally, whenever regression analysis is used, the researcher should examine the simple correlations among the variables with a program like the following.

```
PROC CORR;
    VAR APT ATT ACH5 ACH6;
```

will generate the following output:

VARIABLE	N	MEAN	STD DEV	SUM	MINIMUM	MAXIMUM
ACH6	20	6.1100	0.97867	122.200	4.6000	7.5000
ACH5	20	4.9250	0.92274	98.500	3.6000	6.6000
APT	20	104.0000	12.82678	2080.000	84.0000	136.0000
ATT	20	53.0000	7.74597	1060.000	41.0000	74.0000
INCOME	20	35.0500	16.18471	701.000	19.0000	84.0000

CORRELATION COEFFICIENTS / PROB > |R| UNDER HO:RHO=0
/ N = 20

	ACH6	ACH5	APT	ATT	INCOME
ACH6	1.00000	0.81798	0.62387	0.42559	0.31896
	0.0000	0.0001	0.0033	0.0614	0.1705
ACH5	0.81798	1.00000	0.56297	0.51104	0.36326
	0.0001	0.0000	0.0098	0.0213	0.1154
APT	0.62387	0.56297	1.00000	0.49741	0.09811
	0.0033	0.0098	0.0000	0.0256	0.6807
ATT	0.42559	0.51104	0.49741	1.00000	0.62638
	0.0614	0.0213	0.0256	0.0000	0.0031
INCOME	0.31896	0.36326	0.09811	0.62638	1.00000
	0.1705	0.1154	0.6807	0.0031	0.0000

An examination of the simple correlations often leads to a better understanding of the more complex regression analyses. Here we can see why ATT, which shows a fairly good correlation with ACH6, was never included in a final model. It is highly related to INCOME (r=.626) and also to APT (r=.497). Whatever relationship it had with ACH6 was redundant with APT and INCOME. Also notice that INCOME and APT are unrelated, which contributes to their being included in the regressions. The simple correlations also protect against misinterpretation of "suppressor variables." These are a little too complex to discuss here. However, they can be spotted when a variable is not significantly correlated with the dependent variable but in the multiple regression has a significant regression coefficient (usually negative). You should get help (from Pedhazur or from another text or a consultant) with interpreting such a variable.

PROBLEMS

9-1. We want to test the effect of light level and amount of water on the yield of tomato plants. Potted plants receive 3 levels of light and 2 levels of water. The yield, in pounds, is recorded. The results are as follows:

YIELD	LIGHT	WATER	YIELD	LIGHT	WATER
12	1	1	20	2	2
9	1	1	16	2	2
8	1	1	16	2	2
13	1	2	18	3	1
15	1	2	25	3	1
14	1	2	20	3	1
16	2	1	25	3	2
14	2	1	27	3	2
12	2	1	29	3	2

Write a SAS program to read these data and perform a multiple regression (use PROC REG).

9-2. We want to estimate the number of books in a college library. Data are collected from colleges across the country of the number of volumes, the student enrollment (in thousands), the highest degree offered (1=B.A., 2=M.A., 3=Ph. D.), and size of the main campus (in acres). Results of this (hypothetical) study are displayed below:

BOOKS (in millions)	STUDENT ENROLLMENT (in thousands)	DEGREE	AREA (acres)
4	5	3	20
5	8	3	40
10	40	3	100
1	4	2	50
.5	2	1	300
2	8	1	400
7	30	3	40
4	20	2	200
1	10	2	5
1	12	1	100

Using a forward stepwise regression, show how each of the 3 factors affects the number of volumes in a college library.

9-3. We want to predict a student's success in college by a battery of tests. Graduating seniors volunteer to take our test battery and their final grade point average is recorded. Using a MAX-R^2 technique, develop a prediction equation for final grade point average using the test battery results. The data are as follows:

GPA	HS GPA	COLLEGE BOARD	IQ TEST
3.9	3.8	680	130
3.9	3.9	720	110
3.8	3.8	650	120
3.1	3.5	620	125
2.9	2.7	480	110
2.7	2.5	440	100
2.2	2.5	500	115
2.1	1.9	380	105
1.9	2.2	380	110
1.4	2.4	400	110

9-4. Take a sample of 25 people and record their height, waist measurement, the length of their right leg, the length of their right arm, and their weight. Write a SAS program to create a SAS data set of these data and compute a correlation matrix of these variables. Next, run a stepwise multiple regression, using weight as the dependent variable and the other variables as independent.

9-5. What's wrong with this program?

```
1       DATA MULTREG;
2       INPUT HEIGHT WAIST LEG ARM WEIGHT;
3       CARDS;
        (data lines)
4       PROC CORR;
5          VAR HEIGHT -- WEIGHT;
6       PROC REG;
7          MODEL WEIGHT = HEIGHT WAIST LEG ARM /
                          SELECTION=STEPWISE;
8       RUN;
```

CHAPTER 10

THE SAS INPUT STATEMENT

A. INTRODUCTION

Throughout the examples in the Statistics Section of this book, we have seen some of the power of the SAS INPUT statement. In this chapter, the first in a section on SAS Programming, we will explore the power of the INPUT statement.

B. LIST DIRECTED INPUT

SAS can read data values separated by one or more spaces. This form of input is sometimes referred to as "list directed." The rules here are that we must read **every** variable on a line, the data values must be separated by one or more spaces, and missing values are represented by periods. A simple example is shown below:

```
DATA QUEST;
INPUT ID SEX $ AGE HEIGHT WEIGHT;
CARDS;
1 M 23 68 155
2 F . 61 102
3   M  55  70      202
RUN;
```

Notice that character variables are followed by a $. The multiple spaces between the data values in the third line of data will not cause a problem. Sometimes we are given data that are **comma** delimited (i.e. separated by commas) instead of the spaces that SAS is expecting. We have two choices here: we can use an editor and replace all the commas with blanks or we can leave the commas in the data and use the DLM= option of the INFILE statement to make the comma the data delimiter. (See chapter 11 for details on the INFILE statement and its options.) As an example, suppose you were given a file on a floppy diskette called SURVEY.DTA. All the data values are separated by commas. The first two lines are shown next:

```
001,M,23,68,155
002,F,.,61,102
```

To read this file we code:

```
DATA HTWT;
INFILE 'A:SURVEY.DTA' DLM=',';
INPUT ID SEX $ AGE HEIGHT WEIGHT;
RUN;
```

The INFILE statement directs the INPUT statement to read an external file called SURVEY on the floppy diskette in drive A and to use commas as the data delimiter.

Using Formats with List Directed Reads

We may have data such as date values which we want to read with a date format, but still want to use the list directed form of input. We have two choices here. One is to precede the INPUT statement with an INFOR-MAT statement, assigning an informat to each variable. An INFORMAT statement uses the same syntax as a FORMAT statement but is used to supply an **input** format instead of an **output** format for a variable. An example of an INFORMAT statement is shown below:

```
DATA INFORM;
INFORMAT DOB VISIT MMDDYY8.;
INPUT ID DOB VISIT DX;
CARDS;
1 10/21/46 6/5/89 256.20
2 9/15/44 4/23/89 232.0
   etc.
```

An alternative to the INFORMAT is to supply the formats directly in the INPUT statement. We do this by following the variable name with a colon, followed by the appropriate format. A program using this method with the same data set is shown next:

```
DATA FORM;
INPUT ID DOB : MMDDYY8. VISIT : MMDDYY8. DX;
CARDS;
1 10/21/46 6/5/89 256.20
2 9/15/44 4/23/89 232.0
   etc.
```

Either method can also be used to override the default 8 character limit for character variables. So, to read a file containing last names (some longer than 8 characters) we could use either of the next two programs:

*Example with an INFORMAT statement;

```
DATA LONGNAME;
INFORMAT LAST $20.;
INPUT ID LAST SCORE;
CARDS;
1 STEVENSON 89
2 CODY 100
3 SMITH 55
4 GETTLEFINGER 92
     etc.
```

*Example with INPUT formats;

```
DATA LONGNAME;
INPUT ID LAST : $20. SCORE;
CARDS;
1 STEVENSON 89
2 CODY 100
3 SMITH 55
4 GETTLEFINGER 92
     etc.
```

Before we leave "list directed" reads, there is one more "trick" you should know about. Suppose you wanted to read a first and last name into a single variable. If we used spaces as data delimiters, we could not have a blank between the first and last name. However, the very clever people at the SAS institute thought about this problem and came up with the & sign in a list directed INPUT statement. Using a & instead of a : changes the delimiter to **two** or more spaces. To see how this works, look at the next program:

```
DATA FIRSTLST;
INPUT ID NAME & $30. SCORE1 SCORE2;
CARDS;
1 RON CODY   97 98
2 JEFF SMITH   57 58
   etc.
```

Notice that there are at least **two** spaces between the name and the first score.

C. COLUMN INPUT

Most of the examples in this book used INPUT statements which specified which columns to read for each data value. The syntax is to list the variable names, followed by the column or columns to read. In addition, we follow the variable name by a $ sign if we are reading character values. A simple example is shown here:

```
DATA COL;
INPUT ID 1-3 SEX $ 4 HEIGHT 5-6 WEIGHT 7-11;
CARDS;
001M68155.5
2  F61 99.0
  3M  233.5
etc.
```

Notice that the ID number for subject number 2 is not right adjusted. In most other programming languages this would cause a problem; not so for SAS software. We could have placed the '2' in any of the first 3 columns and it would have been read properly. Notice also that we can include decimal points in numeric fields. Just remember to leave the extra columns for them. Finally, remember that we can simply leave columns blank when we have missing values.

D. POINTERS AND FORMATS

An alternative to specifying the starting and ending columns is to specify a starting column and a length. This is especially useful when we are given a coding layout like the following:

Variable	Starting Column	Length	Type	Description
ID	1	3	NUM	SUBJECT ID
SEX	4	1	CHAR	SEX M=MALE F=FEMALE
AGE	9	2	NUM	AGE IN YEARS
HEIGHT	11	2	NUM	HEIGHT IN INCHES
V_DATE	15	6	DATE	VISIT DATE IN MMDDYY FORMAT

Rather than doing all the high level arithmetic to compute ending columns for each of these variables, we can use a pointer (@ sign) to specify the starting column and a format, which will not only tell SAS how to read the data value, but how many columns to read. Here is the program to read the data layout above:

```
DATA POINT;
INPUT @1 ID 3.
      @4 SEX $1.
      @9 AGE 2.
      @11 HEIGHT 2.
      @15 V_DATE MMDDYY6.;
```

The @ symbol, called a pointer, indicates the starting column for each variable. Some of the pointers are redundant, such as the @4 before SEX. As data are read, the pointer moves along the data line. Since ID started in column 1 and was 3 columns in length, the pointer was ready to read data in column 4 next. We recommend using a pointer before **every** variable as in this example; it makes for a neater program and reduces the possibility of reading the wrong column. The format N. is used for a numeric variable of length N, and $N. is the format used for a character variable of length N. The general form for a SAS numeric format is N.n where N is the number of columns to read and n is the number of digits to the right of the decimal point. For example, the number 123 read with a format 3.2 would be interpreted as 1.23 (we are reading 3 columns and there are two digits to the right of the decimal point). Using this notation, we can read numbers with an "implied" decimal point. By the way, we can also read numbers **with** decimal points. The number 1.23 read with the format 4. (remember the decimal point takes up a column) would be interpreted as 1.23. The format MMDDYY6. was one of the date formats we used in chapter 4 to read date values. We used a separate line for each variable simply as a matter of programming style.

E. READING MORE THAN ONE LINE PER SUBJECT

When we have more than one line of data for each subject, we can use the row pointer, #, to specify which row of data we want to read. Just as with the column pointer, we can move anywhere within the multiple rows of data per subject. Keep in mind that we must have the same number of rows of data for each subject. Below is an example where two lines of data were recorded for each subject:

```
INPUT #1 ID 1-3 AGE 5-6 HEIGHT 10-11 WEIGHT 15-17
      #2 SBP 5-7 DBP 8-10;
CARDS;
001 56    72    202
    140080
002 45    70    170
    130070
RUN;
```

If you have N lines of data per subject but don't want to read data from all N lines, make sure to end your input statement with #N, where N is the number of data lines per subject. For example, if you have 6 lines of data per subject but only want to read 2 lines (as in the example above), you would write:

```
INPUT #1 ID 1-3 AGE 5-6 HEIGHT 10-11 WEIGHT 15-17
      #2 SBP 5-7 DBP 8-10    #6;
```

F. CHANGING THE ORDER AND READING A COLUMN MORE THAN ONCE

It is possible to move the input pointer to any starting column, in any order. Thus, we can read variables in any order and we can read columns more than once. Suppose we had a 6 digit ID where the last 2 digits represented a county code. We could do this:

```
INPUT @1 ID 6. @5 COUNTY 2. etc.;
```

or

```
INPUT ID 1-6 COUNTY 5-6 etc.;
```

We can also read variables in any order. The following INPUT statements are valid:

```
INPUT ID 1-3 HEIGHT 5-6 SEX $ 4 WEIGHT 7-9;
INPUT @1 ID 3. @5 HEIGHT 2. @4 SEX $1. @7 WEIGHT 3.;
```

G. FORMAT LISTS

A real time savings can be realized by using format lists. A typical beginner SAS program may look like this:

```
DATA NOVICE;
INPUT ID 1-3 QUES1 4 QUES2 5 QUES3 6 QUES4 7
   QUES4B 8 QUES4C 9 QUES5 10 QUES6 11 QUES7 12
   QUES8 13 QUES9 14
   @20 DOB MMDDYY6. @26 ST_DATE MMDDYY6.
   @32 END_DATE MMDDYY6.;
```

To use a format list, place a list of variables in parentheses and place the format(s) to be used for these variables in another set of parentheses. The program above, rewritten to use format lists, follows:

```
DATA ADVANCED;
INPUT ID 1-3 @4 (QUES1-QUES4 QUES4B QUES4C
    QUES5-QUES9) (1.)
    @20 (DOB ST_DATE END_DATE) (MMDDYY6.);
```

The format list can also contain something called relative pointer directions. Using + and - signs, we can move the pointer forward or backward in the record. Next, we will show you a novel INPUT statement where relative pointers saved a lot of coding. A researcher coded 12 systolic and diastolic blood pressures (the number was reduced for illustrative purposes) for each subject. They were entered in pairs. A straightforward INPUT statement would be:

```
INPUT ID 1-3 SBP1 4-6 DBP1 7-9 SBP2 10-12 DBP2 13-15 etc.;
```

A more compact method, using relative pointers, is:

```
INPUT ID 1-3 @4 (SBP1-SBP12)(3. +3) @7 (DBP1-DBP12)(3. +3);
```

Thus, we "skip over" the diastolic pressures the first time, set the pointer back to column 7 and repeat the same trick with the diastolic pressures.

H. "HOLDING THE LINE" - SINGLE AND DOUBLE @'S

There are times when we want to read one variable and, based on its value, decide how to read other variables. To do this, we will need more than one INPUT statement. Normally, when SAS finishes an INPUT statement, the pointer is moved to the next line of data. So, if we had more than one INPUT statement, the second INPUT statement would be reading data from the next record. We have two ways to prevent this; the single and double @ symbols. A single @ sign, placed at the end of an INPUT statement, means to "hold the line." That is, do not move the pointer to the next record until the end of the data step is reached. The double @ symbol "holds the line strongly." That is, the pointer will not be moved to the next record, even if a CARDS statement (end of the data step) is encountered. It will move to the next record only if there are no more data to be read on a line. Here are some examples to help make this clear. In the first example, we ran a survey in 1989 and 1990. Unfortunately, in 1990, an extra question was added, **in the middle of the questionnaire** (where else!). We want to be able to combine these data in a single file and read each record according to the data layout for that year. The year of the survey was coded in columns 79 and 80 (89 for 1989 and 90 for 1990). In 1989 we had 10 questions in columns 1-10. In 1990 there was an extra question (let's call it 5B) placed in column 6 and questions 6 through 10 wound up in columns 7-11. We will use a trailing @ to read these data:

```
DATA QUEST;
INPUT YEAR 79-80 @;   * HOLD THE LINE;
IF YEAR = 89 THEN INPUT @1 (QUES1-QUES10)(1.);
   ELSE IF YEAR = 90 THEN INPUT @1 (QUES1-QUES5)(1.)
   @6 QUES5B 1. @7 (QUES6-QUES10)(1.);
CARDS;
```

A simple example where a double @@ is needed is shown next. Suppose we want to read in pairs of X and Y's and want to place several X Y pairs per line. We could read these data with a double trailing @:

```
DATA XYDATA;
INPUT X Y @@;
CARDS;
1 2 7 9 3 4 10 12
15 18 23 67
RUN;
```

The data set XYDATA would contain 6 X,Y pairs (1,2), (7,9), (3,4) (10,12), (15,18), and (23,67). Without the double trailing @, the data set would contain only two X,Y pairs, (1,2) and (15,18).

I. SUPPRESSING THE ERROR MESSAGES FOR INVALID DATA

If invalid data is read by the SAS system (such as character data in a numeric field or two decimal points in a number), an error message is placed in the SAS Log, the offending record is listed, and a missing value is assigned to the variable. Below is an example of a SAS Log where a character value (a) was read into a numeric field:

```
    1    data example;
    2    input x y z;
    3    cards;
NOTE: Invalid data for X in line 5 1-1.
RULE:---+---1---+---2---+---3---+---4---+---5---+---6---+---7---
    5 a 3 4
X=. Y=3 Z=4 _ERROR_=1 _N_=2
    6    run;
NOTE: The data set WORK.EXAMPLE has 2 observations and 3 variables.
NOTE: The DATA statement used 2.00 seconds.
```

Although this information can be very useful, there are times where we know that certain fields contain invalid data values and we want missing values to be substituted for the invalid data. For large files, the SAS Log may become quite large and the processing time will be longer when these error messages are processed. There are two choices to reduce the error message handling. First, a single question mark placed after the variable name will suppress the invalid data message but still print the offending line of data. Two question marks following the variable name will suppress all error messages and prevent the automatic _ERROR_ variable from being incremented. Here is the INPUT statement to suppress error messages when an invalid value is encountered for X:

```
INPUT X ?? Y Z;
```

If you are using column input, you would write:

```
INPUT X ?? 1-2 Y 3-4 Z 5-6;
```

To allow invalid values for X, Y, and Z, we could write:

```
INPUT @1 (X Y Z) (?? 2.);
```

J. READING "UNSTRUCTURED" DATA

Almost all the examples in this text have been either small data sets or balanced data sets that were relatively easy to read using standard INPUT statements. However, in the "real" world, we often encounter data sets that are not so "clean." For example, we might have a varying number of records for each subject in a study. Another example would be an unbalanced design where there were different numbers of subjects in each treatment. As these data sets become large, reading them without error sometimes becomes the most difficult part of the data processing problem. The techniques shown in this section will allow you to read almost any type of unstructured data easily.

The key to all the examples that follow is to embed "tags" in the data to indicate to the program what type of data to read. A t-test example with unequal n's and an unbalanced ANOVA will serve to illustrate the use of tags and stream data input.

Example 1—Unbalanced T-test.

The amount and complexity of the data have been reduced to make the examples short and easy to follow. The strength of the techniques is their use with larger, more complicated data sets.

We want to analyze an experiment where we had 5 control and 3 treatment subjects and we recorded a single variable per subject. The data are shown below:

GROUP

CONTROL	TREATMENT
20	40
25	42
23	35
27	
30	

The simplest, most straightforward method to read these data is shown next:

Example 1-A.

```
*TRADITIONAL INPUT METHOD;
DATA EX1A;
INPUT GROUP $ X @@;
CARDS;
C 20 C 25 C 23 C 27 C 30
T 40 T 42 T 35                    (cont.)
```

```
PROC TTEST;                    (Continued from previous page)
    CLASS GROUP;
    VAR X;
RUN;
```

For larger amounts of data, this program has some problems. It is tedious and time consuming to repeat the group identification before each variable to be read. This can be corrected in two ways: First, we can put the information concerning the number of observations per group in the **program** (Example 1-B) or we can put this information in the **data** itself (Example 1-C). As mentioned above, if the number of observations were large (several hundred or more), a single mistake in counting would have disastrous consequences.

Example 1-B.

```
DATA EX1B;
GROUP='C';
DO I=1 TO 5;
    INPUT X @;
    OUTPUT;
    END;
GROUP='T';
DO I=1 TO 3;
    INPUT X @;
    OUTPUT;
    END;
DROP I;
CARDS;
20 25 23 27 30
40 42 35
PROC TTEST;
    CLASS GROUP;
    VAR X;
RUN;
```

Example 1-C

```
DATA EX1C;
DO GROUP='C','T';
    INPUT N;
    DO I=1 TO N;
        INPUT X @;
        OUTPUT;
        END;
    END;
DROP N I;
CARDS;
5
20 25 23 27 30
3
40 42 35
PROC TTEST;
    CLASS GROUP;
    VAR X;
    RUN;
```

The method we are suggesting for large data sets is shown in Example 1-D below:

Example 1-D.

```
*READING THE DATA WITH TAGS;
DATA EX1D;
RETAIN GROUP;
INPUT TEST $ @@;
IF TEST='C' OR TEST='T' THEN DO;
    GROUP=TEST;
    RETURN;
    END;                              (cont.)
```

```
X=INPUT (TEST,5.0);     (Continued from previous page)
OUTPUT;
DROP TEST;
CARDS;
C 20 25 23 27 30
T 40 42 35
PROC TTEST;
    CLASS GROUP;
    VAR X;
RUN;
```

With this program we can add or delete data without making any changes to our program. The two important points in the program are:

1. All data items are read as **character** and interpreted. If a 'C' or 'T' is found, the variable GROUP is set equal to TEST and the data step returns to read the next number. The RETAIN statement prevents the variable GROUP from being reinitialized to missing each time the INPUT statement reads a new number—it will keep its value of 'C' or 'T' until it gets reset.
2. The **INPUT function** is used to "reread" the data with a numeric format. The INPUT function takes two arguments. The first is the variable to "reread," the second is the format with which to read this value. Thus, although TEST is a character variable, X will be stored as a numeric. We chose the format 5. since we knew it would be larger than any of our data values.

This same program can read data that are not as ordered as Example 1-D. For instance, the data set

```
C 20 25 23 T 40 42
C 30 T 35
```

will also be read correctly. For large data sets, this structure is less prone to error than Examples 1-A through 1-C. (Of course, we pay additional processing costs for the alternative program but the ease of data entry and the elimination of counting errors is probably worth the extra cost.)

Example 2—Unbalanced Two-Way ANOVA.

The next example will be an unbalanced design for which we want to perform an analysis of variance. Our design is as follows:

GROUP

	A	B	C
	20	70	90
	30	80	90
M	40	90	80
	20	90	50
SEX			
	25	70	20
	30	90	20
F	45	90	30
	30	80	
	65	85	
	72		

The straightforward method of entering these data would be:

```
DATA EX2A;
INPUT GROUP $ SEX $ SCORE;
CARDS;
A M 20
A M 30
   etc.
```

This is a lengthy and wasteful data entry method. For small data sets of this type, we could follow the example of the unbalanced t-test problem and enter the number of observations per cell, either in the program or imbedded in the data. A preferable method, especially for a large number of observations per cell where counting would be inconvenient, is shown in Example 2-B below:

```
*FIRST METHOD OF READING ANOVA DATA WITH TAGS;
DATA EX2A;
DO SEX='M','F';
    DO GROUP='A','B','C';
        INPUT TEST $ @;
        DO WHILE (TEST NE '#');
            SCORE=INPUT(TEST,6.0);
            OUTPUT;
            INPUT TEST $ @;
            END;
        END;
    END;
DROP TEST;
CARDS;
20 30 40 20 # 70 80 90 90
# 90 90 80 50 # 25 30 45 30
65 72 # 70 90 90 80 85 # 20 20 30 #
PROC GLM;
    etc.
```

This program reads and assigns observations to a cell until a "#" is read in the data stream. The program then finishes the innermost loop and the next cell is selected. We can read as many lines as necessary for the observations for a given cell.

An improved version of this program is shown next (Example 2-B). With this program, we can read the cells in any order and do not have to supply the program with the cell identification since it is incorporated right in the tags. Let's look over the program first, and then we will discuss the salient features:

```
*MORE ELEGANT METHOD FOR UNBALANCED ANOVA DESIGN;
DATA EX2B;
RETAIN GROUP SEX;
INPUT TEST $ @@;                              (cont.)
```

(Continued from previous page)

```
IF VERIFY (TEST,'ABCMF ') = 0 THEN DO;
 GROUP = SUBSTR (TEST,1,1);
   SEX = SUBSTR (TEST,2,1);
   DELETE;
   RETURN;
   END;
SCORE = INPUT (TEST,6.);
DROP TEST;
CARDS;
AM 20 30 40 20 50
BM 70 80 90
CM 90 80 80 90
AF 25 30 45 30 65 72
BF 70 90 90 80 85
CF 20 20 30
PROC GLM;
   etc.
```

This program allows us to enter the cells in any order and even use as many lines as necessary for the observations from a cell. This form of data entry is also convenient when we will be adding more data at a later time. The analysis can be rerun without any changes to the program. Additional observations can even be added at the end of the original data.

Special features of this program are the use of the **VERIFY** and **SUBSTR** functions. The **VERIFY** function returns 0 if all the characters of the variable TEST can be found as one of the characters in the second argument of the function. Note that a blank is included in argument 2 of the VERIFY function since the length of TEST is, by default, equal to 8 bytes, which means that it will contain two letters and 6 blanks. The SUBSTR function picks off the GROUP and SEX values from the TEST string and the INPUT function converts all character values back to numeric. (See chapter 16 for a more detailed discussion of SAS functions.)

PROBLEMS

10-1. You have 12 subjects in the placebo group and 12 in the drug group. One way to structure your data is like this:

GROUP	SCORE
P	77
P	76
.	
.	
D	80
D	84
.	
.	

(a) Write an INPUT statement to read these data, assuming you have one or more spaces between the group designation and the score.

(b) Suppose you prefer to arrange you values on two lines like this:

```
P 77 P 76 ...
D 80 D 84 ...
```

Write an INPUT statement for this arrangement.

(c) This time, the 12 scores for the placebo group are on the first line and the 12 scores for the drug group are on another like this:

```
77 76 ...
80 84 ...
```

Write a data step to read these data. Be sure the data set contains a GROUP as well as a SCORE variable.

(d) Modify the program in (C) so that each of the 24 subjects has a subject number from 1 to 24.

*10-2. Someone gave you the following data file:

VARIABLE	START COLUMN	LENGTH	DESCRIPTION
ID	1	3	NUMERIC
SEX	4	1	CHAR
DOB	10	6	MMDDYY
VISIT	16	6	MMDDYY
DISCHRG	22	6	MMDDYY
SBP1	30	3	NUMERIC
DBP1	33	3	NUMERIC
HR1	36	2	NUMERIC
SBP2	38	3	NUMERIC
DBP2	41	3	NUMERIC
HR2	44	2	NUMERIC
SBP3	46	3	NUMERIC
DBP3	49	3	NUMERIC
HR3	52	2	NUMERIC

Write an INPUT statement, using format lists, to read these data. See if you can find a way to format the SBP's and DBP's other than the straightforward @30 (SBP1 DBP1)(3.) HR1 2. (SBP2 DBP2)(3.) etc.

CHAPTER 11

EXTERNAL FILES: READING AND WRITING RAW AND SYSTEM FILES

A. INTRODUCTION

New SAS users are often confused by the different ways SAS software can read and write data to external files. This is due to the fact that SAS programs can read and write many different types of data files. For example, simple ASCII files (or EBCDIC text files on a mainframe) are read with INFILE and INPUT statements, while SAS data sets use two-level SAS data set names and do not require INPUT statements. This chapter will discuss several ways that SAS software can read and write a variety of data types. The use of temporary and permanent SAS data sets is discussed along with the advantages and disadvantages of each.

B. DATA IN THE PROGRAM ITSELF

Before we discuss how to read data from **external** files, let's review how SAS reads data lines that are part of the program itself, following a CARDS statement. For example:

```
DATA EX1;
INPUT GROUP $ X Y Z;
CARDS;
CONTROL 12 17 19
TREAT 23 25 29
CONTROL 19 18 16
TREAT 22 22 29
PROC MEANS N MEAN STD STDERR MAXDEC=2;
    TITLE 'MEANS FOR EACH GROUP';
    CLASS GROUP;
    VAR X Y Z;
RUN;
```

The INPUT method used, column specification, formats, pointers, etc. will not change any of our examples, so for the most part, simple list input is used. The CARDS statement tells the program that the data lines will follow. The word CARDS is obviously a throwback to the old days when many of us used actual punch cards in a deck to be read into a card reader. CARDS meant that the data cards were to follow. (An aside: One of us gave a talk to a group of 9th graders the other day and used a SAS program to demonstrate a point. Just out of curiosity, they were asked if any of them knew what data cards were. None did! One can feel very old.) You might ask yourself, how does the program know when the data lines end and the remainder of the SAS program begins? How does the program know that the line "PROC MEANS N MEAN STD STDERR MAXDEC=2;" is not a line of data? Good, we knew you would figure it out. It's the semicolon at the end of the line. While we're on the subject, there are a few special (and rare) cases where we might run into trouble with this instream form of data entry. Suppose we wrote the above program example like this:

```
DATA EX1;
INPUT GROUP $ X Y Z;
CARDS;
CONTROL 12 17 19
TREAT 23 25 29
CONTROL 19 18 16
TREAT 22 22 29
PROC MEANS N MEAN STD
    STDERR MAXDEC=2;
    TITLE 'MEANS FOR EACH GROUP';
    CLASS GROUP;
    VAR X Y Z;
RUN;
```

It might be necessary to use more than one line to write the first SAS statement following the data (suppose we had a long list of options for PROC MEANS). What will happen when we run this program? Well, we just figured out that the program identified the first programming statement following the data by scanning ahead and seeing the semicolon at the end of the line. In the form above, the line "PROC MEANS N MEAN STD" will be read as a data line. The program still thinks that the value of GROUP is "PROC", and will print error messages telling us that the values for X Y and Z are not numeric. Worse yet, the next line "STDERR MAXDEC=2;" will be treated as the first SAS statement following the data (it ends in a semicolon) and, since this line is not a proper SAS statement, an error message will result. This is a fairly rare problem, but if it happens to you, you'll know the cause. Here is the solution. Either place a null statement after the last line of data or follow the data lines with a RUN statement when you do not have a semicolon at the end of the first SAS statement following your data.

```
DATA EX1;
INPUT GROUP X Y Z;
CARDS;
CONTROL 12 17 19
TREAT 23 25 29
CONTROL 19 18 16
TREAT 22 22 29
;
PROC MEANS N MEAN STD
   STDERR MAXDEC=2;
   TITLE 'MEANS FOR EACH GROUP';
   CLASS GROUP;
   VAR X Y Z;
RUN;
```

Before we leave this topic, here is one more (and rare) possibility you may encounter. What happens when your data contains semicolons? For example, suppose you had:

```
INPUT AUTHOR $10. TITLE $40.;
CARDS;
SMITH     The Use of the ; in Writing
FIELD     Commentary on Smith's Book
PROC SORT;
   BY AUTHOR;
```

The program, seeing the semicolon in the first line of data, will treat the line as a SAS statement and generate more error messages than you would like to see. The solution to this rare problem is to use the special SAS statement CARDS4 which requires four semicolons in a row ";;;;" to indicate the end of your data. The corrected example would look like this:

```
INPUT AUTHOR $10. TITLE $40.;
CARDS4;
SMITH       The Use of the ; in Writing
FIELD       Commentary on Smith's Book
;;;;
PROC SORT;
   BY AUTHOR;
```

C. READING ASCII DATA FROM AN EXTERNAL FILE

It's not unusual to be given data in an external file to be analyzed with SAS software. Whether on a floppy diskette, on a microcomputer or on a tape used with a mainframe computer, we will want a way to have our SAS program read data from an external source. For this example, we will assume that the data file is either an ASCII (American Standard Code for Information Interchange) file or a "card image" file on tape (also called "raw" data). To read this file is surprisingly easy. The only changes to be made to the first example are these: 1. Precede the INPUT statement with an INFILE statement; and 2. Omit the CARDS statement, and, of course, the lines of data. An INFILE statement is the way we tell a SAS program where to find external "card image" data. On a mainframe version of SAS software, an INFILE statement will refer to what is called a DDname (DD stands for Data Definition) which gives information on where to find the file. On OS batch systems, the DDname is included in the JCL (Job Control Language). On systems such as CMS, the DDname is defined with a FILEDEF statement. On a microcomputer or UNIX system, the INFILE statement can either name a file directly (placed in single quotes) or it can be a fileref defined with a FILENAME statement. We will show examples of all of these variations.

PC-SAS Example - Reading ASCII data from an External Data File

```
DATA EX2A;
INFILE 'B:MYDATA';
*THIS INFILE STATEMENT TELLS THE PROGRAM THAT OUR
INPUT DATA IS LOCATED IN THE FILE MYDATA ON A FLOPPY
DISKETTE IN THE B DRIVE;
INPUT GROUP $ X Y Z;
PROC MEANS N MEAN STD STDERR MAXDEC=2 ;
   VAR X Y Z;
RUN;
```

File MYDATA (located on the floppy diskette in drive B) looks like this:

```
CONTROL 12 17 19
TREAT 23 25 29
CONTROL 19 18 16
TREAT 22 22 29
```

An alternative way of writing the INFILE statement in the example above is to use a FILENAME statement to create an alias or "fileref" for the file (a short "nickname" which we associate with the file). This is shown below:

```
DATA EX2B;
FILENAME GEORGE 'B:MYDATA';
INFILE GEORGE;
*THIS INFILE STATEMENT TELLS THE PROGRAM THAT OUR
INPUT DATA IS LOCATED IN THE FILE MYDATA ON A FLOPPY
DISKETTE IN THE B DRIVE;
INPUT GROUP $ X Y Z;
PROC MEANS N MEAN STD STDERR MAXDEC=2 ;
   VAR X Y Z;
RUN;
```

Note the difference between these two INFILE statements. The first INFILE statement refers to the external file directly and the filename is placed in single quotes. The second INFILE example defines an alias first with a FILENAME statement and then uses the alias with the INFILE statement. Notice that when we use a fileref it is **not** in single quotes. This point is important since it is the only way that the program can distinguish between an actual file name and a fileref.

A Mainframe Example

The mainframe example which is shown next is basically the same as the microcomputer example shown above. The only difference is in the way we create the fileref. On an OS batch system, we would create the fileref with a DD statement in the JCL like this:

```
//JOBNAME JOB (ACCT,BIN),'RON CODY'
//    EXEC SAS
//SAS.GEORGE DD DSN=ABC.MYDATA,DISP=SHR
//SAS.SYSIN DD *
DATA EX2C;
INFILE GEORGE;
*THIS INFILE STATEMENT TELLS THE PROGRAM THAT THE
FILE ABC.MYDATA CONTAINS OUR EXTERNAL DATA FILE
(ASSUME IT IS CATALOGUED);
INPUT GROUP $ X Y Z;
PROC MEANS N MEAN STD STDERR MAXDEC=2 ;
    VAR X Y Z;
RUN;
```

This example on a CMS system would be the same except that a FILEDEF statement would be used to associate the DDname with the file instead of the DD statement in the JCL. Here it is:

```
CMS FILEDEF GEORGE DISK MYDATA DATA B;
*THE FILE MYDATA DATA IS ON THE B MINIDISK OF MY CMS
SYSTEM;
DATA EX2D;
INFILE GEORGE;
*THIS INFILE STATEMENT TELLS THE PROGRAM THAT THE
DATA IS LOCATED IN THE FILE WITH FILENAME MYDATA,
FILETYPE DATA, AND FILEMODE B.;
INPUT GROUP $ X Y Z;
PROC MEANS N MEAN STD STDERR MAXDEC=2 ;
   VAR X Y Z;
RUN;
```

So, once we know how to create a DDname or a fileref in our computing environment, the SAS statements to read the files are the same. You will need to refer to your manual on how to create a fileref with TSO or VSE. Again, the SAS statements will not change.

D. INFILE OPTIONS

There are a variety of options that can be used with an INFILE statement to control how data are read and to allow the SAS program more control over the input operation. These options are placed after the word INFILE and before the semicolon. We will demonstrate several useful options.

Useful options with INFILE;

```
END=variable name
```

This option will automatically set the value of "variable name" to 0 unless the current observation is the last record in the file. This can be used when you want to read several different files and combine their data. (An alternative is to use the EOF=label option which branches to "label" when the end of file is reached.)

```
DATA EX2E;
*WE WILL FIRST READ DATA FROM OSCAR AND THEN FROM
BIGBIRD.TXT. OSCAR IS AN ASCII FILE ON THE FLOPPY
DISKETTE IN THE B DRIVE AND  BIGBIRD.TXT IS IN A
SUBDIRECTORY NAMED DATA ON OUR HARD DISK (C DRIVE).;
FILENAME X 'B:OSCAR';
FILENAME Y 'C:\DATA\BIGBIRD.TXT';
IF TESTEND NE 1 THEN INFILE X END=TESTEND;
   ELSE INFILE Y;
INPUT GROUP $ X Y Z;
PROC MEANS N MEAN STD STDERR MAXDEC=2;
   VAR X Y Z;
RUN;
```

Notice here that we can conditionally execute an INFILE statement, thus giving us complete control over the file reading operation. This same example would be valid on OS or CMS systems with the only change being the way that the DDnames or filerefs were assigned.

Option MISSOVER

The MISSOVER option is very useful when you have records of different length and have missing values at the end of a record. This is frequently the case when a text file was created with a word processor and the records were not padded on the right with blanks. Suppose our file called MYDATA has a short record and looks like the one below:

```
CONTROL 1 2 3
TREAT 4 5
CONTROL 6 7 8
TREAT 8 9 10
```

The program EX2A or EX2B would have a problem reading the second record of this file. Instead of assigning a missing value to the variable Z, it would go to the next record and read "CONTROL" as the value for Z and print an error message (since CONTROL is not a numeric value). The SAS LOG would also contain a NOTE telling us that SAS went to a new line when the INPUT statement reached past the end of a line. The remainder of the third record would not be read and the next observation in our data set would be GROUP=TREAT, X=8, Y=9, and Z=10. To avoid this problem, use the MISSOVER option on the INFILE statement. This will set all variables to missing if any record is short. The entire program would look like this:

```
DATA EX2F;
FILENAME GEORGE 'B:MYDATA';
INFILE GEORGE MISSOVER;
INPUT GROUP $ X Y Z;
PROC MEANS N MEAN STD STDERR MAXDEC=2 ;
   VAR X Y Z;
RUN;
```

Option - LRECL=reclength

You may need to specify your logical record length if it exceeds the default value for your system. When in doubt, add the LRECL (this stands for logical record length and is pronounced El-Recle) option to the INFILE statement. It will not cause a problem if you specify an LRECL larger than your actual record length. For example, suppose you have an ASCII file on a floppy diskette with 210 characters per line and your system default LRECL is 132. To read this file, you would write the INFILE statement like this:

```
INFILE filename LRECL=210;
```

There are many other INFILE options that allow you more control over how data is read from external files. They can be found in the **SAS Procedures Guide**, or the **SAS User's Guide: Basics** (see chapter 1 for complete references).

There will be times where you have data within the SAS program itself (following a CARDS; statement) and **not** in an external file yet you want to use one or more of the INFILE options to control the input data. You can still use these options by specifying a special fileref or DDname called CARDS, followed by any options you wish. Suppose you want to use MISSOVER and you have included the data within the program. You would proceed as follows:

```
DATA EX2G;
INFILE CARDS MISSOVER;
INPUT X Y Z;
CARDS;
1 2 3
4 5
6 7 8
PROC MEANS;
 etc.
```

E. WRITING ASCII OR "RAW DATA" TO AN EXTERNAL FILE

We may have reason to have our SAS program write data to an external file in "card image" or ASCII format. Writing raw data to a file would have the advantage of being somewhat "universal" in that most software packages would be able to read it. On most microcomputer systems, an ASCII file could be read by a word processing program, a spread sheet program, or a data base management package. Writing raw data to a file is very much like reading data from an external file. We use one statement, FILE, to tell the program where to send the data, and PUT to indicate which variables and in what format to write them. Thus, to read raw data files we use the statements INFILE and INPUT; to write raw data files we use the statements FILE and PUT. Here is a simple example of a program that reads a raw file (MYDATA), creates new variables, and writes out the new file (NEWDATA) to a floppy disk.

```
DATA EX3A;
*THIS PROGRAM READS A RAW DATA FILE, CREATES A NEW
VARIABLE AND WRITES THE NEW DATA SET TO ANOTHER FILE;
FILENAME IN 'C:MYDATA';
FILENAME OUT 'A:NEWDATA';
INFILE IN;
FILE OUT;
INPUT GROUP $ X Y Z;
TOTAL = SUM (OF X Y Z);
PUT GROUP $ 1-10 @12 (X Y Z TOTAL)(5.);
RUN;
```

An alternative form using PC-SAS or UNIX based systems would be to omit the FILENAME statements and indicate the file names in quotes directly in the INFILE and FILE statements. Running this program will produce a new file called NEWDATA which looks like this:

```
CONTROL          12   17   19   48
TREAT            23   25   29   77
CONTROL          19   18   16   53
TREAT            22   22   29   73
```

Notice that we can employ any of the methods of specifying columns or formats that are permissible with an INPUT statement, with the PUT statement. In the example above, we specified columns for the first variable (GROUP) and a format (in a format list) for the remaining four variables. This gives us complete control over the structure of the file to be created. It goes without saying that this example will work just the same on a mainframe under OS or CMS, providing that the correct JCL or FILEDEF statements are issued. Note that on an OS system, if we are creating a new file, we will have to provide all the parameters (such as RECFM, DISP, UNIT, DSN, DCB, etc.) necessary for your system.

F. CREATING A PERMANENT SAS DATA SET

So far, we have seen how to read raw "card image" data and to write the same type of data to an external file. We will now demonstrate how to create a permanent SAS data set. A SAS data set, unlike a raw data file, is not usable by software other than SAS. It contains not only the data, but your variable names, labels, and formats (if any). Before we show you an example, let's first discuss the pros and cons of using permanent SAS data sets. First, here are some cons: As we mentioned, non-SAS programs cannot read SAS data sets. If we are using PC-SAS software, we cannot use a word processor or editor to look at or change anything in a SAS data set. Likewise, on a mainframe, we cannot use any of the editors or utilities to list the contents of the SAS data set. To read, update, or modify a SAS data set requires using SAS software and either writing a program (for example to change a data value) or using SAS/FSP® (Full Screen Product) to display and/or update an observation. When you write a SAS program or use SAS/FSP to modify a SAS data set, you must keep in mind that the original raw data are not modified and you can no longer recreate the SAS data set from the raw data without making the modification again. Finally, in the minus column, SAS data sets typically take up more storage than the original data set and are usually kept in addition to the original raw data, thus more than doubling the system storage requirements.

With all these negatives, why create permanent SAS data sets? Probably the most compelling reason to create and use permanent SAS data sets is speed. We think it is safe to say that typical SAS programs use most of the machine resources in the data step. If you plan to be running many different analyses on a data set that will not be changing often, it is a good idea to make the data set permanent for the duration of the analyses. SAS data sets are also a good way to transfer data to other users providing they have SAS software available. Knowing the data structure is no longer necessary since all the variables, labels, and formats have already been defined. We will see shortly how to use PROC CONTENTS to see what is contained in a SAS data set.

Our first example in this section will be to write a SAS program which has the data in the program itself, and create a permanent SAS data set.

```
LIBNAME FELIX 'C:\SASDATA';
DATA FELIX.EX4A;
*THIS PROGRAM READS DATA FOLLOWING THE CARDS
STATEMENT AND CREATES A PERMANENT SAS DATA SET IN A
SUBDIRECTORY CALLED \SASDATA ON THE C DRIVE;
INPUT GROUP $ X Y Z;
CARDS;
CONTROL 12 17 19
TREAT 23 25 29
CONTROL 19 18 16
TREAT 22 22 29
RUN;
```

The way we distinguish between temporary and permanent SAS data sets is by the SAS data set name. If we have a two-level name (two names separated by a period), we are defining a permanent SAS data set name. With a single level SAS data set name, we are defining a temporary data set which will disappear when we exit the SAS environment.

In PC-SAS the first part of the two-level name (the part before the period) names a subdirectory, defined with a LIBNAME statement, where the SAS data set is to be stored (or read). We can have many SAS data sets contained within a single subdirectory. On a mainframe implementation, the first level name refers to a fileref (defined with the appropriate control statement) or a DDname (defined in the JCL). On mainframe systems, a single OS data set can contain several SAS data sets.

When this program executes, the data set EX4A will be a permanent SAS data set located in the \SASDATA subdirectory of our C disk. On a microcomputer, if we look at a list of files in the \SASDATA subdirectory, there will be a file called EX4A.SSD. The extension SSD is added to all PC-SAS data sets. Note that on any SAS system, the first level name does not remain with the data set; it is only used to point to a SAS library. The only requirement is that the first level name match either the LIBNAME, the fileref, or the DDname within a program.

Now that we have created a permanent SAS data set, let's see how to read it and determine its contents.

G. READING PERMANENT SAS DATA SETS

Once we have created a permanent SAS data set, we can use it directly in a procedure once we have defined a LIBNAME, fileref, or DDname. Following our PC-SAS example where we created a SAS data set called EX4A and placed it in the C:\SASDATA subdirectory, we will now show you a SAS program which uses this permanent data set.

```
LIBNAME ABC 'C:\SASDATA';
PROC MEANS DATA=ABC.EX4A N MEAN STD STDERR MAXDEC=3;
RUN;
```

You can see right away how useful it is to save SAS data sets. Notice that there is no data step at all in the above program. All that is needed is to define a SAS library (where the SAS data set is located) and to use a DATA= option with PROC MEANS to indicate on which data set to operate. First, observe that the fileref ABC is not the same name we used when we created the data set. The fileref ABC is defined with the LIBNAME statement and indicates that we are using the subdirectory C:\SASDATA. Therefore, the first part of the two-level SAS data set name is ABC. The second part of the two-level name tells the system which of the SAS data sets located in C:\SASDATA is to be used. It is important to remember that we **must** use the DATA= option with any procedure where we are accessing previously stored SAS data sets because the program will not know which data set to use (When we create a SAS data set in a DATA step, the system keeps track of the "most recently created data set" and uses that data set with any PROCEDURE where you do not explicitly indicate which data set to use with a DATA= option). Just so that we don't short change the mainframe users, the same program, written on an OS system, would look something like this:

```
//GROUCH JOB (1234567,BIN),'OSCAR THE'
//    EXEC SAS
//SAS.ABC DD DSN=OLS.A123.S456.CODY,DISP=SHR
//SAS.SYSIN DD *
PROC MEANS DATA=ABC.EX4A N MEAN STD STDERR MAXDEC=3;
/*
//
```

Imagine, a one-line SAS program! The DDname was defined in the JCL, indicating my SAS data set was stored in the OS data set called OLS.A123.S456.CODY which was catalogued. On a CMS system, the DDname or first part of a two-level name is what CMS calls the filetype in the general filename filetype filemode method of defining a file. The filename corresponds to the SAS second level name. Thus, without even issuing a FILEDEF command, we could write:

```
PROC MEANS DATA=ABC.EX4A N MEAN STD STDERR MAXDEC=3;
```

as long as we had a filetype of ABC and a filename of EX4A.

H. HOW TO DETERMINE THE CONTENTS OF A SAS DATA SET (PROC CONTENTS)

As we mentioned earlier, we cannot use our system editor to list the contents of a SAS data set. How can we "see" what is contained in a SAS data set? We use PROC CONTENTS. This very useful procedure will tell us the following important information about our data set: the number of observations, the number of variables, the record length, and an alphabetical listing of variables (which includes labels, length, and formats). As an option, you can obtain a list of variables in order of their position in the data

set. Here are the statements to display the contents of the permanent SAS
data set EX4A created above:

```
LIBNAME SUGI 'C:\SASDATA';
PROC CONTENTS DATA=SUGI.EX4A POSITION;
```

Output from this procedure is shown below:

```
SAS                                9:30 Monday, August 8, 1988   1

CONTENTS PROCEDURE

 Data Set Name:  SUGI.EX4A              Type:
 Observations:   4                      Record Len: 36
 Variables:      4
 Label:

-----Alphabetic List of Variables and Attributes-----

 #  Variable  Type  Len  Pos  Label
 1  GROUP     Char   8    4
 2  X         Num    8   12
 3  Y         Num    8   20
 4  Z         Num    8   28

CONTENTS PROCEDURE
----Variables Ordered by Position----

 #  Variable  Type  Len  Pos  Label
 1  GROUP     Char   8    4
 2  X         Num    8   12
 3  Y         Num    8   20
 4  Z         Num    8   28
```

One final point of information: the DATA= option of PROC CONTENTS
can be used to list all the SAS data sets contained in a SAS library instead
of a single data set. Use the form libname._ALL_ instead of libname.dataset-
name, this will display all the SAS data sets stored in the library referred to
by the libname. Of course, if you happen to have SAS/FSP (full screen
product), you can browse and edit a SAS data set with FSBROWSE and
FSEDIT.

I. PERMANENT SAS DATA SETS WITH FORMATS

One special note is needed to caution you about saving permanent SAS data
sets in which you have assigned formats to one or more of the variables in
the DATA step. If you try to use this data set (in a procedure for example),

you will get an error that formats are missing. The important thing to remember is this: if you create a permanent SAS data set which assigns formats to variables, you must make the format library permanent as well. Also, if you give someone else the data set, make sure you give him or her the format library. To make your format library permanent, add the LIBRARY= option to PROC FORMAT. Then, issue a LIBNAME statement with the special library name LIBRARY pointing to the format library when accessing the data set. Since this sounds rather complicated, we will show the code to create a permanent format library and the code to access a permanent data set where formats were used.

Code to Create a Permanent Format Library and Assign the Format to a Variable

```
LIBNAME LIBRARY 'C:\SASDATA';
*THE SAS FORMAT LIBRARY IS LOCATED IN C:\SASDATA;
PROC FORMAT LIBRARY=LIBRARY;
   VALUE $XGROUP 'TREAT'='TREATMENT GRP'
'CONTROL'='CONTROL GRP';
LIBNAME FELIX 'C:\SASDATA';
DATA FELIX.EX4A;
INPUT GROUP $ X Y Z;
FORMAT GROUP $XGROUP.;
CARDS;
CONTROL 12 17 19
TREAT 23 25 29
CONTROL 19 18 16
TREAT 22 22 29
RUN;
```

Program to Read a Permanent SAS Data Set with Formats

```
LIBNAME C 'C:\SASDATA';
LIBNAME LIBRARY 'C:\SASDATA';
PROC PRINT DATA=C.EX4A;
```

J. RENAME WARNING

Before we leave the topic of permanent SAS data sets, one final note concerning SAS data sets created with PC-SAS or UNIX. Do not use the DOS REN (rename) or the UNIX MV (move) command to change the name of a SAS data set (.SSD file). You will not be able to read it if you do. SAS data sets contain the data set name internally and the DOS or UNIX file name and the internal name must match. If you wish to change the name of a SAS data set, use PROC DATASETS with a change statement to do it. For example, to rename the permanent data set EX4A to OSCAR, the appropriate statements would be:

```
LIBNAME XXX 'C:\SASDATA';   *THE LIBRARY WHERE THE
                             DATA SET IS LOCATED;
PROC DATASETS LIBRARY=XXX;
   CHANGE EX4A=OSCAR;        *THE SYNTAX IS CHANGE
                             old name = new name;
```

K. WORKING WITH LARGE DATA SETS

Special consideration needs to be taken when we process large data sets. Of course, large is a relative term. On a small microcomputer, 20,000 observations with 10 variables might be considered large. On a mainframe, users frequently process data sets with millions of observations. A few simple techniques described here can reduce the processing time (and cost if you're paying for it) for processing a large file.

1. Don't read a file unnecessarily. For example:

Inefficient Way:

```
LIBNAME INDATA 'C:\MYDATA';
DATA TEMP;
SET INDATA.STATS;
RUN;
PROC PRINT;
   VAR X Y Z;
RUN;
```

Efficient Way;

```
LIBNAME INDATA 'C:\MYDATA';
PROC PRINT DATA=INDATA.STATS;
   VAR X Y Z;
RUN;
```

The data step in the "Inefficient" example is unnecessary. It simply copies one data set into another so that the PROC PRINT can use the default, most recently created data set. Surprisingly, this is a common error.

    2. Drop all unnecessary variables. Not only do more variables take up more space, they slow down data step processing as well.

Inefficient Way: (If all you want is the quiz average)

```
DATA QUIZ;
INPUT @1 (QUIZ1-QUIZ10)(3.);
QUIZAVE = MEAN (OF QUIZ1-QUIZ10);
CARDS;
```

Efficient Way:

```
DATA QUIZ;
INPUT @1 (QUIZ1-QUIZ10)(3.);
QUIZAVE = MEAN (OF QUIZ1-QUIZ10);
DROP (QUIZ1-QUIZ10);
CARDS;
```

    3. Use a LENGTH statement to assign lengths to your numeric variables. (The length of a numeric variable is **not** the number of digits in the number, but rather, the number of bytes the computer uses to store the number in its internal representation.) The default length is 8 bytes (i.e. double precision). For most applications, 4 bytes will

be sufficient. Changing from 8 to 4 bytes will half the storage requirements and speed up data transfer. When numeric variables are assigned lengths less than 8 bytes, all data step calculations are still done with double precision arithmetic. If you are unfamiliar with how changing the length may affect your results, check with one of your computer guru friends. Unsuspected results can occur when you use lengths of 3 or less, so be careful—don't overdo it. You can also assign lengths to character variables; however, if they were read in with format or columns specified, they will already have their lengths defined.

Inefficient Way:

```
DATA SINGLE;
INPUT A $ B $ X1-X10 Y Z;
etc.
```

Efficient Way:

```
DATA SINGLE;
INPUT A $ B $ X1-X10 Y Z;
LENGTH _NUMERIC_ 4  A $ 2 B $ 4;
etc.
```

In the example above, be sure to place the LENGTH statement **after** the INPUT statement, since the internal name _NUMERIC_ represents the numeric variables that have be previously defined in the data step. Without the lengths assigned to the two character variables, they would both have lengths of 8 bytes, the default.

4. Use a DROP (or KEEP) **option** on the SET statement rather than a DROP (or KEEP) **statement** in the data step. When a DROP option is used, only the variables still in the data set will be brought into the Program Data Vector. This can result in a significant decrease in processing time.

Inefficient Way:

```
DATA NEW;
SET OLD;
DROP X1-X20 A B;
etc.
```

Efficient Way:

```
DATA NEW;
SET OLD (DROP=X1-X20 A B);
etc.
```

5. Reduce the number of sorts.

Inefficient Way: (Data set is already sorted by DAY)

```
PROC SORT DATA=MYDATA;
   BY DAY;
RUN;
PROC MEANS DATA=MYDATA N MEAN STD;
   BY DAY;
   VAR ... ;
RUN;
```

Efficient Way:

```
PROC MEANS DATA=MYDATA N MEAN STD;
   BY DAY NOTSORTED;
   VAR ... ;
RUN;
```

NOTE: Some versions of SAS may not need the keyword NOTSORTED in the BY statement.

As another example, if you need your data in DAY order and know that later in the program you need it in DAY-HOUR order, do the two- level sort first.

Inefficient Way:

```
PROC SORT;
   BY DAY;
RUN;
etc.
PROC SORT;
   BY DAY HOUR;
RUN;
etc.
```

Efficient Way:

```
PROC SORT;
   BY DAY HOUR;
RUN;
etc.
```

6. Think about using a CLASS statement instead of a BY statement with PROC MEANS. This will eliminate the need to sort the data but will require more memory to run.

Inefficient Way:

```
PROC SORT;
   BY DAY;
RUN;
PROC MEANS DATA=MYDATA N MEAN NWAY;
   BY DAY;
   VAR ... ;
RUN;
```

Efficient Way:

```
PROC MEANS DATA=MYDATA N MEAN NWAY;
   CLASS DAY;
   VAR ... ;
RUN;
```

7. When a small subset is selected from a large file, use the WHERE statement instead of an IF statement.

Inefficient Way:

```
DATA ALPHA;
SET BETA;
IF X GE 20;
RUN;
```

Efficient Way:

```
DATA ALPHA;
SET BETA;
WHERE X GE 20;
RUN;
```

8. Use a WHERE statement in a PROC when you only need to run a single procedure on a subset of the data.

Inefficient Way:

```
DATA TEMP;
SET OLD;
WHERE AGE GE 65;
RUN;
PROC MEANS N MEAN STD;
   VAR ... ;
RUN;
```

Efficient Way:

```
PROC MEANS N MEAN STD;
   WHERE AGE GE 65;
   VAR ... ;
RUN;
```

9. Use ELSE IF instead of multiple IF statements.

Inefficient Way:

```
DATA SURVY;
INPUT ID AGE HEIGHT WEIGHT;
IF 0 LE AGE LT 20 THEN AGEGRP=1;
IF 20 LE AGE LT 30 THEN AGEGRP=2;
IF 30 LE AGE LT 40 THEN AGEGRP=3;
IF AGE GE 40 THEN AGEGRP=4;
RUN;
```

Efficient Way:

```
DATA SURVY;
INPUT ID AGE HEIGHT WEIGHT;
IF 0 LE AGE LT 20 THEN AGEGRP=1;
ELSE IF 20 LE AGE LT 30 THEN AGEGRP=2;
ELSE IF 30 LE AGE LT 40 THEN AGEGRP=3;
ELSE IF AGE GE 40 THEN AGEGRP=4;
RUN;
```

10. When using multiple IF statements, place the one most likely to be true first.

Inefficient Way: (Most of the subjects are over 65)

```
DATA SURVEY;
SET OLD;
IF 0 LE AGE LT 20 THEN AGEGRP=1;
ELSE IF 20 LE AGE LT 30 THEN AGEGRP=2;
ELSE IF 30 LE AGE LT 40 THEN AGEGRP=3;
ELSE IF AGE GE 40 THEN AGEGRP=4;
RUN;
```

Efficient Way: (Most of the subjects are over 65)

```
DATA SURVEY;
SET OLD;
IF AGE GE 40 THEN AGEGRP=4;
ELSE IF 30 LE AGE LT 40 THEN AGEGRP=3;
ELSE IF 20 LE AGE LT 30 THEN AGEGRP=2;
ELSE IF 0 LE AGE LT 20 THEN AGEGRP=1;
RUN;
```

11. When checking if a variable is one of several values, use the IN statement (new with Version 6) instead of multiple OR operators.

Inefficient Way:

```
DATA CHECK;
SET OLD;
IF STATE = 'NJ' OR STATE = 'NY' OR STATE = 'PA' THEN
INCLUDE='YES';
    ELSE INCLUDE 'NO ';
RUN;
```

Efficient Way:

```
DATA CHECK;
SET OLD;
IF STATE IN ('NJ', 'NY', 'PA') THEN INCLUDE='YES';
    ELSE INCLUDE 'NO ';
RUN;
```

When we use the IN statement, if any one of the values in the list matches the value of the variable, the system stops looking further in the list. This is not true when we use multiple OR operators. This also means that we should put more likely matches earlier in the list when we use the IN statement. Note that the IN statement can also be used with numeric variables, in which case we do not use the single quotes in the list of possible matches.

12. Save summary statistics in a permanent SAS file if you plan to do further computations with them.

Inefficient Way:

```
LIBNAME C 'C:\MYDATA';
PROC MEANS DATA=C.INDATA;
    CLASS RACE SEX;
    VAR ... ;
RUN;
```

Efficient Way:

```
LIBNAME C 'C:\MYDATA';
PROC MEANS DATA=C.INDATA NWAY;
   CLASS RACE SEX;
   VAR ... ;
   OUTPUT OUT=C.SUMMARY MEAN= ;
RUN;
```

13. Use _NULL_ as a data set name when you only want to process records from a file (such as data cleaning) but do not want to keep the resulting data set.

Inefficient Way:

```
DATA TEMP;
SET OLD;
FILE 'ERRORS';
IF AGE GT 110 THEN PUT ID= AGE= ;
RUN;
```

Efficient Way:

```
DATA _NULL_;
SET OLD;
FILE 'ERRORS';
IF AGE GT 110 THEN PUT ID= AGE= ;
RUN;
```

14. Save your SAS system files if plan to do further processing on the data. Reading a system file is much more efficient than reading raw data.

15. Use "OPTIONS OBS=n" where n is either zero or a small number when testing your code. Remember to set it back with "OPTIONS OBS=MAX" before you do any more processing.
16. Use PROC DATASETS to rename variables or change variable labels.
17. Use PROC APPEND to add new data to a large file.

Inefficient Way:

```
DATA COMBINE;
SET BIGFILE NEWFILE;
RUN;
```

Efficient Way:

```
PROC APPEND BASE=BIGFILE DATA=NEWFILE;
RUN;
```

PROBLEMS

11-1. You are given a text (ASCII) file called FRODO on a floppy diskette. The data layout is as follows:

VARIABLE	COL(S)
ID	1-3
AGE	5-6
HR	8-10
SBP	12-14
DBP	16-18

A few sample records are shown below:

```
123456789|12345678 (Columns listed here, not on the diskette)
001 56  64 130  80
002 44  72 180      Note: No DBP recorded for this ID (short
003 64  78 140  88          record)
```

You place this diskette in the A: drive of your MS-DOS computer. Write a SAS program that will read this file and do the following:

(a) Compute the mean AGE, HR, SBP, DBP, and AVEBP, where AVEBP is defined as two-thirds of the diastolic blood pressure (DBP) plus one- third of the systolic blood pressure (SBP). (This is actually a weighted average of the DBP and SBP with weights of 2/3 and 1/3, since the heart spends more time in diastole than systole.)

(b) Create a SAS system file called BILBO (SSD file) on the floppy.

(c) Create another SAS system file called HIBP which contains only records of subjects with AVEBP greater than or equal to 100.

11-2. You are given a tape with a SAS system file and a format library on it. You copy this tape to a hard disk. The file names are SUR-VEY90.SSD and FORMATS.SCT respectively. Two variables of special interest on this tape are ICD_9 and AGE. The format library contains a format for ICD_9 and this format has been assigned in the data set to ICD_9. Write a SAS program, for a computer system you use (mainframe OS, CMS, MS-DOS, UNIX, etc.) that will read this data set, recognize the format library, and produce a frequency distribution of the ICD_9 codes in decreasing order of frequency (PROC FREQ option ORDER=FREQ). Also, compute descriptive statistics for AGE (n, mean, standard deviation, standard error, minimum, and maximum).

11-3. You have a SAS data set called MESTAKE on a floppy diskette. You are embarrassed and want to correct the spelling of this data set to MISTAKE. The floppy is in the B: drive. Write the SAS program to rename this data set. Remember, you **cannot** use a rename command from your operating system (REN in DOS, MV in UNIX, etc.)

CHAPTER 12
IMPORTING AND EXPORTING DATA

This chapter will discuss ways to move data from such formats as ASCII, Lotus®, and dBASE® to a SAS system file. Included in this discussion will be the moving of SAS system files from other platforms (such as UNIX) to system files on PC's. We will discuss PROC DIF, DBF, CPORT, and CIM-PORT as well as a non-SAS Institute package, DBMS/COPY which translates data between a variety of formats, including SAS system files. The special problems of missing values and incompatible formats is also addressed.

A. READING DATA FROM AN EXTERNAL ASCII FILE.

One common way for SAS users to enter data into a micro-computer is with a word processing package. Several such packages write directly in ASCII format such as PC-WRITE® and WordStar® (non-document mode only). Others use their own proprietary format such as Word Perfect® and Multimate®. These latter packages contain translation routines which can convert their internal format to standard ASCII. In Word Perfect, the choice "Save to DOS Text File" will write ASCII files, while in Multimate, you must run a translate program.

   Another way to create ASCII files is to have a spread sheet program or a database program "print to a file." This technique is similar to sending data to the printer except that the resulting text will reside in a disk file. Be careful that the package you are using does not format the text by adding margins or placing page breaks in the file. In Lotus, be sure to select the "Unformatted" and "Margin" (set left to zero) options in the Print menu before writing out the file. ASCII is a good "common denominator" between other packages and SAS system files when all else fails. Look for details on reading and writing ASCII files in sections C-E of chapter 10.

B. READING DATA FROM A LOTUS® SPREADSHEET VIA DIF FORMAT

One way of converting a Lotus spreadsheet into a SAS system file is via a DIF (Data Interchange Format) file. Once your spreadsheet has been translated to a DIF file, you may use PROC DIF to convert the DIF file into a SAS system file. Let's first discuss the format of the original spreadsheet. You may simply have columns of variables, with the first row of the spreadsheet containing the values for your first observation. Below is a sample of a simple spreadsheet (containing the same values as the sample ASCII file above):

```
                     Lotus Spreadsheet Example 1

                 A         B        C        D        E

        1                  1 M              23       68      160
        2                  2 F              44       62       99
        3                  3 M              29               200
        4                  4 F              27       65
        5                  5 M              66       72      220
        6                  6 F              60       60      100
```

Notice that the numbers are right justified and the character variables are left justified. When this spreadsheet is converted to a SAS system file, the numbers will be SAS numeric (8 byte) variables and the characters will become character variables of length 20. Character values longer than 20 bytes will be truncated when we use the DIF format for our translation.

Another form of the spreadsheet is to have the first row contain column headings. This form is shown next:

```
                     Lotus Spreadsheet Example 2

                 A         B        C        D        E

        1   ID            SEX      AGE     HEIGHT   WEIGHT
        2            1 M              23       68      160
        3            2 F              44       62       99
        4            3 M              29               200
        5            4 F              27       65
        6            5 M              66       72      220
        7            6 F              60       60      100
```

Finally, you may have one or more lines of text or comments in your spreadsheet. An example of this is shown next:

```
                      Lotus Spreadsheet Example 3

               A       B       C       D       E

      1    These lines contain comments that we do not
      2    want to include with our data.
      3    ----------------------------------------------
      4    ID        SEX      AGE     HEIGHT   WEIGHT
      5         1 M                23       68      160
      6         2 F                44       62       99
      7         3 M                29              200
      8         4 F                27       65
      9         5 M                66       72      220
     10         6 F                60       60      100
```

There are two ways of dealing with examples 2 and 3. First, before we enter the Lotus translate program, we can use the "RANGE" command of Lotus and name a range that includes only the data. We can then translate only the range and create a DIF file that will be identical to the one from Example 1. The other alternative is to translate the spreadsheet intact and use the SKIP option of PROC DIF to skip the first n lines of the spreadsheet.

Now that we have translated our WK1 file to a DIF file, we are ready to see how PROC DIF works. The syntax for PROC DIF is:

```
PROC DIF DIF=fileref OUT=sas_file SKIP=n;
```

where fileref = a file reference to the .DIF file

sas_file = name of the newly created SAS system file

n = number of lines of the spreadsheet to skip

For example, suppose our original worksheet file was called LOTUS.WK1. The translated DIF file will be named LOTUS.DIF (the .DIF is added automatically by the translate routine). If we want our SAS system file to be called LOTUSAS, the following PROC statements can be used:

```
FILENAME IN 'LOTUS.DIF';
PROC DIF DIF=IN OUT=LOTUSAS;
```

The variables in the resulting SAS data set would be named COL1, COL2, COL3, etc. You could rename these variables using PROC DATASETS such as:

```
PROC DATASETS;
   MODIFY LOTUSAS;
      RENAME COL1=ID COL2=SEX COL3=AGE COL4=HEIGHT
             COL5=WEIGHT;
```

C. READING DATA FROM A LOTUS SPREADSHEET VIA DBF FORMAT

An alternate method of converting a Lotus spreadsheet to a SAS system file is by first converting the spreadsheet to DBF format (choose dBase III from the Lotus translate screen) and to then use PROC DBF to create the SAS system file. There are advantages and disadvantages to this method. First, the Lotus translate routine expects that the first row of the spreadsheet contains variable names and subsequent rows contain data values. If there are extraneous rows or columns in your spreadsheet, use the "range" command in Lotus to name a range where your variable names and values are located. The Lotus to DBF conversion is more particular than the Lotus to DIF conversion. The translate routine insists that the second row of the spreadsheet (the first row of data) either contain data values or be formatted. After the conversion is completed, the resulting SAS system file will have the same variable names as the column headings. Therefore, we must be careful to choose column headings which are valid SAS variable names. If we have column headings that are too long, they will be truncated to 8 bytes. If they contain invalid characters (such as blanks or -), they will be converted by PROC DBF into valid SAS variable names. The resulting SAS system file will use 8 bytes for the numeric variables and the Lotus spreadsheet column width for the character variables. Empty cells will be converted to **zeros** by the Lotus to DBF conversion. Therefore, if zero is a valid value for a variable, you must put a missing value code (such as 9999) in the empty cells of these variables. After the SAS system file is created, you can convert the missing value codes back to SAS missing values.

The syntax for PROC DBF is shown next:

```
PROC DBF DB3=dbase_fileref OUT=sas_file;
```

where dbase_fileref = the fileref for the .DBF file, created with the FILENAME statement

```
sas_file = the name of the SAS system file.
```

For our example, suppose that the Lotus spreadsheet was converted to a .DBF file with the name LOTUS.DBF. The SAS programming statements to convert a DBF file to a SAS system file are shown below:

```
FILENAME GARFIELD 'LOTUS.DBF';
PROC DBF DB3=GARFIELD OUT=LOTUSAS;
```

If we had missing values in our spreadsheet and zero was not a valid data value, we would next have to convert to zeros to SAS missing values. One method, using ARRAYS is shown here:

```
DATA NEWSAS;
SET LOTUSAS;
ARRAY XXX[*] _NUMERIC_;
DO I = 1 TO DIM(XXX);
   IF XXX[I] = 0 THEN XXX[I] = .;
   END;
DROP I;
RUN;
```

Notice that missing values for character variables converted correctly to SAS missing values. Also, had zero been a valid data value, you would have had to place a unique missing value (9999 for example) in the spread sheet and converted that value to missing in the same way that zero was converted in the example above. In case you are not familiar with the DIM function, it returns the length of the array (i.e. the number of elements in the array) so we do not have to count how many numeric variables we had in our data set.

D. CONVERTING DBASE III FILES TO SAS SYSTEM FILES

Converting dBase III files to SAS system files is accomplished the same way we converted Lotus to SAS via DBF format, from the point that the spreadsheet was converted to a dBase file. The cautions concerning missing values still pertain.

E. CONVERTING LOTUS SPREADSHEETS TO SAS SYSTEM FILES VIA DBMS/COPY

A third party software package called DBMS/COPY®, available from Conceptual Software (P.O. Box 56627, Houston, TX, 77256 - telephone (800)STAT-WOW) can be used to convert system files between most of the major database, spreadsheet, and statistical packages, including SAS. Some of the more common packages supported are: Lotus, Quatro, Clipper, Dataease, dBase, Informix, Ingres, Oracle, Paradox, PC-File, Prodas, Rbase, Reflex, Smart, ASCII, ACT!, Datalex, ABstat, Bass, BMDP, CSS, 4CaST/2, Forecast Pro, MicroStat-II, NCSS, Probe, RATS, SigmaPlot, StatGraphics, Sygraph, Excel, Autobox, Gauss, Glim, Minitab, NCSS, SAS, SCA, Soritex, SPSS, Stata, StatPac, and Systat. In addition, DBMS/COPY can convert SAS transportable files to SAS system files (more about this later). DBMS/COPY is "menu driven," that is, just call up the program and on-screen instructions will direct you to select a source and destination file. Translation choices are grouped logically into spreadsheet, DBMS, and statistical categories. This is one of the best conversion packages we have seen and if you have need to import data from any other system to or from a SAS system file, the price of this package is well worth it. When we use DBMS/COPY to convert a Lotus spreadsheet to a SAS system file, we have the choice of using column headings as SAS variable names. When the translation is done, the spreadsheet will be shown on the screen and we can choose the data and variable name areas. DBMS/COPY will even convert multiple row headings into valid SAS variable names! Missing values of the spreadsheet will also be converted correctly to SAS missing values. This is by far the easiest way to convert spreadsheets to SAS system files.

F. CONVERTING SAS SYSTEM FILES FROM UNIX TO PC-SAS:

SAS system files are not compatible across hardware platforms (such as UNIX to PC-SAS). To migrate a SAS system file from one platform to another, you must first convert the system file to a transportable file using PROC CPORT, transfer the file to your PC (over a network or telecommunications line), and then run PROC CIMPORT to convert the transportable file back to a system file on the PC. We will show how this is done with a simple example of a single SAS system file on a UNIX system which we want to move to a PC. (Note: PROC CPORT and CIMPORT are capable of transporting an entire library or catalog as well.) Suppose our original UNIX file is called MYSAS.SSD in a subdirectory called SASDATA. Here are the steps we should follow:

1. Program to run on the UNIX system.

```
LIBNAME XXX '/USERS/CODY/SASDATA';
*Note: the actual name of this subdirectory may be
       slightly different;
FILENAME TRANS '/USERS/CODY/SASDATA/MYTRANS';
PROC CPORT DATA=XXX.MYSAS FILE=TRANS;
RUN;
```

2. Download the transportable file (MYTRANS) to your PC. We use KERMIT which provides an error free transmission protocol.
3. Run the following program on your PC:

```
LIBNAME YYY 'C:\SASDATA'; *The subdirectory where
                           you want the SAS system
                           file to reside;
FILENAME IN 'MYTRANS';
PROC CIMPORT DATA=YYY.NEWSAS INFILE=IN;
RUN;
```

The DATA option of CPORT provides the name of the SAS system file that you want to convert to a transportable format. OUT= defines the filename of the transportable file you want to create. PROC CIMPORT is similar to CPORT except that DATA= will provide the name of the SAS system file you want to recreate on the PC and INFILE= gives the filename of the transportable file you downloaded to your PC. Information about CPORT and CIMPORT can be found in the **SAS Procedures Guide** release 6.03 or, in more detail, in the Technical Report: P-176 Using the SAS System.

G. TO CONVERT FROM ALMOST ANYTHING TO ANYTHING ELSE

Use DBMS/COPY.

PROBLEMS

12-1. You ran a procedure to convert a spreadsheet into a SAS system file called HTWT.SSD (using PROC DIF). The resulting data set has variable names COL1-COL5. You would like the names ID, AGE, SEX, HEIGHT, and WEIGHT instead. The data set is in the subdirectory SASDATA on your D: disk (the same place you invoked SAS from). Write a program to rename these variables. Do not create another SAS data set.

CHAPTER 13
WORKING WITH ARRAYS

A. INTRODUCTION

SAS® arrays are a facility that can reduce the amount of coding in a data step. Although often thought of as an advanced programming tool, there are many applications of arrays that can be easily mastered. This chapter will demonstrate some of the more common uses of SAS arrays. In the simplest form, an array is a list of SAS variable names. We can use an array to replace multiple lines of SAS code where the only changes from line to line are the variable names used. The original implementation of ARRAYS (prior to Version 5) used what is called implicit subscripting. We will discuss this older form of arrays later, but for now, we will concentrate on the explicit form.

B. USING AN ARRAY TO SUBSTITUTE A SAS MISSING VALUE FOR 999

We will start off with a simple example. We have a data set where a value of 999 was used to represent a missing value (probably coded by an SPSS programmer). Our goal is to change all values of 999 to the SAS missing value.

Here is a SAS data step that does not use an array:

```
DATA EX1;
INPUT A B C D E;
IF A=999 THEN A=.;
IF B=999 THEN B=.;
IF C=999 THEN C=.;
IF D=999 THEN D=.;
IF E=999 THEN E=.;
CARDS;
(data lines)
RUN;
```

Here is the same program, using arrays:

```
DATA EX1;
INPUT A B C D E;
ARRAY X[5] A B C D E;
DO I=1 TO 5;
   IF X[I]=999 THEN X[I]=.;
   END;
DROP I;
CARDS;
(data lines)
RUN;
```

Without even knowing how arrays work, you can see that we did not do much to reduce the size of our program. If we had a hundred variables rather than five, the size differential would have been more obvious. Now to explain what we did. First, the form of the array statement we used is:

```
ARRAY arrayname[n] sas_variables;
```

(where n is the number of elements and sas_variables is a list of SAS variables) The statement begins with the word ARRAY, followed by an array name. Valid array names meet the same criteria as SAS variable names. However, an array name may not be the same as the name of a variable in your data set. Following the array name, in square brackets (in PC/SAS, {} brackets may also be used; on some other systems, regular parentheses are used— check with your computer center or just try it out), is the number of elements (variables) which the array is to represent. An asterisk "*" may be substituted for this number if you do not care to do the counting yourself. (Note: We almost always use the form [*] since we do not count too well.) Finally, following the number of elements, is a list of SAS variable names. The SAS variable name conventions - and -- may be used as well as the reserved SAS names _NUMERIC_ , _CHARACTER_, and _ALL_. It is important to note that among these conventions, except for the single - notation, a list of variables must have been previously defined, either by placing the ARRAY statement after the input statement or by some other mechanism (such as a LENGTH or RETAIN statement). In our example above, the array name X will represent the five variables A, B, C, D, and E. With this form of the array statement we can tell the data step which element of the array we want to process by using a subscript (also called an index). Thus, X[1] (the first element of the X array) is equivalent to the variable name A; X[2] will represent B and so forth. To make this equivalence clear, the two statements which follow are identical once our array has been defined.

```
SUM = A + B + D;
```

is equivalent to

```
SUM = X[1] + X[2] + X[4];
```

We usually find it convenient to use our arrays in some sort of iterative process. Our first example uses a DO statement. The syntax of a DO loop is:

```
DO counter = start TO end BY increment;
      (lines of SAS code)
   END;
```

The SAS statements between the DO and END statement will be repeated according the directions specified in the DO statement. Our simple example used "I" as the counter, 1 as the start value, 5 as the end value, and no value specified for the increment (which then defaults to 1). So, any SAS lines of code between our DO and END statement will be repeated five times, with the value of "I" taking on values of 1,2,3,4, and 5. We had the SAS statement

```
IF X[I]=999 THEN X[I]=.;
```

inside our loop, the first time through the loop, "I" has a value of 1. So the line of SAS code is:

```
IF X[1]=999 THEN X[1]=.;
```

Remember that this is equivalent to:

```
IF A=999 then A=.;
```

The next time through the loop, "I" will have a value of 2 and the line will be interpreted as:

```
IF X[2]=999 THEN X[2]=.;
```

which is equivalent to:

```
IF B=999 THEN B=.;
```

OK, do you have the picture? You can now see why the two programs above are equivalent. As a matter of fact, the best way to begin using arrays is to write out a few lines of SAS code without using arrays. Then, noticing that the lines all look the same except for the variable names, you write an ARRAY statement to represent your variables, substituting the array name for the variable name that changes in each line. Next, place the line in a DO loop so that the process will be repeated for each element in the array list. You should also notice in our first example, that we DROPPED the counter variable "I." If we forget to do this, each observation in our data set will have an "I" variable with a value of six. Why six? Because DO loops increment the counter before they check if the resulting value is greater than the ENDING value, at which time the iteration stops. We will show you later how to generalize this program to change the missing value from '999' to '.' for all our numeric variables. But first, here is another good example of array processing.

C. ENGLISH TO METRIC CONVERSION EXAMPLE

In this example, we will convert some weights and heights from English units to metric units.

Program without arrays:

```
DATA EX2;
INPUT WEIGHT1-WEIGHT5 HEIGHT1-HEIGHT5;
WEIGHT1=WEIGHT1/2.2;
WEIGHT2=WEIGHT2/2.2;
WEIGHT3=WEIGHT3/2.2;
WEIGHT4=WEIGHT4/2.2;
WEIGHT5=WEIGHT5/2.2;
HEIGHT1=2.54*HEIGHT1;
HEIGHT2=2.54*HEIGHT2;
HEIGHT3=2.54*HEIGHT3;
HEIGHT4=2.54*HEIGHT4;
HEIGHT5=2.54*HEIGHT5;
CARDS;
(data lines)
RUN;
```

Program with arrays;

```
DATA EX2;
INPUT WEIGHT1-WEIGHT5 HEIGHT1-HEIGHT5;
ARRAY WEIGHT[*] WEIGHT1-WEIGHT5;
ARRAY HEIGHT[*] HEIGHT1-HEIGHT5;
DO J=1 TO 5;
    WEIGHT[J]=WEIGHT[J]/2.2;
    HEIGHT[J]=2.54*HEIGHT[J];
    END;
DROP J;
CARDS;
(data lines)
RUN;
```

Notice that we used an asterisk in place of the number of elements so we did not have to count. We defined an array for the weights and one for the heights. Please realize that the array names WEIGHT and HEIGHT are arbitrary. We could have named them FRED and GEORGE. It is convenient to use the above convention when naming arrays. It's easy to remember that the elements of the array WEIGHT are your WEIGHTn variables. Be sure, however, that you do not have a variable in your data set with the same name. In our example, we could not have also had variables called WEIGHT and HEIGHT.

D. USING AN ARRAY TO CREATE NEW VARIABLES

So far, our arrays have represented variables that were listed in the INPUT statement. This is not necessary. We can define an array with a list of variables that are not included as INPUT variables. We will modify the above program to demonstrate this. Instead of converting the original WEIGHTn and HEIGHTn variables to metric values, we want to create ten new variables which will have metric values. Thus, we will be able to use either the English or metric variables in any procedures that follow. Here is the code:

```
DATA EX3;
INPUT WEIGHT1-WEIGHT5 HEIGHT1-HEIGHT5;
ARRAY WEIGHT[*] WEIGHT1-WEIGHT5;
ARRAY HEIGHT[*] HEIGHT1-HEIGHT5;
ARRAY WTKG[*] WTKG1-WTKG5;
ARRAY HTCM[*] HTCM1-HTCM5;
DO J=1 TO 5;
   WTKG[J]=WEIGHT[J]/2.2;
   HTCM[J]=2.54*HEIGHT[J];
   END;
DROP J;
CARDS;
(data lines)
RUN;
```

The resulting data set will contain the original five weight and five height variables as well as the five metric weight and five metric height ones.

E. REPLACING 999 WITH SAS MISSING VALUES FOR ALL NUMERIC VARIABLES

We now want to expand the example in section B to replace missing values of 999 with SAS missing values for all numeric variables.

```
DATA EX4;
INPUT A B C X1-X20;
ARRAY X[*] _NUMERIC_ ;
DO I=1 TO DIM(X);
   IF X[I]=999 THEN X[I]=.;
   END;
DROP I;
CARDS;
(data lines)
RUN;
```

The first change is to substitute the SAS internal variable _NUMERIC_ for the variable list of the ARRAY statement. This internal SAS name is available anywhere in a SAS program, in either a DATA or PROC step. It means "use all numeric variables." Note also that the internal name _CHARACTER_ is available and, as you would expect, it refers to all character variables. We used an asterisk in the ARRAY statement since we did not want to count how many numeric variables there were in our data set. Since the number of array elements is unknown, we used the DIM function (DIM stands for Dimension) in the next line. This function, whose argument is an array name (in this case X) returns the number of elements in the array (in this case, the number of numeric SAS variables). The remainder of the program is identical to the example in section B. This is a good example of an array that can save a considerable amount of SAS coding, especially in a data set with a lot of numeric variables.

F. ARRAYNAME[*] NOTATION IN A DATA STEP

A little used, obscurely documented, but very useful feature of arrays is the ability to refer to all elements of an array with the ARRAYNAME[*] notation. To see how this works, look at the following example:

```
DATA EX5;
ARRAY X[*] A B C D E;
INPUT X[*];
S = SUM (OF X[*]);
CARDS;
(data lines)
RUN;
```

We used the asterisk notation both in the INPUT statement and as the argument of the SUM function.

G. TRANSFORMING A DATA SET FROM ONE OBSERVATION PER SUBJECT TO MORE THAN ONE PER SUBJECT

In this example, we will use an array where the index of the array becomes a useful variable in our data set. Let's look at the problem of transforming a data set where each SAS observation contains several measurements on each subject at different times. We want a program that will transform this data set into one where each observation contains data on one subject at a single time. In addition, this new data set should contain a variable (which we will call TIME) that indicates at which time the measure was taken. To clarify this, here is a diagram of the original data set:

SUBJ	X1	X2	X3
1	10	11	13
2	5	6	8
etc.			

where X1 is a measure taken at time=1, X2 is the same measure taken at time=2 etc. We want the new data set to look like this:

SUBJ	TIME	X
1	1	10
1	2	11
1	3	13
2	1	5
2	2	6
2	3	8

We could program this without arrays like this:

```
DATA EX6;
SET oldname;
TIME=1;
X=X1;
OUTPUT;
TIME=2;
X=X2;
OUTPUT;
TIME=3;
X=X3;
OUTPUT;
DROP X1-X3;
RUN;
```

The same program using arrays is shown below:

```
DATA EX6;
SET oldname;
ARRAY XX[3] X1-X3;
DO TIME=1 TO 3;
   X=XX[TIME];
   OUTPUT;
   END;
DROP X1-X3;
RUN;
```

Notice the efficiency of using TIME as the index of our DO loop, thus saving us the problem of setting a value for TIME manually. Also notice that the array could not have been named X since we used X as a variable in our data set. Obviously with more levels of TIME, this use of arrays becomes even more advantageous.

H. TRANSFORMING A DATA SET FROM MANY OBSERVATIONS PER SUBJECT TO ONE PER SUBJECT

In this next example, you will see where arrays are used to transform a data set with multiple observations per subject into a data set with a single observation per subject. We will transform a data set from the form shown directly below to one that has all measurements for one subject in one observation. The objective here is just the opposite of that done in the example above. One possible reason for this transformation would be to use the REPEATED statement in PROC GLM. Here is the original data set:

SUBJ	TIME	X	Y	Z
1	1	5	6	7
1	2	6	7	8
1	3	6	6	6
1	4	3	4	5
1	5	7	8	9
2	1	4	5	6
2	2	4	5	7
2	3	5	7	9 (cont.)

2	4	5	8	8
2	5	8	8	9

The transformed data set would look like this:

SUBJ	X1	X2	X3	X4	X5	Y1	Y2	Y3	Y4	Y5	Z1	Z2	Z3	Z4	Z5
1	5	6	6	3	7	6	7	6	4	8	7	8	6	5	9
2	4	4	5	5	8	5	5	7	8	8	6	7	9	8	9

The program which does the transformation, uses an array for each of the variables X, Y, and Z and the RETAIN statement to prevent the variables from being set to missing each time a new observation from the original data set is read.

```
DATA MULTIPLE;
INPUT SUBJ TIME X Y Z;
CARDS;
1 1 5 6 7
1 2 6 7 8
1 3 6 6 6
1 4 3 4 5
1 5 7 8 9
2 1 4 5 6
2 2 4 5 7
2 3 5 7 9
2 4 5 8 8
2 5 8 8 9
RUN;
PROC SORT DATA=MULTIPLE;
   BY SUBJ TIME;
RUN;
DATA ONEPER;
SET MULTIPLE;
   BY SUBJ TIME;
ARRAY XX[*] X1-X5;
ARRAY YY[*] Y1-Y5;
ARRAY ZZ[*] Z1-Z5;
RETAIN X1-X5 Y1-Y5 Z1-Z5;               (cont.)
```

```
                           (Continued from previous page)
IF FIRST.SUBJ THEN DO I=1 TO 5;
    XX[I]=.; YY[I]=.; ZZ[I]=.;
    END;
XX[TIME]=X;
YY[TIME]=Y;
ZZ[TIME]=Z;
IF LAST.SUBJ THEN OUTPUT;
KEEP SUBJ X1-X5 Y1-Y5 Z1-Z5;
RUN;
```

The best way to understand this program is to picture an observation in the new data set ONEPER. Each time the program reads in an observation from MULTIPLE, one column of the table is filled in.

T I M E

	1	2	3	4	5
X					
Y					
Z					

Let's follow this program in detail to see how it works. The first observation from data set MULTIPLE has SUBJ=1, TIME=1, X=5, Y=6, and Z=7. FIRST.SUBJ is TRUE so we set the three arrays (and therefore the values of X1-X5, Y1-Y5, and Z1-Z5) to missing. If we did not do this, a subject with a missing observation (i.e. no data taken at TIME n) would be assigned the values from the previous subject for that time. Next, since TIME=1, XX[TIME] is equal to XX[1] which represents the variable X1 which gets set to 5, the value of X. In the same manner, Y1 will be set to 6 and Z1 will be assigned the value 7. Since LAST.SUBJ is not true, we do not output; we return to read the next observation from MULTIPLE. By using the RETAIN statement, the values of X1-X5, Y1-Y5, and Z1-Z5 will not be reset to missing each time a new observation is read. Thus we can imagine filling in the boxes in the diagram above. The internal SAS variable LAST.SUBJ is TRUE when the last observation for a subject is read. So when LAST.SUBJ is TRUE, we OUTPUT the observation to the new data set. This program will also work if there are missing observations in the original data set.

I. CHARACTER ARRAYS

So far, we have made arrays of numeric variables. Character variable arrays are also possible. If a variable has already been identified as a character variable (in a LENGTH or INPUT statement for example), then an array can be set up just the same as the arrays of numeric variables we have already seen. However, if the array statement is placed in the DATA step before the variables have been defined (such as directly after the DATA statement), the array statement must include a $ after the array name to indicate that the variables being assigned to the array are to be character. As a good programming practice, you should include a $ for all character arrays. Here is an example of a character array:

```
DATA EX7;
ARRAY X[*] $ A B C;
INPUT A $ 1-2 B $ 3-4 C $ 5-6;
DO I = 1 TO 3;
   IF X[I]='XX' THEN X[I]=' ';
   END;
DROP I;
CARDS;
(data lines)
RUN;
```

J. INITIAL VALUES AND ATTRIBUTES

Besides declaring an array as character, we can define the variable lengths and initial values with the ARRAY statement. The general form is:

```
ARRAY arrayname[n or *] $ length
      list of vars (initial values);
```

For example, to declare an array of numeric variables to all be length 4, we would have:

```
ARRAY ABC[*] 4 X Y Z;
```

To assign initial values of 0, 1, and 3 to X, Y, and Z respectively, we would add:

```
ARRAY ABC[*] 4 X Y Z (0 1 3);
```

K. TEMPORARY ARRAYS

A temporary array, as the name implies, has only temporary variables which can be referred to only as ARRAYNAME[index]. This can be of value when speed and memory are of concern. As an example, at the Robert Wood Johnson Medical School, we had a very large test scoring program which could unscramble multiple versions of a test before performing an item analysis. The mapping of each version to the main version was accomplished using temporary arrays. Using arrays with real variables would have added hundreds of variables to the data set and exceeded memory capacity on a PC. Here is an example where the elements of a temporary array are used to hold the passing scores on each of ten tests.

```
DATA TEST;
ARRAY X[10] _TEMPORARY_
(65 60 60 65 70 62 66 67 64 60);
*X[1] TO X[10] HOLD PASSING SCORES ON
TESTS;
ARRAY SCORE[10] SCORE1-SCORE10;
INPUT ID SCORE1-SCORE10;
NUMPASS=0;
DO I = 1 TO 10;
    IF SCORE[I] GE X[I] THEN NUMPASS+1;
    END;
DROP I;
CARDS;
001 90 60 60 90 90 90 90 90 90 61
002 40 50 60 70 80 90 80 70 60 50
RUN;
PROC PRINT NOOBS;
RUN;
```

In this example, the variables X[1] to X[10] exist only as subscripted elements of the array X. Notice that there are no Xn variables in the data set and none in the DROP statement. Whenever you need variables only in the data step (ie. you would have DROPPED them anyway) and you want an array, use the _TEMPORARY_ attribute to save memory and time.

L. SPECIFYING ARRAY BOUNDS

So far, all of our array indices have run from 1 to n (where n is the number of variables in the variable list). There are times when it is useful to be able to specify lower and upper bounds on the array index. One of the best examples is one used in the SAS Language Guide. This example uses variable names such as cost88, cost89, and cost90 where the numeric part refers to the year. An array statement such as:

```
ARRAY COST[3] COST88-COST90;
```

is fine except that you have to remember that COST[1] refers to 1988, COST[2] refers to 1989 and COST[3] refers to 1990. By specifying bounds:

```
ARRAY COST[88:90] COST88-COST90;
```

you have the advantage that COST[88] refers to 1988 and so forth.

Another useful example concerns variables that were measured over time where we want to call the value of X at time 0, X0; the value of X at time 1, X1, etc. It is confusing to have an array of X's where X[1] is the value of X at time 0. Much more convenient is to set the lower bound of the array to 0. Your DO loops can also start counting from 0.

M. MULTIDIMENSIONAL ARRAYS

SAS allows for multidimensional arrays. In the example that follows, the scores for five tests are kept for each of three classes. The first dimension will tell us which class the scores are for, the second, the test within class. So, on the data line, the first five scores are for class one, the second five for class two, and the third five for class three. A diagram of the data for one subject is shown in table I below:

	TEST 1	TEST 2	TEST 3	TEST 4	TEST 5
CLASS 1	90	90	100	100	95
CLASS 2	80	80	80	90	90
CLASS 3	70	70	70	60	70

Table I

Here is the program using arrays:

```
DATA EX8;
ARRAY X[3,5] X1-X15;
ARRAY AVE[3] AVE1-AVE3;
*NOTE FIRST DIMENSION IS CLASS NUMBER
 SECOND IS TEST NUMBER (IE. 5 TESTS FOR
 EACH OF 3 CLASSES);
INPUT X[*] @;
DO CLASS=1 TO 3;
   DO TEST=1 TO 5;
 AVE[CLASS]+X[CLASS,TEST]/5;
 END;
   END;
DROP TEST CLASS X1-X15;
CARDS;
90 90 100 100 95  80 80 80 90 90
70 70 70 60 70
(data for other students)
RUN;
```

The first DO loop used CLASS as its index. CLASS is first set to 1. Then while CLASS is held at 1, the inner loop (DO TEST) executes for all five tests. Inside this loop, the statement AVE[CLASS]+X[CLASS,TEST]/5 adds each of the five tests scores (divided by 5) so that after the inner loop has executed five times, AVE[CLASS] will be the average for one of the three classes. If you have not seen nested DO loops before, this may seem confusing. To help clarify this, Table II shows the actual 15 computations performed by the nested loops:

AVE[1]+X[1,1]/5; CLASS=1,	TEST=1	AVE[1] = 0 + 90/5
AVE[1]+X[1,2]/5;	TEST=2	AVE[1] = 18 + 90/5
AVE[1]+X[1,3]/5;	TEST=3	AVE[1] = 36 + 100/5
AVE[1]+X[1,4]/5;	TEST=4	AVE[1] = 56 + 100/5
AVE[1]+X[1,5]/5;	TEST=5	AVE[1] = 76 + 95/5
AVE[2]+X[2,1]/5; CLASS=2,	TEST=1	etc.
AVE[2]+X[2,2]/5;	TEST=2	
AVE[2]+X[2,3]/5;	TEST=3	
AVE[2]+X[2,4]/5;	TEST=4	
AVE[2]+X[2,5]/5;	TEST=5	
AVE[3]+X[3,1]/5; CLASS=3,	TEST=1	
AVE[3]+X[3,2]/5;	TEST=2	
AVE[3]+X[3,3]/5;	TEST=3	
AVE[3]+X[3,4]/5;	TEST=4	
AVE[3]+X[3,5]/5;	TEST=5	

Table II

N. IMPLICITLY SUBSCRIPTED ARRAYS

Before we leave the topic of arrays, we should mention the alternate type of array which does not explicitly show the subscript when you refer to an array element in the data step. This was the original form of the array statement in version 5 that was superceded by the explicit subscript form that we have discussed until now. We strongly recommend that you use the explicit form. However, since the implicit form is still supported and you may have to maintain older SAS code that contains this type of array, we will briefly show you how it works. The form of the ARRAY statement is:

```
ARRAY arrayname(index variable)
      list of SAS variables;
```

Length and $ attributes are also available and placed before the list of SAS variables. When using the array name in a data step, the index variable is first set (usually by a DO loop) and the array name is used without a subscript. Here is an example:

```
DATA EX9;
ARRAY MOZART(I)  A  B  C  D  E;
INPUT A B C D E;
DO I = 1 TO 5;
    IF MOZART=999 THEN MOZART=.;
    END;
DROP I;
CARDS;
(data lines)
```

Notice that inside the DO loop, the array name MOZART is used without a subscript. When I=1, MOZART will represent the variable name A; when I=2, MOZART will represent B, and so forth. A default subscript _I_ will be used if no subscript is indicated in the ARRAY statement. The DO loop would then read "DO _I_ = 1 to 5." A very useful form of the DO loop, "DO OVER" is available when the implicit subscript form of the array is used. DO OVER is equivalent to "DO subscript = lower bound TO upper bound" but saves us the trouble of using the DIM function or knowing how many elements are in the array. Furthermore, if you use the default subscript _I_, you don't even have to remember to DROP it since it is an internal SAS variable and not a variable in the data set. The example above could therefore be rewritten as:

```
DATA EX10;
ARRAY MOZART  A  B  C  D  E;
INPUT A B C D E;
DO OVER MOZART;
    IF MOZART=999 THEN MOZART=.;
    END;
CARDS;
(data lines)
```

As convenient as this may seem, we still recommend the explicit arrays of version 6.

O. CONCLUSIONS

Yes, we can live without ARRAYS, but a thorough understanding of ARRAYS can substantially reduce the size of a SAS program. We hope that the examples offered here will give you the courage to try using ARRAYS in your next program. Good luck[!].

PROBLEMS

13-1. Rewrite this program, using arrays:

```
DATA PROB13_1;
INPUT (HT1-HT5)(2.)  (WT1-WT5)(3.);
DENS1 = WT1 / HT1**2;
DENS2 = WT2 / HT2**2;
DENS3 = WT3 / HT3**2;
DENS4 = WT4 / HT4**2;
DENS5 = WT5 / HT5**2;
CARDS;
```

13-2. Rewrite the following program, using arrays:

```
DATA OLDMISS;
INPUT A B C X1-X3 Y1-Y3;
IF A=999 THEN A=.;
IF B=999 THEN B=.;
IF C=999 THEN C=.;
IF X1=999 THEN X1=.;
IF X2=999 THEN X2=.;
IF X3=999 THEN X3=.;
IF Y1=777 THEN Y1=.;
IF Y2=777 THEN Y2=.;
IF Y3=777 THEN Y3=.;
CARDS;
```

*13-3. We have a data set called FROG which looks like this:

ID	X1	X2	X3	X4	X5	Y1	Y2	Y3	Y4	Y5
01	4	5	4	7	3	1	7	3	6	8
02	8	7	8	6	7	5	4	3	5	6

We want a data set that has an observation for each subject (ID) at each time interval (X1 represents X at time 1, etc.). Write a program, using arrays, to accomplish this. The new data set (TOAD) should look like this:

ID	TIME	X	Y
01	1	4	1
01	2	5	7
01	3	4	3
01	4	7	6
01	5	3	8
02	1	7	5
02	2	7	4
02	3	8	3
02	4	6	5
02	5	7	6

*13-4. We have data set (called STATE) that contains an ID variable, and up to 5 states (2 letter codes) which an individual may have visited in the last year. Three observations from this data set are shown next:

ID	STATE1	STATE2	STATE3	STATE4
1	NY	NJ	PA	GA
2	NJ	CA	XX	XX
3	PA	XX	XX	XX

As you can see, "XX" was used as a missing value. First, write a program to read these records and replace the values of "XX" with blanks. Next, write the necessary SAS statements to compute frequency counts showing now many people visited each state. Present the frequency list in decreasing order of frequency (use the ORDER=FREQ option of PROC FREQ).

*13-5. You inherited an old SAS program (shown below) and want to convert it to one using explicit array subscripts. Rewrite the program to do this.

```
DATA OLDFASH;
SET BLAH;
ARRAY JUNK(J) X1-X5 Y1-Y5 Z1-Z5;
DO OVER JUNK;
   IF JUNK = 999 THEN JUNK=.;
   END;
DROP J;
RUN;
```

CHAPTER 14

DATA SET SUBSETTING, CONCATENATING, MERGING, AND UPDATING

A. INTRODUCTION

This chapter covers some basic data set operations. Subsetting is an operation where we select a subset from one data set to form another. Another common requirement is to combine data from several files into a single SAS data set. There are several ways of combining information from different files as well. Let's take these topics one at a time.

B. SUBSETTING

We have already seen some examples of data subsetting. The key here is the SET statement which "reads" observations from a SAS data set to form a new SAS data set. As we process the records from the original data set, we can modify any of the values, create new variables, or make a decision whether or not to include the observation in the new data set. A simple example follows:

```
DATA WOMEN;
   SET ALL;
   IF SEX = 'F';
RUN;
```

In this example, data set ALL contains a variable, SEX, which has values of M and F. The IF statement, used in this context, is called a subsetting IF. To those of you familiar with other programming languages, this is a "funny" looking IF statement—there is no THEN clause. This form of an IF statement in SAS has an implied THEN clause which is: THEN OUTPUT. Any record satisfying the conditions of the IF statement will be written to the new data set WOMEN. An equivalent expression is:

```
IF SEX NE 'F' THEN DELETE;
```

We can use any boolean expression in the IF statement to subset the data set. For example, we could have:

```
DATA OLDWOMEN;
SET ALL;
IF SEX = 'F' AND AGE > 65;
RUN;
```

With the release of version 6 of SAS software, an alternative to the IF statement became available, called the WHERE statement. Although there are several subtle differences between using IF and WHERE statements, we can subset a data set just as easily by substituting WHERE for IF in the programs above. When the data set we are creating is a small subset of the original data set, the WHERE statement will be faster and more efficient. In addition, we also have the option of using the WHERE statement **in a SAS PROCEDURE.** So, to compute frequencies of RACE and INCOME only for females, we could write:

```
PROC FREQ DATA=ALL;
   WHERE SEX = 'F';
   TABLES RACE INCOME;
RUN;
```

If we want to run a procedure for **all** levels of a variable, we should use a BY statement instead. We have found the WHERE statement particularly useful when we run t-tests or ANOVAs and we want to eliminate one or more groups from the analysis. Suppose the variable GROUP has 3 levels (A,B, and C) and we want to run a t-test between groups A and B. Using the WHERE statement greatly simplifies the job:

```
PROC TTEST DATA=dataset;
   WHERE GROUP='A' OR GROUP='B';
   CLASS GROUP;
   VAR ...;
```

C. COMBINING SIMILAR DATA FROM MULTIPLE FILES

Assume that we have several files, each containing the **same** variables. To create a SAS system file from multiple SAS system files, just use the SET statement to name each of the files to be combined. For example:

```
DATA ALLDATA;
SET MEN WOMEN;
RUN;
```

Data set ALLDATA will contain all the observations from the data set MEN, followed by all the observations from the data set WOMEN.

D. COMBINING DIFFERENT DATA FROM MULTIPLE FILES

In this section, we will demonstrate how to combine different information from multiple files. Suppose we have a master student file that contains SS numbers and student names. We then give a test and create a file that contains student SS numbers and test scores. We now want to print out a list of student numbers, names, and scores. Below are sample master and test files:

SS	NAME	
123456789	CODY	
987654321	SMITH	
111223333	GREGORY	Master File
222334444	BERNHOLC	
777665555	CHAMBLISS	

SS	SCORE	
123456789	100	
987654321	67	Test file
222334444	92	

To merge the student names in the MASTER file with the SS numbers in the TEST file, we first **sort** both files by SS:

```
PROC SORT DATA=MASTER;
   BY SS;
RUN;
PROC SORT DATA=TEST;
   BY SS;
RUN;
```

To merge these two files into a new data set we use a MERGE statement:

```
DATA BOTH;
MERGE MASTER TEST (IN=FRODO);
   BY SS;
IF FRODO;
FORMAT SS SSN11.;
RUN;
```

The IN= option following the data set name TEST instructs the program to include only those students whose SS number is in the TEST file. (Notice that there are SS numbers in the MASTER file for students who did not take the test.) When the merge takes place, the variable following the IN= option will have a value of **true** if the data set contributed data to the current observation. To limit the merged data set to only those students in the TEST file, we use a subsetting IF statement on the next line to insure that the student had a record in the TEST file. The merged data set (BOTH) is shown next:

SS	NAME	SCORE
123-45-6789	CODY	100
222-33-4444	BERNHOLC	92
987-65-4321	SMITH	67

The general syntax for the MERGE statement is:

```
MERGE file_one (IN=var_name) file_two (IN=var_name);
   BY match_vars;
```

Where file_one and file_two are the two files to be merged and the IN= option that follows each file name, if used, can control which observations will be included in the merged data set. The BY statement will tell the program how to select observations from the two data sets. If the BY variable has a different variable name in one of the files, you can use a RENAME option in the MERGE statement. For example, if SS were called ID in the TEST file, we would write:

```
MERGE MASTER TEST (IN=INTEST, RENAME=(ID=SS));
```

NOTE: ID is renamed to SS in file TEST before the merge.

We should mention that MERGE can be used **without** a BY statement. When that is done, the observations are combined in the order they appear in the two data sets. This is extremely risky and we recommend that you never do it.

E. TABLE LOOK UP

This section will explore some other ways that merging can be used to perform a "table look up." By table look up, we mean that one can pull information from a data set based on one or more criteria and add that information to the current data set. Some simple examples will make this clear. We have one file which contains ID numbers, YEAR, and white blood count (WBC). Some sample records are shown here:

ID	YEAR	WBC
1	1940	6000
2	1940	8000
3	1940	9000
1	1941	6500
2	1941	8500
3	1941	8900

Data set WORKER

Next, we have a file that tells us the benzene exposure for these subjects for each year. This file is shown next:

YEAR EXPOSURE

1940	200
1941	150
1942	100
1943	80

Data set EXP

What we want is to add the correct exposure to each record in the WORKER file. This part of the problem is identical to the SS and NAME problem above. The SAS statements to perform the merge are:

```
PROC SORT DATA=WORKER;
   BY YEAR;
RUN;
PROC SORT DATA=EXP;
   BY YEAR;
RUN;
DATA BOTH;
MERGE WORKER (IN=INWORK) EXP;
   BY YEAR;
IF INWORK;
RUN;
```

The resulting data set, BOTH is shown next:

ID	YEAR	WBC	EXPOSURE
1	1940	6000	200
2	1940	8000	200
3	1940	9000	200
1	1941	6500	150
2	1941	8500	150
3	1941	8900	150

Data set BOTH

We will now extend this problem to a real "table look up" problem. We will want to assign an exposure based on the YEAR and the WORK assignment. Our look up table consists of years, work codes, and exposures. Here is the look up table:

YEAR	WORK	EXPOSURE	
1940	MIXER	190	
1940	SPREADER	200	
1941	MIXER	140	
1941	SPREADER	150	Data set EXP
1942	MIXER	90	
1942	SPREADER	100	
1943	MIXER	70	
1943	SPREADER	80	

The WORKER file now contains the YEAR, WORK code, and WBC counts:

ID	YEAR	WORK	WBC	
1	1940	MIXER	6000	
2	1940	SPREADER	8000	
3	1940	MIXER	9000	Data set WORKER
1	1941	MIXER	6500	
2	1941	MIXER	8500	
3	1941	SPREADER	8900	

To add the correct exposure to each record in the WORKER file, we have to "look up" the exposure for the correct YEAR and WORK code. A MERGE statement with two BY variables will accomplish this for us:

```
PROC SORT DATA=WORKER;
   BY YEAR WORK;
RUN;
PROC SORT DATA=EXP;
   BY YEAR WORK;
RUN;
MERGE WORK (IN=INWORK) EXP;
   BY YEAR WORK;
IF INWORK;
RUN;
```

The merged file (BOTH) is shown next:

ID	YEAR	WORK	WBC	EXPOSURE
1	1940	MIXER	6000	190
3	1940	MIXER	9000	190
2	1940	SPREADER	8000	200
1	1941	MIXER	6500	140
2	1941	MIXER	8500	140
3	1941	SPREADER	8900	150

F. UPDATING A MASTER FILE FROM AN UPDATE FILE

In many business applications, we will have a master file that needs to be updated with new information. For example, we might have part numbers and prices in the master file. The update file would contain part numbers and new, updated prices. Typically, the update file would be smaller than the master file and contain observations only for those part numbers with new prices. In addition, the update file may contain part numbers that are not present in the master file. Here is an example:

PART_NO	PRICE	
1	19	
4	23	MASTER file
6	22	
7	45	

PART_NO	PRICE	
4	24	UPDATE file
5	37	

We sort both files by PART_NO and then perform the UPDATE:

```
DATA NEWMASTR;
UPDATE MASTER UPDATE;
   BY PART_NO;
```

The result is:

PART_NO	PRICE
1	19
4	24
5	37
6	22
7	45

NEWMASTR file

CHAPTER 15

SELECTED PROGRAMMING EXAMPLES

This chapter contains a number of common applications. It serves two functions: one is to allow you to use any of the programs here, with modification, if you have a similar application; the other is to demonstrate SAS programming techniques.

A. EXPRESSING DATA VALUES AS A PERCENT OF THE GRAND MEAN

A common problem is to express data values as percents of the grand mean, rather than in the original raw units. In this example, we have recorded the heart rate (HR), systolic blood pressure (SBP), and diastolic blood pressure (DBP) for each subject. We want to express these values as percents of the mean HR, SBP, and DBP for all subjects. For example, in the data set below, the mean heart rate for all subjects is 70 (mean of 80, 70, and 60). The first subject's score of 80, expressed as a percentage, would be 100% x 80 / 70 =114.28%. The approach here will be to use PROC MEANS to compute the means and to output them in a data set which we will then merge with the original data so that we can perform the needed computation.

```
1     DATA TEST;
2     INPUT HR SBP DBP;
3     CARDS;
      80 160 100
      70 150 90
      60 140 80
4     RUN;
5     PROC MEANS NOPRINT DATA=TEST;
6        VAR HR SBP DBP;
7        OUTPUT OUT=MOUT MEAN=MHR MSBP MDBP;
8     RUN;
9     DATA NEW (DROP=MHR MSBP MDBP _FREQ_ _TYPE_);
10    SET TEST;
11    IF _N_ = 1 THEN SET MOUT;
12    HRPER=100*HR/MHR;
13    SBPPER=100*SBP/MSBP;
14    DBPPER=100*DBP/MDBP;
15    RUN;                                    (cont.)
```

```
                    (Continued from previous page)
 16    PROC PRINT NOOBS;
 17        TITLE 'LISTING OF NEW DATA SET';
 18    RUN;
```

Description:

We use the NOPRINT option with PROC MEANS because we do not want the procedure to print anything but, rather, to create a data set of means. In this case, the output data set from PROC MEANS will consist of one observation. The variables _TYPE_ and _FREQ_ are added to the output data set by the MEANS procedure. _TYPE_ is useful when a CLASS statement is used with PROC MEANS. We will show examples of this later. The _FREQ_ variable shows how many observations were used in the computation of the mean (or any other statistic we request). The single observation in the data set MOUT is shown below:

OBS	_TYPE_	_FREQ_	MHR	MSBP	MDBP
1	0	3	70	150	90

We want to add the three variables MHR, MSBP, and MDBP to every observation in the original data set so that we can divide each value by the mean and multiply by 100%. Since our original data set has three observations and the mean data set contains only one observation, we use a trick: we use the SAS internal variable _N_ (the observation counter) to conditionally execute the SET statement. The Program Data Vector now contains the variables HR, SBP, DBP, _TYPE_, _FREQ_, MHR, MSBP, and MDBP. We can now divide HR by MHR, SBP by MSBP, and DBP by MDBP. Each time we bring in another observation from the original (TEST) data set, the values of MHR, MSBP, and MDBP will remain in the Program Data Vector (they are automatically RETAINED). The final data set created by this program (NEW) is shown next:

HR	SBP	DBP	HRPER	SBPPER	DBPPER
80	160	100	114.286	106.667	111.111
70	150	90	100.000	100.000	100.000
60	140	80	85.714	93.333	88.889

B. EXPRESSING A VALUE AS A PERCENT OF A GROUP MEAN

This example is an extension of the previous problem. Here we have two groups (A and B) and we want to express each measurement as a percentage of the **GROUP** mean.

```
DATA TEST;
INPUT GROUP $ HR SBP DBP @@;
CARDS;
A 80 160 100 A 70 150 90 A 60 140 80
B 90 200 180 B 80 180 140 B 70 140 80
RUN;
PROC SORT;
    BY GROUP;
RUN;
PROC MEANS NOPRINT DATA=TEST NWAY;
    CLASS GROUP;
    VAR HR SBP DBP;
    OUTPUT OUT=MOUT MEAN=MHR MSBP MDBP;
RUN;
DATA NEW (DROP=MHR MSBP MDBP _FREQ_ _TYPE_);
MERGE TEST MOUT;
    BY GROUP;
HRPER=100*HR/MHR;
SBPPER=100*SBP/MSBP;
DBPPER=100*DBP/MDBP;
RUN;
PROC PRINT NOOBS;
    TITLE 'LISTING OF NEW DATA SET';
RUN;
```

Description:

Since the output data set from PROC MEANS contains GROUP, we can MERGE it with the original data set, using GROUP as the BY variable. Data set MOUT will contain two observations, one for each value of GROUP. The contents of MOUT are shown below:

OBS	GROUP	_TYPE_	_FREQ_	MHR	MSBP	MDBP
1	A	1	3	70	150.000	90.000
2	B	1	3	80	173.333	133.333

Data set NEW, which contains both the original values and the percentage values is shown next:

GROUP	HR	SBP	DBP	HRPER	SBPPER	DBPPER
A	80	160	100	114.286	106.667	111.111
A	70	150	90	100.000	100.000	100.000
A	60	140	80	85.714	93.333	88.889
B	90	200	180	112.500	115.385	135.000
B	80	180	140	100.000	103.846	105.000
B	70	140	80	87.500	80.769	60.000

C. PLOTTING MEANS WITH ERROR BARS

When we plot a set of means, we may want to include error bars which represent one standard error above and below the mean. The program below shows how we can use PROC MEANS to output the standard errors and then use PROC PLOT to plot the means and the error bars.

```
DATA ORIG;
INPUT SUBJ TIME DRUG DBP SBP;
CARDS;
(data lines)
RUN;
PROC MEANS NOPRINT DATA=ORIG NWAY;
   CLASS DRUG TIME;
   VAR SBP DBP;
   OUTPUT OUT=MEANOUT MEAN= STDERR=SE_SBP SE_DBP;
RUN;
DATA TMP;
SET MEANOUT;
SBPHI=SBP+SE_SBP;
SBPLO=SBP-SE_SBP;
DBPHI=DBP+SE_DBP;                              (cont.)
```

```
                              (Continued from previous page)
DBPLO=DBP-SE_DBP;
RUN;
PROC PLOT DATA=TMP;
    PLOT SBP*TIME=DRUG SBPHI*TIME='-' SBPLO*TIME='-'
    / OVERLAY BOX;
    PLOT DBP*TIME=DRUG DBPHI*TIME='-' DBPLO*TIME='-'
    / OVERLAY BOX;
    TITLE 'Plot of mean Blood Pressures for Placebo
           and Drug';
    TITLE2 'Error bars represent +- 1 standard
            error';
RUN;
```

Description:

The original data set contained variables DRUG and TIME as well as the two blood pressures (SBP and DBP). The data set produced by PROC MEANS (with the CLASS statement) would have as many observations as there were combinations of DRUG and TIME (note the NWAY option). We are seeking a plot of mean SBP (and DBP) versus time with DRUG as the plotting symbol. The data set TMP adds and subtracts the standard errors from the means so that we can plot them along with the means. We are using a "-" as a plotting symbol to represent error bars.

D. USING A MACRO VARIABLE TO SAVE CODING TIME

Programmers are always looking for a way to make their programs more compact (and to avoid typing). While there is an extensive **macro** language as part of the SAS system, we will only use a macro variable in this example. Macro statements begin with % signs. A macro variable is defined with a %LET function. The expression to the right of the = sign will be assigned to the macro variable. We precede the macro variable name with an ampersand (&) in the program so that the system knows we are referring to a macro variable. In this example, we are using a macro variable to take the place of a variable list. Any time we want to refer to the variables ONE, TWO and THREE, we can use the macro variable LIST instead.

```
DATA TEST;
%LET LIST=ONE TWO THREE;
INPUT &LIST FOUR;
CARDS;
1 2 3 4
4 5 6 6
RUN;
PROC FREQ;
    TABLES &LIST;
RUN;
```

E. COMPUTING RELATIVE FREQUENCIES

In this example, we have an ICD (International Classification of Diseases) code for each year. We want to know what percent of the observations contain a particular code for each year. That is, we want to express each ICD code as a percent of all observations for that year.

```
DATA ICD;
INPUT ID YEAR ICD;
CARDS;
001 1950 450
002 1950 440
003 1951 460
004 1950 450
005 1951 300
RUN;
PROC FREQ;
    TABLES YEAR*ICD / OUT=ICDFREQ NOPRINT;
*DATA SET ICDFREQ CONTAINS THE COUNTS FOR EACH CODE
  IN EACH YEAR;
RUN;
PROC FREQ DATA=ICD;
    TABLES YEAR / OUT=TOTAL NOPRINT;
RUN;                                    (cont.)
```

```
                               (Continued from previous page)
*DATA SET ICD CONTAINS THE TOTAL NUMBER OF OBS FOR
 EACH YEAR;
DATA RELATIVE;
MERGE ICDFREQ TOTAL (RENAME=(COUNT=TOT_CNT));
BY YEAR;
RELATIVE=100*COUNT/TOT_CNT;
DROP PERCENT;
RUN;
PROC PRINT;
    TITLE 'RELATIVE FREQUENCIES OF ICD CODES BY YEAR';
RUN;
```

Description:

The first PROC FREQ creates an output data set (ICDFREQ) that looks like the following:

ICDFREQ data set

YEAR	ICD	COUNT	PERCENT
1950	440	1	20
1950	450	2	40
1951	300	1	20
1951	460	1	20

Notice that the data set created by PROC FREQ contains all the TABLES variables as well as the two variables COUNT and PERCENT. The COUNT variable in this data set tells us how many times a given ICD code appeared in each year.

Next, we need the **total** number of ICD codes for each year to be used in the denominator to create a relative incidence of each ICD code for each year. Running PROC FREQ with only YEAR as a TABLE variable will give us the number of ICD codes for each year. Data set TOTAL is shown next:

YEAR	COUNT	PERCENT
1950	3	60
1951	2	40

All we have to do now is to merge the two data sets so that we can divide the COUNT variable in the ICDFREQ data set by the COUNT variable in the TOTAL data set. When we do the merging, we will rename COUNT in the TOTAL data set to TOT_CNT since we can't have two values for a single variable in one observation. Finally, we can divide COUNT by TOT_CNT to obtain our desired result.

RELATIVE FREQUENCIES OF ICD CODES BY YEAR

YEAR	ICD	COUNT	TOTAL	RELATIVE
1950	440	1	3	33.3333
1950	450	2	3	66.6667
1951	300	1	2	50.0000
1951	460	1	2	50.0000

F. COMPUTING COMBINED FREQUENCIES ON DIFFERENT VARIABLES

In this example, questionnaires are issued to people to determine which chemicals they are sensitive to. Each subject replies yes or no (1 or 0) to each of the ten chemicals on the list. We want to list the chemicals in decreasing order of sensitivity. If we compute frequencies on each of the ten variables, we will be unable to display a list showing the chemicals in decreasing order of frequency. Our first step will be to restructure the data set into one with up to ten observations per subject. Each observation will include a chemical number (from 1 to 10) indicating which chemical was selected. Here is the program:

```
PROC FORMAT;
   VALUE CHEMICAL 1='WATER' 2='INK' 3='SULPHUR'
                  4='IRON' 5='TIN' 6='COPPER' 7='DDT'
                  8='CARBON' 9='SO2' 10='NO2';
RUN;
DATA SENSI;
INPUT ID 1-4 (CHEM1-CHEM10)(1.);            (cont.)
```

(Continued from previous page)

```
ARRAY CHEM[*] CHEM1-CHEM10;
DO I=1 TO 10;
   IF CHEM[I]=1 THEN DO;
      CHEMICAL=I;
      OUTPUT;
      END;
   END;
KEEP ID CHEMICAL;
FORMAT CHEMICAL CHEMICAL.;
CARDS;
00011010101010
00021000010000
00031100000000
00041001001111
00051000010010
RUN;
PROC FREQ ORDER=FREQ;
   TABLES CHEMICAL;
RUN;
```

Description:

For a more detailed description of how to restructure data sets using arrays, see the relevant section of chapter 13. Data set SENSI will have as many observations per person as the number of 1's on the list of chemicals (CHEM1 to CHEM10). The variable CHEMICAL is set equal to the DO loop counter, I, which tells us which of the ten chemicals was selected. The observations from data set SENSI are shown here to help clarify this point:

ID	CHEMICAL
1	WATER
1	SULPHUR
1	TIN
1	DDT
1	SO2
2	WATER

2	COPPER
3	WATER
3	INK
4	WATER
4	IRON
4	DDT
4	CARBON
4	SO2
4	NO2
5	WATER
5	COPPER
5	SO2

Notice that the formatted values for CHEMICAL are displayed since we assigned a format to the variable. A simple PROC FREQ will now tell us the frequencies for each of the 10 chemicals. The ORDER=FREQ option of PROC FREQ will produce a frequency list in decreasing order of frequencies. The output from PROC FREQ is shown next:

CHEMICAL	Frequency	Percent	Cumulative Frequency	Cumulative Percent
WATER	5	27.8	5	27.8
SO2	3	16.7	8	44.4
COPPER	2	11.1	10	55.6
DDT	2	11.1	12	66.7
INK	1	5.6	13	72.2
SULPHUR	1	5.6	14	77.8
IRON	1	5.6	15	83.3
TIN	1	5.6	16	88.9
CARBON	1	5.6	17	94.4
NO2	1	5.6	18	100.0

G. COMPUTING A MOVING AVERAGE

Suppose we record the COST of an item each day. For this example, we want to compute a moving average of the variable COST for a three day interval. On day 3, we will average the COST for days 1, 2, and 3; on day 4, we will average the COST on days 2, 3, and 4, etc.

```
*Program to compute a moving average;
DATA MOVING;
INPUT COST @@;
DAY+1;
COST1=LAG(COST);
COST2=LAG2(COST);
IF _N_ GE 3 THEN MOV_AVE = MEAN (OF COST COST1
COST2);
DROP COST1 COST2;
CARDS;
1 2 3 4 . 6 8 12 8
RUN;
PROC PRINT;
RUN;
```

The data set MOVING is shown next:

OBS	COST	DAY	MOV_AVE
1	1	1	.
2	2	2	.
3	3	3	2.00000
4	4	4	3.00000
5	.	5	3.50000
6	6	6	5.00000
7	8	7	7.00000
8	12	8	8.66667
9	8	9	9.33333

Description:

The LAGn function returns the value of the function argument from the nth previous observation. Thus, LAG (which is equivalent to LAG1) will return the value from a previous observation; LAG2 will return the value from the next earlier observation, and so forth. Notice how the use of a moving average "smooths out" the abrupt change on day 8.

H. SORTING WITHIN AN OBSERVATION

We use PROC SORT to sort **observations** in a SAS data set. However, we may have occasion to sort **within** an observation. In the example that follows, we have recorded five values (L1-L5) for each subject. We want to arrange the five values from highest to lowest. The method used here is known as a "bubble sort," because the highest (or lowest) values "bubble" or move closer to the top each time the program returns to the computation loop.

```
1    *PROGRAM TO SORT WITHIN AN OBSERVATION;
2    DATA TEST;
3    INPUT ID L1-L5;
4    CARDS;
     1 1 2 3 4 5
     2 1 3 5 2 4
     3 . 7 9 . .
5    RUN;
6    DATA NEW;
7    SET TEST;
8    ARRAY L[5] L1-L5;
9    LOOP:FLAG=0;
10   DO I=1 TO 4;
11      IF L[I+1] GT L[I] THEN DO;
12         HOLD=L[I];
13         L[I]=L[I+1];
14         L[I+1]=HOLD;
15         FLAG=1;
16         END;
17      END;
18   IF FLAG=1 THEN GO TO LOOP;
19   DROP I FLAG HOLD;
20   RUN;
```

Description:

Line 9 contains a SAS labeled statement. A statement in a SAS program can be labeled by a one to eight character label followed by a colon. We can then use a GOTO statement to control the logical flow of the program. Lines 10 through 17 run through the data values pairwise, reversing the order of a pair if two values are not in descending order. A flag then gets set, so that the program knows to repeat the process until no more pair reversals are made. Notice that we have 5 variables to be sorted and the DO loop runs from 1 to 4, since we have I+1 as a subscript inside the loop. To reverse the sorting order, substitute a LT operator for the GT operator in line 13.

I. TEST SCORING, ITEM ANALYSIS, AND TEST RELIABILITY

This example solves a common problem (scoring a test) and uses many SAS features that cause difficulty for SAS users. First, we will write a program to score a test. The first line of data will be an **answer key** followed by student responses. The method here is to read the answer key differently from the student responses.

```
1      *PROGRAM TO SCORE A TEST;
2      DATA SCORE;
3      RETAIN KEY1-KEY10;
4      ARRAY KEY[*] KEY1-KEY10;
5      ARRAY ANS[*] ANS1-ANS10; *ANS ARE STUDENT ANS;
6      ARRAY S[*] S1-S10; *THE S'S ARE SCORED RESPONSES;
7      IF _N_ = 1 THEN DO;
8         INPUT @11 (KEY1-KEY10)(1.);
9         DELETE;
10        END;
11     ELSE DO;
12        INPUT SS 1-9 @11(ANS1-ANS10)(1.);
13        DO I = 1 TO 10;
14           IF KEY[I] = ANS[I] THEN S[I]=1;
15           ELSE S[I]=0;
16           END;
17        RAW=SUM (OF S1-S10);
18        PERCENT=100*RAW/10;
19        DROP I KEY1-KEY10;
20        END;
21     FORMAT SS SSN11.;                           (cont.)
```

```
22    CARDS;                    (Continued from previous page)
      ANS KEY    1234554321
      102231324 1234323321
      101202333 3334254321
      102010222 1233544211
                 etc.
23    PROC SORT;
24       BY SS;
25    PROC PRINT;
26       TITLE 'STUDENT ROSTER';
27       ID SS;
28       VAR RAW PERCENT;
29    PROC MEANS MAXDEC=2 N MEAN STD RANGE MIN MAX;
30       TITLE 'CLASS STATISTICS';
31       VAR RAW PERCENT;
32    PROC CHART;
33       TITLE 'HISTOGRAM OF STUDENT SCORES';
34       VBAR PERCENT / MIDPOINTS=50 TO 100 BY 5;
35    PROC FREQ;
36       TITLE 'FREQUENCY DISTRIBUTION OF STUDENT ANS';
37       TABLES ANS1-ANS10;
38    RUN;
```

Description:

Line 3 instructs the program to "RETAIN" the variables KEY1-KEY10 for each observation. This is necessary since SAS programs will, by default, set all variables to **missing** before each observation is read. Since the values for the KEY variables are read only once, the RETAIN statement prevents the program from setting the values of the retained variables to missing. The variables KEY1 to KEY10 maintain their values throughout the entire data step. The answer key is read separately from the student answers by use of the "observation counter," which is designated by $\_N\_$. This is a "built-in" SAS variable that has the value of the present observation number. Thus, when $\_N\_$ is 1 we are reading the key. For all other values of $\_N\_$, we are reading student answers. Notice the DELETE statement in line 9. We include this since we do not want the first observation (the answer key) to be part of the output data set. (When $\_N\_$ equals 1, the variables ANS1-ANS10 have missing values since we haven't read any student scores yet.) The test scoring is done in lines 13 through 16. It simply states that if the student answer is equal to the answer key then the scoring variable should be set to 1, otherwise it is set to 0.

Since the raw score on a test is the number of correct responses, the SUM function in line 17 computes each student's raw score. The next line converts the raw score to a percentage score. Next we make use of the built-in format SSN11. to print the student social security numbers in standard format (this also ensures that any leading zeros in the number are printed).

The first several PROCs are straightforward. We want a student roster in SS number order (lines 23-28), the class statistics (lines 29- 31), a histogram (lines 32-34), and the frequencies of 1's, 2's, etc. for each of the questions on the test (lines 35-37).

Selected output from these procedures is shown below:

```
STUDENT ROSTER


          SS    RAW    PERCENT
 101-20-2333    7        70
 102-01-0222    6        60
 102-23-1324    7        70
 112-34-6765    5        50
 223-44-3232    9        90
 453-54-5353    8        80
CLASS STATISTICS

N Obs  Variable  N    Minimum     Maximum      Range       Mean
------------------------------------------------------------------
   6   RAW       6       5.00        9.00        4.00       7.00
       PERCENT   6      50.00       90.00       40.00      70.00
------------------------------------------------------------------


N Obs  Variable     Std Dev
------------------------------
   6   RAW            1.41
       PERCENT       14.14
------------------------------
```

```
HISTOGRAM OF STUDENT SCORES

FREQUENCY BAR CHART
FREQUENCY

  2 +                           ****
    |                           ****
    |                           ****
    |                           ****
    |                           ****
  1 +    ****      ****         ****          ****      ****
    |    ****      ****         ****          ****      ****
    |    ****      ****         ****          ****      ****
    |    ****      ****         ****          ****      ****
    |    ****      ****         ****          ****      ****
    -----------------------------------------------------------
                                                            1
         5      5      6      6      7      7      8      8      9      9      0
         0      5      0      5      0      5      0      5      0      5      0
                               PERCENT MIDPOINT


FREQUENCY DISTRIBUTION OF STUDENT ANS

                              Cumulative   Cumulative
ANS1    Frequency   Percent   Frequency    Percent
-------------------------------------------------------
   1        4        66.7          4          66.7
   2        1        16.7          5          83.3
   3        1        16.7          6         100.0

                              Cumulative   Cumulative
ANS2    Frequency   Percent   Frequency    Percent
-------------------------------------------------------
   1        1        16.7          1          16.7
   2        4        66.7          5          83.3
   3        1        16.7          6         100.0
```

We can produce a compact table showing answer choice frequencies using PROC TABULATE. To do this efficiently, we will restructure the data set so that we will have a variable called QUESTION, which is the question number, and CHOICE, which is the answer choice for that question for each student. We will be fancy and create CHOICE as a character variable that shows the letter choice (A,B,C,D, or E) with an asterisk (*) next to the correct choice for each question. Again, we offer the program here without much explanation for those who might find the program useful or those who would like to figure out how it works. One of the authors (Smith) insists that good item analysis includes the mean test score for all students choosing each of the multiple choice items. Therefore, the code to produce this statistic is included as well. The details of TABULATE are too much to describe here and we refer you to the **SAS Guide to Tabulate Processing,** available from the SAS Institute, Cary, NC. This is one of the best manuals from the SAS Institute and if you plan to use PROC TABULATE (it's very powerful), we recommend this manual highly.

The complete program to restructure the data set and produce the statistics described above is shown next:

```
1.    *PROGRAM TO SCORE A TEST;
2.    OPTIONS LS=64 PS=59 NOCENTER;
3.    PROC FORMAT;
4.       PICTURE PCT LOW-<0=' ' 0-HIGH='00000%';
5.    DATA SCORE;
6.    LENGTH Q1-Q10 $ 2;
7.    RETAIN KEY1-KEY10;
8.    ARRAY KEY[*] KEY1-KEY10;
9.    ARRAY ANS[*] ANS1-ANS10; *ANS ARE STUDENT ANS;
10.   ARRAY Q[*] $ Q1-Q10; *CHARACTER VARS USED WITH
                            PROC TABULATE;
11.   ARRAY S[*] S1-S10;    *THE S'S ARE SCORED
                            RESPONSES;
12.   IF _N_ = 1 THEN DO;
13.       INPUT @11 (KEY1-KEY10)(1.);
14.       DELETE;
15.       END;
16.   ELSE DO;
17.       INPUT SS 1-9 @11 (ANS1-ANS10)(1.);
18.       DO I = 1 TO 10;
19.          Q[I] = LEFT(TRANSLATE (ANS[I],'ABCDE',
                              '12345'));
20.          IF KEY[I] = ANS[I] THEN DO;
21.             S[I]=1;
22.             SUBSTR(Q[I],2,1)='*';
23.             END;
24.          ELSE S[I]=0;
25.          END;
26.       RAW=SUM (OF S1-S10);
27.       PERCENT=100*RAW/10;
28.       DROP I KEY1-KEY10;
29.       END;
30.   FORMAT SS SSN11.;                          (cont.)
```

```
31.    CARDS;              (Continued from previous page)
       ANS KEY   1234554321
       102231324 1234323321
       101202333 3334254321
       102010222 1233544211
       123456789 1234112345
       343212323 2213554115
              etc.
32.    DATA TEMP;
33.    SET SCORE;
34.    KEEP QUESTION CHOICE PERCENT;
35.    ARRAY Q[*] $ 2 Q1-Q10;
36.    DO QUESTION=1 TO 10;
37.        CHOICE=Q[QUESTION];
38.        OUTPUT;
39.        END;
40.    PROC TABULATE;
41.        CLASS QUESTION CHOICE;
42.        VAR PERCENT;
43.        TABLE QUESTION*CHOICE
44.        ,PERCENT=' '*(PCTN<CHOICE>*F=PCT.
           MEAN*F=PCT.
45.        STD*F=10.2)    / RTS=20 MISSTEXT=' ';
46.        KEYLABEL ALL='TOTAL' MEAN='MEAN SCORE'
           PCTN='FREQ'
47.                   STD='STANDARD DEVIATION';
48.    RUN;
```

A brief explanation of the program follows:

Lines 3 and 4 create a format to be used with PROC TABULATE so that percentage scores will be printed with the "%" sign. Lines 5 through 18 are the same as the previous program, with the exception of the Q variables. The Q's are character variables of length 2 which hold the student's answer choice. The first byte of this variable is a letter A,B,C,D, or E. The second byte is either a blank or an asterisk (*), representing the correct answer for a particular question. Line 19 uses the TRANSLATE function which translates the numerical responses (1,2,3,4,5) to letters (A,B,C,D,E) and left justifies it (with the LEFT function). Line 22 places an asterisk in the second position of the correct answer choice. Lines 32 through 39 restructure the data set as mentioned earlier. This data set contains n observations per student, where n is the number of items on the test. Careful, you cannot use this data set to compute the test standard deviation! The original data set must be used for that purpose.

Selected portions of the output from these procedures are shown in the tables below:

		FREQ	MEAN SCORE	STANDARD DEVIATION
QUESTION	CHOICE			
1	A*	36%	52%	23.60
	B	15%	30%	10.00
	C	15%	53%	37.86
	D	15%	16%	5.77
	E	15%	33%	23.09
2	CHOICE			
	A	5%	20%	
	B*	47%	54%	22.97
	C	10%	45%	35.36
	D	15%	33%	23.09
	E	21%	17%	9.57
3	CHOICE			
	A	10%	30%	14.14
	B	21%	20%	8.16
	C*	36%	64%	13.97
	D	21%	35%	31.09
	E	10%	20%	0.00

The frequency column shows the percentage of students selecting each item choice. The frequency next to the correct answer (marked by an *) is the item difficulty (percent of students answering the item correctly). The column labeled MEAN SCORE shows the mean test score for all students answering the indicated answer choice. For example, for item 1, 36% of the class chose A, the correct answer, 15% chose B, and so forth. The mean score of the students who chose A was 52%; for B, 30%, etc.

Computing test reliability is shown next. This program computes a test statistic called coefficient alpha, which, for a test item that is dichotomous, is equivalent to the Kuder-Richardson formula 20. This statistic is now available in PROC CORR with option ALPHA (Cronbach's alpha). You may still want to use the code below to compute your KR-20. At the very least, it serves as a good programming example. The formula for Cornbach's alpha is:

$$\text{alpha (or KR-20 if dichotomous)} = \frac{k}{k-1} \times \left[1 - \frac{(\text{sum item variances})}{\text{test variance}} \right]$$

Where k is the number of items on the test.

The key here is to output a data set that contains the item and test **variances.** Here is the program:

```
1       PROC MEANS NOPRINT DATA=SCORE;
2          VAR S1-S10 RAW;
3          OUTPUT OUT=VAROUT VAR=VS1-VS10 VRAW;
4       DATA _NULL_;
5       FILE PRINT;
6       SET VAROUT;
7       SUMVAR = SUM (OF VS1-VS10);
8       KR20 = (10/9)*(1-SUMVAR/VRAW);
9       PUT KR20= ;
10      RUN;
```

We use PROC MEANS to output a data set containing the item variances. The keyword VAR= computes variances for the variables listed in the VAR statement. This data set contains only one observation. In order to sum the item variances, we need to use another data step. You may not be familiar with the special SAS data set name _NULL_ in line 4. This reserved data set name instructs the SAS system to process the observations as they are encountered but **not** to write them to a temporary or permanent SAS data set. This saves time and, perhaps, money. Line 7 computes the sum of the item variances, and line 8 is the formula for coefficient alpha. We get the program to print the results for us by using a PUT statement (line 9). The results of this PUT are sent to the same place that normal SAS output goes, because of the FILE PRINT statement in line 5.

CHAPTER 16
REVIEW OF SAS FUNCTIONS

A. INTRODUCTION

Throughout this book, we have used functions to perform a variety of tasks. We used a LOG function to transform variables and various DATE functions to convert a date into an internal SAS date. We will see in this chapter that the SAS programming language has a very rich assortment of functions that can greatly simplify some very complex programming problems. Take a moment to browse through this chapter to see what SAS functions can do for you.

B. ARITHMETIC AND MATHEMATICAL FUNCTIONS

The functions you are probably most familiar with are ones which perform arithmetic or mathematical calculations. Remember that **all** SAS functions are recognized as such because the function name is always followed by a set of parentheses, containing one or more arguments. This way, the program can always differentiate between a **variable name** and a **function**. Here is a short program which computes a new variable, called LOGLOS which is the natural log of LOS (length of stay). This is a common way to "pull in the tail" of a distribution skewed to the right. We have:

```
DATA FUNC_EG;
INPUT ID SEX $ LOS HEIGHT WEIGHT;
LOGLOS = LOG(LOS);
CARDS;
    etc.
```

The new variable (LOGLOS) will be in the data set FUNC_EG and its values will be the natural (base e) log of LOS. Note that a zero value for LOS will result in a missing value for LOGLOS. When zeros are possible values and you still want a log transformation, it is common to add a small number (usually .5 or 1) to the variable before taking the log.

We will now list some of the more common arithmetic and mathematical functions and their purpose:

Function Name	Action
LOG	Base e log
LOG10	Base 10 log
SIN	Sine of the argument (in radians)
COS	Cosine
TAN	Tangent
ARSIN	Arcsine (inverse sine) of argument Result is in radians
ARCOS	Arccosine
ARTAN	Arctangent
FLOOR	Drops off the fractional part of a number
SQRT	Square root

Some functions take more than one argument. For example, the ROUND function has two arguments, separated by commas. The first argument is the number to be rounded and the second argument indicates the roundoff unit. Here are some examples:

```
ROUND (X,1)      Round X to the nearest whole number
ROUND (X,.1)     Round X to the nearest tenth
ROUND (X,100)    Round X to the nearest hundred
```

Other functions operate on a list of arguments. A good example of this is the MEAN function. If we have a series of variables (say X1 to X5) for each subject and we want the **mean** of these 5 numbers, we write:

```
MEAN_X = MEAN (OF X1-X5):
```

We may use any variable list following the word OF. An important difference between the MEAN function and the alternative expression:

```
MEAN_X = (X1 + X2 + X3 + X4 + X5)/5;
```

is that the MEAN function returns the **mean** of the **nonmissing** values. Thus, if we had a missing value for X5, the function would return the mean of X1, X2, X3, and X4. Our equation for the mean above would return a missing value if any of the X values were missing.

The SUM, STD, and STDERR functions work the same way as the MEAN function except that a **sum, standard deviation,** or a **standard error** is computed instead of a **mean.**

Two very useful functions are N and NMISS. They return, as you would expect, the number of nonmissing (N) or the number of missing (NMISS) values in a list of variables. Suppose we have recorded 100 scores for each subject and want to compute the mean of these 100 scores. We will allow each subject to be missing 25 or fewer scores and still be included in the calculation. Without the N function, we would have to do a bit of programming. Using the N function, the computation is much simpler:

```
DATA EASYWAY;
INPUT (X1-X100)(2.);
IF N(OF X1-X100) GT 75 THEN AVE = MEAN(OF X1-X100);
CARDS;
    etc.
```

The NMISS function is used in a similar fashion.

C. RANDOM NUMBER FUNCTIONS

We saw in chapter 6 how we could use random numbers to assign subjects to groups. Two functions, UNIFORM and RANUNI, generate uniform random numbers in the range from 0 to 1. Random number generators (more properly called **pseudo** random number generators) require an initial number, called a seed, which they use to calculate the first random number. From then on, each random number is used in some way to generate the next. In either of these functions, a zero seed will cause the function to use a seed derived from the time clock, thus generating a different random series each time it is used. RANUNI can also be seeded with any number of your choosing; UNIFORM requires a 5,6,or 7 digit odd number as a seed. In either case, if you supply the seed, the function will generate the **same** series of random numbers each time. A simple example follows in which we use a uniform random number to put a group of subjects in random order:

```
DATA SHUFFLE;
INPUT NAME : $20.;
X = RANUNI(0);
CARDS;
CODY
SMITH
MARTIN
LAVERY
THAYER
RUN;
PROC SORT;
   BY X;
RUN;
PROC PRINT;
   TITLE 'Names in Random Order';
   VAR NAME;
RUN;
```

To generate a series of random numbers from n to m, we need to scale our 0 to 1 random numbers accordingly. To generate a series of random numbers from 1 to 100, we could write:

```
X = 1 + 99 * RANUNI(0);
```

For purposes of statistical modeling, we might also want a series of random numbers chosen from a normal distribution (mean=0, variance=1). The RANNOR function will generate such variables. The allowable seeds for RANNOR follow the same rules as for RANUNI.

D. TIME AND DATE FUNCTIONS

We saw some examples of date functions in chapter 4. We will summarize the time and date functions here.

There are several extremely useful date functions. One, MDY (month, day, year) will convert a month, day, and year value into a SAS date variable. Suppose, for example, that we want to know a subject's age as of July 15, 1990 and we know his date of birth. We could use the MDY function to compute the age like this:

```
AGE = (MDY(7,15,90) - DOB)/365.25;
```

A more efficient method would be to use a SAS date variable as shown below:

```
AGE = ('15JUL90'D - DOB)/365.25;
```

Another possible use of the MDY function would be when date information is not recorded in one of the standard methods for which SAS has a date format. As long as we can read the month, day, and year into variables, we can then use the MDY function to compute the date. For example:

```
INPUT ID 1-3 MONTH 4-5 DAY 10-11 YEAR 79-80;
DATE = MDY(MONTH,DAY,YEAR);
DROP MONTH DAY YEAR;
FORMAT DATE MMDDYY8.;
etc.
```

There are several date functions which extract information from a SAS date. For example, the YEAR function returns a four digit year from a SAS date. The MONTH function returns a number from 1 to 12, which represents the month for a given date. There are two functions which return day information. The DAY function returns the day of the **month** (i.e., a number from 1 to 31) and the WEEKDAY function returns the day of the **week** (a number from 1 to 7; 1 being Sunday). As an example, suppose we want to see distributions by month and day of the week for hospital admissions. The variable ADMIT is a SAS date variable:

```
PROC FORMAT;
    VALUE DAYWK 1='SUN' 2='MON' 3='TUE' 4='WED' 5='THU'
        6='FRI' 7='SAT';
    VALUE MONTH 1='JAN' 2='FEB' 3='MAR' 4='APR' 5='MAY'
        6='JUN' 7='JUL' 8='AUG' 9='SEP' 10='OCT' 11='NOV'
        12='DEC';
DATA HOSP;                                        (cont.)
```

```
                              (Continued from previous page)
INPUT @1 ADMIT MMDDYY6. etc. ;
DAY = WEEKDAY(ADMIT);
MONTH = MONTH(ADMIT);
FORMAT ADMIT MMDDYY8. DAY DAYWK. MONTH MONTH.;
CARDS;
(data lines)
PROC CHART;
   VBAR DAY / DISCRETE;
   VBAR MONTH / DISCRETE;
RUN;
```

Look for a shortcut method for producing the day of the week or month name in the discussion of the PUT function later in this chapter.

Besides working with date values, SAS has a corresponding set of functions to work with times. For example, we can read a time in hh:mm:ss (hours, minutes, seconds) format using the time8. format. We can then extract hour, minute, or second information from the time variable using the HOUR, MINUTE, or SECOND **functions**, just the way we used the YEAR, MONTH, and WEEKDAY functions above.

Before we leave the date and time functions, let's discuss two very useful functions, INTCK and INTNX. They may save you pages of SAS coding. INTCK returns the number of intervals between any two dates. Valid, interval choices are: DAY, WEEK, MONTH, QTR, YEAR, HOUR, MINUTE, and SECOND. The syntax of the INTCK function is:

```
INTCK (interval, start, end);
```

where interval is one of the choices above, placed in single quotes, start is the starting date, and end is the ending date. As an example, suppose we want to know now many quarters our employees have worked. If START is the SAS variable that holds the starting date, the number of quarters worked would be:

```
NUM_QTR = INTCK ('QTR',START,TODAY());
```

NOTE: The TODAY function, which has no argument, returns today's date.

Since the algorithms used to compute the number of intervals can be confusing, we recommend reading the section on SAS functions in the appropriate SAS manual.

The INTNX function can be thought of as the inverse of the INTCK function; it returns the date, given an interval, starting date, and the number of intervals elapsed. Suppose know the date of hire and want to compute the date representing the start of the third quarter. You would use:

```
DATE3RD = INTNX ('QTR',HIRE,3);
FORMAT DATE3RD MMDDYY8.;
```

If HIRE were 01/01/90, 01/05/90, or 03/30/90, the value of DATE3RD would be 10/01/90. If a person were hired on April 1, 1990, his third quarter date would be 01/01/91.

E. THE INPUT AND PUT FUNCTIONS: CONVERTING NUMERICS TO CHARACTER AND CHARACTER TO NUMERIC VARIABLES

While the INPUT and PUT functions have many uses, one common application is to convert between numeric and character values.

The PUT function uses the formatted value of a variable to create a new variable. For example, suppose we have recorded the AGE of each subject. We also have a format which groups the ages into four groups:

```
PROC FORMAT;
   VALUE AGEGRP LOW-20='1' 21-40='2'
         41-60='3' 61-HIGH='4';
RUN;
DATA PUTEG:
INPUT AGE @@;
AGE4 = PUT (AGE,AGEGRP.);
CARDS;
5 10 15 20 25 30 66 68 99
RUN;
```

In this example, the variable AGE4 will be a character variable with values of '1','2','3', or '4'. As another example, suppose we want a variable to contain the three letter day of the week abbreviations (MON, TUE, etc.). One of the SAS built-in formats is WEEKDATEn. which returns values such as: WEDNESDAY, SEPTEMBER 12, 1990 (if we use WEEKDATE29.). The format WEEKDATE3. will be the first three letters of the day name (SUN, MON, etc.). To create our character day variable, we can use the PUT function:

```
DAYNAME = PUT(DATE,WEEKDATE3.);
```

There are some really useful tricks that can be accomplished using the PUT function. Consider one file that has social security numbers as 9 digit numerics. Another file has social security numbers coded as 11 digit character strings (123-45-6789). Our job is to merge the two files based on social security number. There are many ways to solve this problem, either pulling out the three numbers between the dashes and recombining them to form a numeric, or converting the 9 digit number to a character string and placing the dashes in the proper places using the appropriate string functions. By far the easiest method is to use the fact that SAS has a built in function, SSN11., which formats 9 digit numerics to 123-45-6789 style social security numbers. Therefore, using the PUT function, we can create a character variable in the form 123-45-6789 like this:

```
SS = PUT (ID,SSN11.);
```

In general, to convert a numeric variable to a character variable, we can use the PUT function, with the appropriate format. If we have a file where group is a numeric variable and we want a character variable instead, we can write:

```
GROUPCHR = PUT (GROUP,1.);
```

We use the INPUT function in a similar manner, except that we can "reread" a variable according to a new format. The most common use of this function is to convert character values into numeric values. There are several examples of this in the last section of chapter 10, reading unstructured data. We will show you a simple example here. In this example, we will read either a group code (character) or a score (numeric). Since we don't know if we will be reading a character or a number, we will read every value as a character and test if it is a valid group code. If not, we will assume it is a score and use the INPUT function to convert the character variable to numeric. Here is the code:

```
DATA FREEFORM;
INPUT TEST $ @@;
RETAIN GROUP;
IF TEST = 'A' OR TEST='B' THEN DO;
   GROUP = TEST;
   DELETE;
   RETURN;
   END;
ELSE SCORE = INPUT (TEST,5.);
DROP TEST;
CARDS;
A 45 55 B 87 A 44 23 B 88 99
RUN;
PROC PRINT;
RUN;
```

To help make this example clearer, the data set formed by running this program is shown below:

OBS	GROUP	SCORE
1	A	45
2	A	55
3	B	87
4	A	44
5	A	23
6	B	88
7	B	99

As you can see, the INPUT function opens up a very flexible way of reading data.

F. STRING FUNCTIONS

We can hear you asking, "what's a string?" Well, computer people have their own jargon and a string, to a computer programmer, is a string of characters. Thus, ABCDE is a string as is 12345 (read as character data). We will only touch on some of the major string functions here—there are lots of them.

First, it's useful to extract a piece of a string. Suppose we had character ID numbers in a SAS system file. The numbers are 8 characters long and the last two characters of the ID number represent a two digit state code. We want to create a new variable, STATE, which contains these two digits. The SUBSTR (pronounced substring) function will do this. The syntax is:

```
SUBSTR (char_variable, starting_position, length);
```

So, if we want to extract the last two digits (positions 7 and 8) we can use:

```
STATE = SUBSTR (ID,7,2);
```

Another very commonly used character function is UPCASE. As the name implies, this function converts the argument to upper case. This can really come in handy when a questionnaire or other source of data was entered in both upper and lower case (by accident). When this happens, we can use the UPCASE function to convert all the strings to upper case. Below is an example of how this could be used:

```
DATA SURVEY;
INPUT ID 1-3 @5 (QUES1-QUES20) ($1.);
ARRAY QUES[20] QUES1-QUES20;
DO I = 1 TO 20;
   QUES[I] = UPCASE(QUES[I]);
   END;
DROP I;
etc.
```

The VERIFY function can be used to test if any element of one string is located anywhere in another. A common use for this function is in data verification. Although the VERIFY function is more general, we will show a partial definition below:

```
VERIFY (char_variable, verify_string);
```

This function will return the position in the char_variable that is **not** present in the verify_string. If all the characters of the char_variable are present in the verify_string, then a 0 is returned. Here are some examples:

```
SCORE='A   '   VERIF=' ABCDE'   VERIFY(SCORE,VERIF)=0
SCORE='X   '   VERIF=' ABCDE'   VERIFY(SCORE,VERIF)=1
SCORE='ABXD'   VERIF=' ABCDE'   VERIFY(SCORE,VERIF)=3
```

Suppose that valid values for X were A,B,C,D, or E. A quick way to check for invalid data would be:

```
CHECK = ' ABCDE';
IF VERIFY(X,CHECK) NE 0 THEN PUT 'ERROR IN RECORD '
    _N_  X= ;
```

Notice the blank in the character string assigned to CHECK. If X were a one byte character variable, the blank in CHECK would be unnecessary. If X were longer than one byte, the value would be "left adjusted" and padded on the right with blanks. The VERIFY function would then return the position of the first blank in the X string if we did not include a blank in the CHECK string.

While we are discussing strings, we should mention the concatenation operation. Although this is not a function, it is a useful string operation and this seems as good a place as anywhere to tell you about it! In computer jargon, concatenate means to join. So, if we concatenate the string 'ABC' with the string 'XYZ' the result is 'ABCXYZ'. Pretty clever, eh? Things can get a bit sticky if we forget that SAS character variables are padded on the right with blanks to fill out the predefined length of the variable. If this is the case, we can use the TRIM function to remove trailing blanks before we concatenate the strings. The concatenation operator is || (two vertical bars). Suppose we had social security numbers in a file and, instead of the usual "-" separators, the digit groups were separated by colons, 123:45:6789 for example. One way to read this string and convert it into the more common format would be:

```
DATA CONVERT;
INPUT PART1 $ 1-3 PART2 $ 5-6 PART3 $ 8-11;
SS = PART1 || '-' || PART2 || '-' || PART3;
KEEP SS;
CARDS;
123:45:6789
etc.
```

The compulsive programmer in one of us (Cody) will not let this program stand without mentioning that the TRANSLATE function discussed next would be a better way to solve this problem. (Your humble second author, Smith, cannot believe anyone is actually reading this section.) The last string function we will discuss is TRANSLATE. This very useful function is used to, as the name implies, translate or convert one set of characters into another. This function may save you writing lots of IF statements. Suppose we have one data set where responses to a questionnaire were coded as A,B,C,D, and E. Another set of data from the same questionnaire was coded 1,2,3,4, and 5 by the data entry person. Assuming that we read the responses as characters, we could write five IF statements to convert the numbers to letters, or use the TRANSLATE function.

The syntax for TRANSLATE is:

```
TRANSLATE (variable, convert_to_string, convert_from_string);
```

For example, to translate 1,2,3,4,5 (character data) to A,B,C,D,E we would write:

```
TRANSLATE (variable,'ABCDE','12345');
```

In the example below, assume that we have variable names QUES1-QUES50 ($1. format) and want to convert the 1-5 to A-E:

```
DATA TRANS;
ARRAY QUES[*] $ QUES1-QUES50;
INPUT (QUES1-QUES50)($1.);
DO I = 1 TO 50;
   QUES[I] = TRANSLATE (QUES[I],'ABCDE','12345');
   END;
DROP I;
etc.
```

The solution to the social security problem above is:

```
INPUT SS $ 1-11;
SS = TRANSLATE (SS,'-',':');
```

G. THE LAG FUNCTION

A lagged value is one from an earlier time. In SAS, we may want to compare a data value from the current observation with a value in the previous observation. We may also want to look back several observations. Without the LAG function, this is a difficult task—with it, it's simple. If we have a variable (X in our data set) the value LAG(X) is the value of X from the previous observation. The value LAGn(X), where n is a number, is the value from the nth previous observation. A common application of the LAG function is to take differences between observations. Suppose each subject was measured twice and each measurement was entered as a separate observation. We want to take the value of X at time 1 and subtract it from the value of X at time 2. We proceed as follows:

Data set ORIG looks like this:

SUBJ	TIME	X
1	1	4
1	2	6
2	1	7
2	2	2
	etc.	

To subtract the X at time 1 from the X at time 2, we write:

```
DATA LAGEG;
SET ORIG;
*NOTE: DATA SET ORIG IS SORTED BY SUBJ AND TIME;
DIFF = X - LAG(X);
IF TIME=2 THEN OUTPUT;
RUN;
```

You could shorten this program even further by using the DIFn function which returns the difference between a value from the current observation and the nth previous observation. The calculation above would be:

```
DIFF = DIF(X);
```

You may also want to look at section G of chapter 15 where we use the LAG function to compute moving averages.

APPENDIX A

REVIEW OF MICROCOMPUTERS AND MS-DOS™

This appendix presents an overview of microcomputer architecture and a review of MS-DOS (also PC-DOS) commands. For those SAS users who are running under other operating systems, feel free to skip this chapter or just read the overview of microcomputers. In order to run PC-SAS on a microcomputer under the MS-DOS operating system, it would be useful to review some of the basic commands of MS-DOS as well as the directory file structure.

A. AN OVERVIEW OF MICROCOMPUTERS

At the time this third edition was being written, PC-SAS version 6.04 was the current version. Version 6.04 runs under the MS-DOS or PC-DOS operating systems on IBM compatible microcomputers. Versions of SAS software which run under Windows® 3.0 and OS/2® are in the planning stages. However, even when SAS software is released for these operating systems, we feel that there will still be many SAS users running under DOS.

First, here is a brief review of the basic components of a microcomputer. The CPU or Central Processing Unit, is the "brain" of the machine. It is a collection of electric circuits, placed on a single chip, which can perform a number of computer instructions. Most of the CPU chips that power IBM compatible microcomputers are manufactured by Intel® Corporation. The manufacturer's number describing the chip, such as 80286, 80386 or 80486, indicates how powerful the chip is. In the list given here, the higher numbers represent the more advanced processor chips. Thus, an 80486 (called a 486 for short) will be more powerful, in general, than a 286 or a 386. As far as the user of the machine is concerned, the way that programs run on the machine will be independent of the CPU present. Except for some differences in the way memory is used, there is no difference in the way that programs run on these machines, except for speed.

The next major component in a microcomputer is disk storage. Microcomputers store data and programs on magnetic surfaces called disks. Any microcomputer that is capable of running SAS software will be equipped with two types of disk drives. One, called a "floppy" disk drive, reads and writes data on a removable disk called a floppy disk (also called a diskette, take your choice). At the present time, floppy diskettes come in two sizes, 3 1/2 inches and 5 1/4 inches in diameter. To make things more complicated, the 3 1/2 inch disks are either double sided, double density (DSDD) which can store 720K (K stands for thousand - actually 1024) bytes or characters of information, or high density (HD) which can store 1.44M (M stands for million) bytes of information. The 5 1/4 inch floppy diskettes come in 360K (DSDD) and 1.2M (HD) versions. The other type of disk drive is called a hard disk. This disk drive is usually located inside the computer itself and is not accessible without removing the cover of the machine. Hard disks store more data than floppy diskettes. Typical configurations are 20M (20 million bytes) up to several hundred megabytes. We recommend a 40M hard drive as a minimum for the PC-SAS user since your SAS programs can take from 10 to almost 30 megabytes of a hard disk.

Finally, a microcomputer must have memory. As you would expect, memory chips store programs and data while the machine is running so that the CPU can read instructions or data from memory, perform manipulations on these instructions or data, and place the results back in memory. The CPU can read and write only to memory. In order to operate on data that is stored on a floppy diskette or a hard disk, it must first be copied to memory. In order for a computer to function, it must have a basic set of instructions that tell it how to perform basic tasks such as copying files and running programs. MS-DOS (called PC-DOS on IBM brand computers) is the operating system that we will be discussing in this chapter. DOS stands for Disk Operating System. The name comes from the fact that the operating system, which is actually a collection of computer programs, resides on the hard disk. The maximum amount of memory that DOS can access directly is 640K. It is because of this limitation that alternative operating environments such as Windows and OS/2 were developed. It turns out that many SAS programs are larger than 640K and, in order to run under DOS, must be "overlayed." This is a technical term that means that only a portion of the program is placed into memory at one time. As the program runs and a memory location is requested that is outside the present piece of program in memory, another portion of the program is read from the disk and "overlayed" on top of a portion of the program presently in memory. The necessity of overlaying the SAS code, as you would expect, slows down its execution. There is a type of memory called expanded memory which is available on IBM compatible computers which can help overcome this problem. If you have expanded memory installed, SAS software can be loaded into it (without overlays) and will run much faster and more efficiently. In addition, when you use expanded memory, more of the base 640K memory is available for the SAS procedures. This will allow your SAS data sets to contain more variables and for your statistical models to be larger.

B. AN OVERVIEW OF DOS

In order to work with SAS software running under DOS, it is necessary to know some basic DOS commands as well as the file directory structure that DOS uses. When you turn on you computer (called "booting the system" in computer lingo), certain portions of the operating system are read into memory. When this portion of the operating system has been loaded and the computer is ready to receive instructions, it will display a prompt. The disk drives in your computer are referred to by letters. If you have one floppy drive, it will be called the A drive. A second drive will be B, etc. The hard drive is usually referred to as the C drive, even if you only have one floppy drive. The usual DOS prompt is a disk drive letter followed by a > sign. So, if you are a typical SAS user and your computer has a hard drive designated by the letter C, you will see a C prompt on your screen. Many DOS users will alter the prompt to relay information about your location in the file directory. We will tell you how to do that shortly. If you take our advice and modify the prompt, you will see C:\ on your screen instead of the usual C prompt. At the prompt (either C or C:\), you are free to issue instructions to the computer. These instructions may be requests to run programs or commands to list, copy, or delete files. Word processing documents, data, and programs are stored in files. Under DOS, file names are restricted to eight characters in length and cannot contain blanks or any of the following characters: . " / \ [ ] : | <>+ = ; , * or ?. In addition to the eight character names, there can be an extension of up to three characters which follows the file name and is separated from the file name by a period. Thus, ABCDE, STOP, X123, HELP.DOC and PROGRAM.SAS are all valid DOS file names. It should be mentioned that certain extensions such as SYS, COM, EXE and BAT have special meanings and should not be used for other purposes. It is useful if you develop good programming skills and choose file names and extensions that help you find your program and data files easily. For example, we recommend that you use the extension .SAS for all your SAS programs, .DTA for all your data files, and .LST for listings of SAS output that you have saved. (Recall that permanenet SAS data sets have the extension .SSD.)

C. DOS COMMANDS

We will show you a few of the more common DOS commands next. Following this is a reference list of these commands with examples. To get a list of the files that you have saved, use the DIR (directory) command. The syntax is: DIR [filespec] where the [ ] indicate that a file specification is optional. If no file specification is given, all the files on the default drive (the drive letter shown in the prompt) will be listed. So, if the prompt is A and you type DIR, you will see a list of all the files on the floppy diskette in drive A. A very useful form of the DIR command is to use a file specification containing "wildcards." The two wildcard characters are * and ?. Most useful is the * wildcard character which takes the place of any string of characters. So, if you want to see a directory of all files that begin with the letter X, you could type:

```
C> DIR X*.*
```

This means to list the directory of any file that starts with the letter X (followed by anything or nothing) and has any (or no) extension (the part after the period). What is the command to see all the files that have a .SAS extension? Did you say DIR *.SAS? If so, you're correct. Do you see now why it is so convenient to use a little thought in naming your files? The question mark wildcard "?" is similar to the "*" wildcard except that each "?" in a file specification takes the place of one character. Thus the file specification BUGS???? refers to all files that start with the letters BUGS followed by up to four characters. Valid matches would be BUGS0001, BUGSABCD, BUGS or BUGS01. The file specification BUGS?? would only match the files BUGS and BUGS01 from the previous list. The file specification can also include a drive designation. To indicate a drive other than the one shown in your prompt, you type the drive letter, followed by a colon, followed by a filename. If you have a C prompt and want to see all the files that begin with X on your B drive, you would enter:

```
C> DIR B:X*.*
```

To list all files on the A drive, you could enter:

```
C> DIR A:
```

Remember that the colon designates a drive. Had we typed:

```
C> DIR A
```

DOS would think we were asking to list the directory of a file called A, not the files on drive A. If you want to change the default prompt, type the drive letter, followed by a colon. So, if you have a C and want to make the A drive the default, enter:

```
C> A:
```

A frequently used command is COPY. To copy a program from one location (called the source) to another destination (called the destination), the general command is:

```
C> COPY source destination
```

where source and destination are valid file specifications. If you have a C and want to copy a file called TRIFID.SAS to your floppy in drive A, the command would be:

```
C> COPY TRIFID.SAS A:
```

Notice that we did not specify a file name in the destination field, only the drive letter. With the file name missing, the operating system will assume you want to use the same file name as on the source drive. So, if you wanted to copy TRIFID.SAS to the A drive and rename it FRED.ABC, the command would be:

```
C> COPY TRIFID.SAS A:FRED.ABC
```

If we follow the COPY command with a single file specification, DOS will interpret it to be the source. The destination will be the drive indicated in the prompt. So, if we have a C and we want to copy all the files from the A drive to our C drive, we would enter:

```
C> COPY A:*.*
```

To delete a file, the command DEL (or ERASE) is used. To delete the file TRIFID.SAS you would type:

```
C> DEL TRIFID.SAS
```

As with DIR and COPY, the file specification may include wildcards. The command

```
C> DEL *.SAS
```

will delete all the files with a .SAS extension; the command

```
C> DEL A:*.*
```

will delete all the files on the floppy diskette in the A drive. When you ask to delete all files on any drive, DOS will prompt you to ask if you are sure. Reply "y" (yes) if you want to proceed with the deletion. Obviously, care is required with this command. For example, had we typed:

```
C> DEL *.*
```

by mistake, the entire root directory of the C drive would be deleted and DOS does not have an UNDELETE command! Because of this omission in DOS, we recommend one of the utility programs, such as The Norton Utilities®, which allows you to UNDELETE a file that was deleted by mistake.

D. THE CHKDSK/F COMMAND

One command that is rarely used by most DOS users but is essential for the SAS programmer is the CHKDSK/F command. This rather cryptic command stands for "check disk" and, when used with the F (fix) option, removes "lost clusters" from your hard disk. What are lost clusters, you may ask? You don't really want to know. You just don't want them on your hard disk. Suffice it to say that when you leave the SAS system abnormally (such as rebooting without exiting first), it will leave lost clusters on the disk. Before you run the SAS system again, enter the CHKDSK/F command at the C:\ prompt. If there are lost clusters, you will receive a message to that effect and be asked,"Convert lost chains to files (Y/N)?." Reply with an "N". (One of the authors is a certified English teacher and knows full well where periods belong within quotes. However, we didn't want you to type N. instead of just an N, since this would get your computer angry.) In appendix B, we will tell you about the SAS Display Manager. If you are in a DOS shell invoked from the Display Manager, DO NOT EVER ISSUE A "CHKDSK/F" command. It may permanently scramble your disk!

E. FORMATTING A DISK

Before any disk, either a floppy diskette or a hard disk, can be used, it must first be formatted. Disks store information on a magnetic surface. As the disk spins, a read/write head moves along the radius to access or record information. In order to locate information, the disk surface is divided into tracks and sectors. Tracks run around the circumference in concentric circles and sectors are pie shaped divisions of the disk's surface. By knowing the track and sector location of a file, it can be found quickly. The track and sector locations are recorded on the disk's surface by a process called formatting. It is likely that your hard disk was already formatted by the manufacturer or by the retail store that sold you the unit. Most floppy diskettes do not come preformatted and need to be formatted before they are used for the first time. The command to format a diskette is:

```
FORMAT drivespec
```

where drivespec is the letter of the drive where the formatting is to take place. As an example, if we have a floppy diskette in the A drive, the command to format this diskette would be:

```
C:> FORMAT A:
```

It is very important to remember that the process of formatting a disk erases all the information on the disk. Therefore it is of extreme importance that the FORMAT command be used with caution. As an example of what can go wrong, suppose that you haven't had your morning coffee yet and you typed the above command as:

```
C:> FORMAT
```

by mistake, leaving out the drive specification. Since the computer is showing a C prompt and you are not specifying a drive, the operating system will assume that you want to format the hard disk! With most versions of MS-DOS, the system would issue a statement such as:

```
Warning! The data in drive C: will be destroyed. Do
you want to continue the format (Y/N)?
```

If it is not your intention to format the hard disk, reply with an "N" to this prompt. Some versions of MS-DOS protect you even further by asking for a volume label of the disk before proceeding.

Before we leave the subject of formatting, here is some useful information on formatting floppy diskettes of different densities. If your A: drive is a 1.2M (HD) 5 1/4 inch drive and you place a 360K (DSDD) diskette in that drive and ask DOS to format the disk, the computer will assume that a high density diskette is in the drive. The computer cannot distinguish between 360K and 1.2M diskettes or between 720K and 1.44M 3 1/2 inch diskettes. Depending on the quality of the low density diskette, the system may or may not be able to perform a successful format. Even if it works, the disk may not be reliable and data may be lost if stored on the improperly formatted diskette. There are options to the FORMAT command to correctly format low density diskettes in high density drives. To format a 360K, 5 1/2 inch diskette in a high density drive, use the command:

```
FORMAT A: /4
```

To format a 720K 3 1/2 diskette in a 1.44M drive, use the command:

```
FORMAT A: /t:80 /n:9
```

Since these commands are so complicated and formatting is such a dangerous activity, we highly recommend alternatives to the DOS FORMAT command. One such program, called Safe Format, can be found in a set of programs called the Norton Utilities®. This program will not only format different density diskettes, but it will notify a user if a diskette already contains data and will format such a diskette so that the old data can be salvaged. In fact, the Norton Utilities (also the Mace Utilities® and PC-Tools®) can UNFORMAT a hard disk and recover its data.

F. SUBDIRECTORY COMMANDS

This seems like a good time to tell you about the hierarchical file structure under DOS. Since a hard disk can store thousands of programs and data files, we need a method of keeping groups of files together. Imagine typing a DIR command and waiting while several thousand file names run by. DOS allows us to define subdirectories on our hard drive. Each subdirectory can contain files or other subdirectories. Directory names follow the same rules as DOS files names (1 to 8 characters in length, containing letters, numerals, and a few of the special characters) but do not have three character extensions. To create a subdirectory we use the MD (make directory) command. So, to make a directory called DATA on our C drive, we would type:

```
C> MD DATA
```

Before we go on, let us introduce the DOS PROMPT command. The form of the command that we recommend is:

```
C> PROMPT $P$G
```

This command changes the simple C prompt to a prompt that contains the name of the subdirectory in which we currently reside. More conveniently, place this command in your AUTOEXEC.BAT file. (See your DOS manual if you are unfamiliar with this file.) Since we start out in the root directory (i.e., the top level under which we create other directories), our initial prompt will look like this:

```
C:\>
```

The backslash (\) symbol, followed by nothing, tells us that we are in the root directory. Suppose we want to move from the root directory into the DATA subdirectory we have just created. The command to change directories is:

```
C:\> CD directory name
```

So, to change to the DATA subdirectory, we would type:

    C:\> CD DATA

The result would be a prompt that looked like this:

    C:\DATA>

Notice that the C: prompt is followed by the subdirectory in which we are located. To get back to the root directory, we would enter:

    C:\DATA> CD \

that is, the change directory command with just a backslash as the directory name. It is useful to picture a subdirectory structure as an inverted tree.

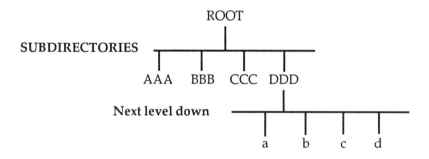

The solid trunk is on top—this represents the root directory. Coming off the main branch are several branches. Each branch represents a subdirectory and each subdirectory can contain files or more subdirectories below it. To change from one subdirectory to another subdirectory, it is necessary to go back up to a level higher than the level you want to go to. For example, if we want to change from the subdirectory labeled AAA above to one called DDD, we would have to go up to the root directory first and then back down to DDD. Now this sounds very complicated at first, but in a short time you will be jumping between directories with ease. In the example above, to move from a subdirectory called AAA to one called DDD, you would enter:

    C:AAA\> CD \DDD

Notice that the backslash preceding the name DDD, indicates that we are to follow a path from the root to DDD. We usually find it easier to always include the \ in front of a subdirectory name, even when we don't need it. So, to change from the root directory to one called SASDATA, we could type:

```
C:\> CD \SASDATA
```

instead of:

```
C:\> CD SASDATA
```

They will both bring you to the SASDATA subdirectory. Now, once you are in a subdirectory, commands like DIR and COPY, unless they include subdirectory names, will operate as though the only files you have are the ones in the present subdirectory. If the subdirectory SASDATA contains two files (ONE.DTA and TWO.DTA), the command DIR when issued from the SASDATA subdirectory will list only these two files. Each subdirectory on the hard disk is like having a separate disk drive with the drive designation being the drive letter followed by a \ and the subdirectory name. If we have a C:\ prompt and want to see a directory of the files in the SASDATA subdirectory, we can either issue a

```
C:\> CD SASDATA
```

command followed by a DIR command or, more simply type:

```
C:\> DIR \SASDATA
```

right from the C:\> prompt.

The only remaining subdirectory command is one to Remove Directories. It is: RD \subdirectory name. Before you issue this command, all files in the subdirectory must be removed. This is accomplished either by entering the command "DEL *.*" from within the subdirectory (careful, if you enter this command from the root directory or from another subdirectory, you will be deleting the wrong files!) or deleting the files in the subdirectory while in the root directory. For example, to delete all files in the subdirectory SASDATA, you would type:

```
DEL \SASDATA
```

Once this is accomplished, you could proceed with removing the directory (RD). Note that the command DEL *.*, when issued from a subdirectory, deletes only those files in the subdirectory. One reason we like the prompt to display the subdirectory name is to make sure you know which subdirectory you are in, especially if you decide to globally delete files.

Whenever you run SAS software, it creates two additional subdirectories of its own: SASWORK and SASUSER. If you are in a subdirectory, SASWORK and SASUSER will be subdirectories of your subdirectory. That is, if you invoked SAS software from a subdirectory called SASDATA, you will have two new subdirectories that look like:

SASDATA\SASWORK and SASDATA\SASUSER

This is important to know in case you decide to delete the SASDATA subdirectory. DOS insists that you remove all subdirectories underneath the one you want to delete. So, if you ran SAS programs from your SASDATA subdirectory, before removing it, you would first have to remove SASDATA\SASWORK and SASDATA\SASUSER.

G. SOME COMMON DOS COMMANDS WITH EXAMPLES

Some of the other DOS commands that you will find useful are listed in the reference table below. For a more thorough discussion of MS-DOS, we recommend An Introduction to MS-DOS by Peter Norton. The square brackets [ ] in the descriptions below indicate optional parameters. Do not type the [ ] symbols as part of the command. One final piece of advice: if learning computer languages is not your idea of a great way to spend leisure time, we would not recommend trying to learn DOS from an IBM or MS-DOS manual. These are meant to be reference manuals, not instructional guides.

Summary of MS-DOS Commands

COMMAND/EXAMPLE	MEANING
A:	A PROMPT
A:	Change to drive A as the default drive. That is, you will see a A: prompt and any subsequent DOS command that does not specify a drive will assume the command pertains to the A drive.

DIR [drive:[filename]]   DIRECTORY

DIR	List the directory of the current drive.
DIR B:	List the directory of drive B.
DIR *.SAS	List all files on the default drive that have a SAS extension.
DIR C:A*.*	List all files on the C drive that start with the letter A.

COPY source [destination]   COPY

COPY A:*.* B:	Copy the contents of the disk in drive A to drive B.
COPY MYFILE A:	Copy "MYFILE" on the default drive to the floppy in drive A.
COPY A:DATA	Copy the file "DATA" on the disk in the A drive to to default drive.

CHKDSK [/F]   CHECK DISK

CHKDSK/F	Run the program called CHKDSK and fix lost clusters. Run this any time you have left the SAS display manager abnormally. Reply to the prompt (it may differ slightly): CONVERT LOST CLUSTERS TO FILES (Y/N)? with an N.

DEL file(s)   DELETE

DEL MYFILE	Delete the file "MYFILE" on the default drive.
DEL A:ABC	Delete the file ABC on the floppy disk in drive A.
DEL A:*.*	Delete all files on the floppy in drive A.

PRINT file   PRINT

PRINT MYFILE	Send the contents of the file "MYFILE" to the printer.

MD   MAKE DIRECTORY

     MD TEMP   Make a directory called TEMP on the default drive.

CD   CHANGE DIRECTORY

     CD \TEMP   Change to the TEMP subdirectory. Note, this is the same as CD TEMP if you are already in the root directory. However, if you are already in a subdirectory, the command with the backslash will move to a subdirectory one level below the root directory. The version without the backslash will move to a subdirectory of the current directory. (Hope that's clear!)

     CD \   Return to the root directory.

RD   REMOVE DIRECTORY

     RD \TEMP   Remove the TEMP subdirectory. Note: The sub-directory must be empty and have no directories below it before it can be removed.

CLS   CLEAR SCREEN

FORMAT   FORMAT A DISK

     FORMAT A: Format the floppy in drive A. Note, this will destroy any existing files on this diskette.

     FORMAT   DO NOT USE ***** This will reformat (and erase) the default drive. If typed from the C:\ prompt this will erase the entire disk.

TYPE   TYPE

     TYPE FRED   List the contents of the file FRED to the screen. This is a quick way to see the contents of text files. The listing will run off the screen if it is longer than 24 lines. This can be prevented by entering a control S (hold

down the CTRL key and type an S) to stop
and start the listing. Another method is to
use something called the MORE filter. Use
the command TYPE FRED | MORE to have
DOS pause at the end of each screen.

PROBLEMS

A-1. Match the disk storage with the appropriate diskette type.

Size	Type
1. 360K	A. 3 1/2 inch DSDD
2. 720K	B. 3 1/2 inch HD
3. 1.2M	C. 5 1/4 inch DSDD
4. 1.44M	D. 5 1/4 inch HD

A-2. You have a floppy diskette in drive B and your computer is showing
a C:\ prompt. What single command do you type to see a list of files
on the floppy diskette in drive B?

A-3. At a C:\DOCUMENT prompt, you issue a DIR command and see
the following list of files:

ABC.TXT	FRED.TXT
PROG1.SAS	PROG2.SAS
PROG3.	PROGRAM.SAS
MEMO.	LETTER.OCT
LETTER.NOV	

(a) What command will delete all the files in this subdirectory?

(b) What command will delete all the .TXT files?

(c) What command will delete all files that start with "P"?

(d) What single command will delete PROG1.SAS and PROG2.SAS?

A-4. (a) You have a file called RON.CDY on the floppy in drive B. You
want to copy this file to a diskette in drive A. What command(s) do
you type? (You can assume the floppy in drive A is already formatted.)

(b) There is another file called KERMIT.FRG on the floppy in drive

A. You want to copy this to a subdirectory called BIOSTAT on your C drive. The subdirectory does not yet exist. What commands will accomplish this?

A-5. At the C:\ prompt, what command will format a HD 3 1/2 inch diskette in your high density, 3 1/2 inch B drive?

A-6. What will happen if, at the C:\ prompt, you type:

```
C:\> FORMAT
```

A-7. You have a file called MYDATA on a floppy in the A drive. Show the command(s) to copy this file to the hard disk in the SASDATA subdirectory. Assume that you are presently in the root directory (i.e. C:\ prompt) and the SASDATA subdirectory already exists.

A-8. In the middle of running a SAS program, you accidentally hit the RESET key on your computer. When you reboot and are back to the C:\ prompt, what command should you issue before running anything else?

A-9. You have a C:\ prompt on your screen. Show the command you would type to change the prompt to: C:\SASDATA.

A-10. You ran a SAS program from the C:\SASPROG subdirectory. Now, you want to delete all the files in \SASPROG and remove the directory. What commands will accomplish this? Hint: Remember that two subdirectories of \SASPROG, SASUSER and SASWORK, will have been created by SAS.)

A-11. Indicate the command(s) to delete the subdirectory MYDATA and all the files within it.

A-12. You are in the C:\SASPROG\SASWORK subdirectory and want to change to the C:\OSCAR subdirectory. What command will do this?

APPENDIX B

THE SAS® DISPLAY MANAGER

A. INTRODUCTION

The SAS Display Manager (DM), an interactive window environment first developed for running SAS software on microcomputers, is now the standard interactive environment for the SAS system on all machines. Some users, for example those on mainframes running in a batch environment, will be running SAS programs without the Display Manager. Users on UNIX, MS-DOS machines, and most other platforms also have the option of running SAS programs without the Display Manager, to conserve memory or to run a large program in background (i.e. the computer will process the job when it has a few spare moments) to minimize the impact of a CPU intensive job on other users of the system.

B. THE SAS® DISPLAY MANAGER

Those users running SAS software under MS-DOS or UNIX will usually want to enter a subdirectory before invoking the Display Manager. For example, on an MS-DOS machine, if you have a subdirectory called SASDATA, you would enter:

```
C:\> CD \SASDATA
```

before invoking the SAS system. To enter the SAS Display Manager, type:

```
C:\SASDATA> SAS
```

When you do this, your screen will be divided into three "windows." On a color monitor, the upper window is pale blue, the middle window is gray, and the bottom window is dark blue (the default colors under MS-DOS). Each of these three windows has a separate function.

The bottom (dark blue) window is the **PROGRAM** window. You can enter your SAS program here or issue commands to bring in a SAS program from a file on your disk. This window contains an editor which allows you to write and edit your program. There are also commands to save your program permanently on your disk. When complete, you can submit (run) your program with a command or by pressing the appropriate function key.

The middle window is the SAS LOG window. The LOG window displays the program lines as the program executes, prints out messages about your data sets as they are created, and gives error messages as errors are detected. On a color monitor, the messages about your data sets are in black, the program lines are in blue, and the error messages are in red. PC-SAS makes such effective use of color that we recommend a color monitor for frequent users of SAS software. One of the authors thought that color was frivolous, but after running SAS programs on a color monitor, never returned to the world of monochrome again.

On top, the OUTPUT window displays the output or results from your SAS program. Again, this will scroll by as the SAS program is executing, allowing you to monitor the progress of the program. To leave the Display Manager and return to the DOS prompt, enter **BYE** on the command line of any window.

```
-OUTPUT----------------------------------------------------------------------
|Command ===>                                                               |
|                                                                           |
|                                                                           |
|                                                                           |
|                                                                           |
-LOG-------------------------------------------------------------------------
|Command ===>                                                               |
|                                                                           |
|NOTE: Copyright(c) 1985,86,87 SAS Institute Inc., Cary, NC                 |
|      27512-8000, U.S.A.                                                    |
|NOTE: SAS (r) Proprietary Software Release 6.04                            |
|      Licensed to xxx Site nnn.                                            |
|NOTE: AUTOEXEC processing completed.                                       |
|                                                                           |
-PROGRAM EDITOR--------------------------------------------------------------
|Command ===>                                                               |
|                                                                           |
|00001                                                                      |
|00002                                                                      |
|00003                                                                      |
|00004                                                                      |
-----------------------------------------------------------------------------
```

The SAS Display Manager (opening screens)

We will now give you the details of each of these windows and the commands you will need to make effective use of the SAS Display Manager. Please refer to the manuals specific to your operating environment, listed in chapter 1 of this book, for the complete reference to the Display Manager. This chapter is intended only as a quick reference to get you started.

One important note on the use of function keys: IBM Compatible microcomputers have either ten or twelve function keys which can be used to perform Display Manager tasks. Other systems may use differing numbers of function keys or PF keys. To make this discussion universal, you can always enter any Display Manager command on the COMMAND line of any window. However, since PC-SAS is so widely available, we will also mention the appropriate function key in parentheses after the command name is first discussed. You may also use CTRL and ALT key combinations to perform Display Manager commands.

C. THE PROGRAM WINDOW

When you first invoke the SAS system, by typing "SAS," the cursor will be located on the **Command** line of the **PROGRAM WINDOW**. To enter commands while in the Display Manager, you will either type the commands on the command line or press the appropriate function, ctrl, or alt keys. If the cursor is not currently on the command line and you wish to enter a command, you can move the cursor to the command line manually with the arrow keys or by pressing the appropriate key. On a PC, the HOME key will move the cursor to the command line of the window in which the cursor is located. You can **zoom** (i.e., fill the screen with the current window, making the other windows temporarily disappear) with the ZOOM command (F7 key). This command (function key) is a "toggle"— each time you enter it, the display will alternate between the three-window display and the full screen display. To begin typing a program, first "zoom" the display, then press the RETURN key to move the cursor to the first numbered line of the PROGRAM WINDOW. Now you can type SAS statements, pressing the RETURN key at the end of each line. (The SAS editor does not "wrap" lines automatically.) If you make a typing mistake, use the backspace key to erase the error. You may also use the arrow keys to position the cursor and use the "Del" key to edit your text. The SAS editor, by default, is in "overwrite" mode; that is, any text you type will overwrite existing text on that line. If you prefer an "insert" or "pushright" mode where any text you type pushes any existing text to the right, press the "Ins" key (or enter the INSERT command on the command line). You will then notice the "I" on the bottom right corner of the screen, indicating that you are in "Insert" mode. This key is also a "toggle;" press it again to change to "overwrite" mode.

As a test, try entering the following program:

```
00001 DATA TEST;
00002 INPUT X Y Z;
00003 CARDS;
00004 1 2 3
00005 4 5 6
00006 RUN;
00007 PROC PRINT;
00008 RUN;
```

When you have finished entering your program, you will want to submit it. To do this, type SUBMIT on the command line (F10). If you can't remember which function key does what, try the KEYS command (F2) which will show the command(s) associated with the function, ctrl, and alt keys. Also, the HELP command (F1) key, will provide you with help on all aspects of the SAS system, including Display Manager commands. If you move to a special window such as the KEYS or HELP window, use the END command to close the window and return to where you were.

Once you've submitted your program, the display will automatically "unzoom" to the three-window display. Next, you will see your program as it passes through the LOG window. This window will inform you that you have two observations and three variables. It will also display the time it took (in seconds) to process each step. Finally, your output will scroll by in the OUTPUT window. There are two ways to examine these two windows. One way is to place the cursor anywhere in a window you want to examine and then zoom the screen by entering the ZOOM command (F7). This will cause the window that contains the cursor to fill the screen. You can now use the PgUp and PgDn keys to browse through the LOG or OUTPUT screens. A faster way to select a window is by using function or control keys. On a PC, the F4 key (or ctrl-o) will select the OUTPUT window, the F3 key (ctrl-l) will select the LOG window, and the F6 key (ctrl-p) will select the PROGRAM window. On other systems, use the KEYS command to find out which function keys, ctrl, or alt keys perform these functions.

Suppose you made a mistake in entering the program. Below is the original program with an error introduced:

```
00001 DATA TEST;
00002 INPUT X Y Z;
00003 CARDS;
00004 1 2 3
00005 4 5 6
00006 RUN;
00007 PROC PRINY;
00008 RUN;
```

When you submit (F10) this program, an error message will appear in the SAS LOG (in red on a color display). At this point you will want to correct the program and run it again. You will probably want to look at the LOG window first to make sure you understand the error message. You can do this by moving to the LOG window (F3 or ctrl-l) and then zooming (F7) the screen. Then, using the PgUp and PgDn keys, you can read the messages in the SAS LOG. You can then go back to the PROGRAM window (F6) to correct the program. Notice two things: one, the screen remains zoomed when you changed windows and, two, **your program has disappeared!** Don't panic—this is normal. As program statements are **submitted**, they are removed from the program window. To **recall** the portion of the program that was just submitted, use the RECALL command (F9) to bring back the lines of code that were just submitted. Your program has returned. Now, using the PgUp, PgDn, and cursor arrow keys, locate the line of the program that contains the error (in our case, the PROC PRINT line, entered incorrectly as PROC PRINY). Correct the error by moving the cursor to the "Y" in PROC PRINY and replacing it with a "T." You can now submit the program again using the submit (F10) key.

A summary of the PC-SAS function keys (default settings) are shown below:

Action	Function Key
Help	F1
Key definition	F2
LOG window	F3

OUTPUT window	F4
NEXT	F5
PROGRAM window	F6
Zoom key	F7
Recall program	F9
Submit program	F10

Knowing how to stop a SAS program while it is executing is useful, especially if you have written a long program with many procedures and notice an error as the program executes. To stop a SAS program, enter a control C (i.e., hold down the control key while typing a "C"). The following message will appear:

```
==BREAK===================================
| Press Y to cancel submitted statements, |
| T to halt data step/proc, N to continue.|
==========================================
```

Simply follow the directions to cancel all the following statements, to halt the currently executing data or proc step, or to continue.

A few more editing commands that you will need are described next. You may want to insert one or more lines between existing lines of your program. To do this, place the cursor anywhere within the line number of the line after which you want the new line or lines to go. To insert a single line, type an "i" and press the return key (with PC-SAS you may enter an alt-i anywhere on a program line to insert a new line). A new line will be created and all lines below will be renumbered automatically. By default, the insert command will insert the new line after the current line. If you would like to place a new line or lines before the current line, use the command "ib" (insert before). This form of the command is especially useful when you want to enter a new line before the first line of the program. To insert more than one line, type an "i," a space, and the number of lines to insert. For example, to insert 4 lines, type "i 4" and press the return key. An insert function is illustrated below:

```
00001 DATA TEST;
00002 INPUT X Y Z;
00003 CARDS;
00004 1 2 3
00005 4 5 6              (Before insert)
00006 RUN;
00007 PROC PRINT;
00008 RUN;
```

```
00001 DATA TEST;
00002 INPUT X Y Z;
00003 CARDS;
00004 1 2 3
01005 4 5 6        ("i" placed in number field)
00006 RUN;
00007 PROC PRINT;
00008 RUN;
```

```
00001 DATA TEST;
00002 INPUT X Y Z;
00003 CARDS;
00004 1 2 3
00005 4 5 6              (After insert)
00006 _                  (Enter new line at 00006)
00007 RUN;
00008 PROC PRINT;
00009 RUN;
```

In a similar manner, single lines can be **deleted** with a "d" in the number field (alt-d anywhere on the line for PC-SAS). To delete several lines, place "dd" in the first line to be deleted and move the cursor to the last line to be deleted and place a "dd" in the number field of that line. All lines from the first "dd" to and including the last "dd" will be deleted.

D. MORE EDITOR COMMANDS

Two more useful commands are **move** and **copy**. First, to move a single program line, place an "m" in the number field of the line to be moved and press the return key. Next, move the cursor to a destination line. Enter an "a" in the number field if you want the moved line to be placed **after** the line you are on; place a "b" in this field if you want the moved line to be placed **before** the current line. To move more than one line at a time, first place an "mm" in the number field of the first line to be moved. Move the cursor to the last line to be moved and place another "mm" there. You can now move this **block** of lines to a new location with an "a" (after) or a "b" (before) in the place where you want to place this block of lines. As an example, suppose we have the following program in the editor window:

```
00001 DATA TEST;
00002 INPUT X Y Z;
00003 CARDS;
00004 1 2 3
00005 4 5 6
00006 RUN;
00007 PROC PRINT;
00008 RUN;
00009 PROC MEANS MAXDEC=2 N MEAN STD;
00010 VAR X Y;
00011 RUN;
```

and we want to move the lines 00009 through 00011 to be placed after line 00006. We first place an "mm" in line 00009:

```
00001 DATA TEST;
00002 INPUT X Y Z;
00003 CARDS;
00004 1 2 3
00005 4 5 6
00006 RUN;
00007 PROC PRINT;
00008 RUN;
00mm9 PROC MEANS MAXDEC=2 N MEAN STD;
00010 VAR X Y;
00011 RUN;
```

The system will say: "NOTE: Pending Line Command," between the command line and line 00001. Now move the cursor to line 00011 and enter the second "mm." Finally, move the cursor to line 00006 and enter an "a."

```
00001 DATA TEST;
00002 INPUT X Y Z;
00003 CARDS;
00004 1 2 3
00005 4 5 6
0a006 RUN;
00007 PROC PRINT;
00008 RUN;
00mm9 PROC MEANS MAXDEC=2 N MEAN STD;
00010 VAR X Y;
00mm1 RUN;
```

The final result is shown next:

```
00001 DATA TEST;
00002 INPUT X Y Z;
00003 CARDS;
00004 1 2 3
00005 4 5 6
00006 RUN;
00007 PROC MEANS MAXDEC=2 N MEAN STD;
00008 VAR X Y;
00009 RUN;
00010 PROC PRINT;
00011 RUN;
```

To copy lines of code, use "c" or "cc" in place of "m" and "mm" respectively.

A complete description of the SAS program editor can be found in the **SAS Language Guide** in the chapter on the Display Manager. (See list of references in the Introduction.)

E. WRITING FILES TO MS-DOS OR YOUR PRINTER

One of the first file operations you will want to perform is saving your program for future use. To do this, first **recall** the program if it was already submitted. Then, move the cursor to the **command** line. Now, issue the **FILE** command as follows:

FILE 'filename'   where filename is a legal DOS filename
                    (may include drive and path)

Valid examples are:

FILE 'XXX.SAS'

FILE 'A:MYPROG'

FILE '\SASDATA\TEST1.SAS'

FILE 'PROB1'

Note that if you enter a filename without a path, such as:

FILE 'PROB1'

your program will be saved in a file with the name PROB1 in the subdirectory from which you invoked the SAS system. So, in our example where we changed to a subdirectory called \SASDATA before we entered the SAS Display Manager, the file PROB1 would be located in the \SASDATA subdirectory.

Another use for the FILE command is to write SAS **output** to a file so that it may be printed later or edited with your word processor. To do this, simply go to the command line of the OUTPUT window (F4, HOME) and enter the FILE command, just as you did in the PROGRAM window. A special file name **'PRN'** will send your output directly to your printer.

FILE 'PRN'   (sends contents of current window to
                    your printer.)

F. READING FILES INTO THE DISPLAY MANAGER PROGRAM WINDOW

Suppose you were working on a program, saved it to a DOS file with the FILE command, and then exited the system. Now at some future time, you enter the Display Manager again and want to do further work on the program. You must first "bring in" the program into the program window. To do this, use the **INCLUDE** command. The syntax is the same as the **FILE** command we just discussed. Thus, if we used the FILE command and saved our program in a file called EX1.SAS, we would issue the command:

```
INCLUDE 'EX1.SAS'
```

to bring the file into the program window. Keep in mind that you are making a **copy** of the DOS file and any changes you make will **not** be made to the DOS file unless you use the FILE command to copy the changed version back out to the DOS file. As we mentioned in the section on DOS file names, we recommend that you use the extension .SAS on all your SAS programs so that it is easy to list and find your SAS programs (e.g., DIR *.SAS).

Before we leave the subject of files, you may find it useful to write your SAS programs **outside** of the SAS Display Manager, using your favorite word processor. As long as you can produce an ASCII file with your word processor (either directly or through a conversion routine), you can take advantage of this feature. First, create the ASCII file containing the SAS program. Next, enter the SAS Display Manager. On the **command** line of the **program window**, type **INCLUDE 'filename'**, where filename is the name of your ASCII file. Remember that the filename can include drive and path attributes. For example, suppose we just created a SAS program with our word processor, and the file is called MYPROG.SAS, and it is located in a subdirectory called MYSUB on the C drive. You would type

```
INCLUDE 'C:\MYSUB\MYPROG.SAS'
```

on the command line to bring the program into the **program window**. If you invoked SAS software from the same subdirectory, the simpler form:

```
INCLUDE 'MYPROG.SAS'
```

could be used. You can then SUBMIT the program (F10) or edit it further with the SAS editor.

G. SUMMARY OF DISPLAY MANAGER COMMANDS

There are a few more Display Manager Commands that may come in handy. They are listed here, along with all the commands already discussed, with definitions and examples:

COMMAND	DEFINITION
BYE	Ends your SAS session.
CLEAR	Clears the contents of a window used in the Program, Log, and Output windows.

END	Closes special windows. For example, if you went to the HELP window and wanted to return to where you were before you typed HELP, use the END command. END is also used to exit the DIR and VAR windows.
NEXT	Used to move the cursor to the next active window.
X	An X entered on a command line will invoke a DOS or UNIX shell. The Display Manager screens will temporarily disappear and the DOS prompt will appear. At this point you may issue normal DOS commands such as DIR or COPY. DO NOT ISSUE THE CHKDSK/F COMMAND WHILE IN A DOS SHELL! You may cause irreparable damage to your disk. To go back to the Display Manager, type EXIT at the DOS prompt. Also, make sure you are in the same subdirectory you were in when you invoked SAS, when you EXIT. On a PC, a CTRL-X from anywhere works the same as an X on the command line.
X 'DOS command'	Allows you to issue a DOS or UNIX command from the Display Manager. Unlike the X command above, you will automatically return to the Display Manager when the command is completed.
e.g. ==> X 'DIR A:'	Issue a DOS command to list the files on the floppy diskette in drive A.
==> X 'LS *.SAS'	In UNIX, list all files with a .SAS extension.
ZOOM	Zoom or unzoom the windows.
TOP	Go to the top of the text in the window.
BOTTOM	Go to the bottom of the window.
RIGHT n	If text extends past the right side of the screen, shift the screen right by n spaces.
e.g. ==> RIGHT 20	Shift the screen 20 spaces to the right.
LEFT n	Shift left n spaces.
CLOCK	Display the time in the top of the screen.

FILE 'filename'   Send the contents of a window to an external file.

e.g. ==> FILE 'PROG.SAS'
                           Copy the contents of the current window to a file called PROG.SAS.

e.g. ==> FILE 'PRN'   Send the contents of the window to the printer.

INCLUDE 'filename'   Bring in a file from the outside into a window.

e.g. ==> INCLUDE 'PROG.SAS'
                           Bring in the file PROG.SAS to the current window.

FIND text   Find the first occurrence of text from the current cursor position.

e.g. ==> FIND print   Move the cursor to the first occurrence of the word "print" from the current cursor position. Note that the command is case sensitive.

RFIND   Find the same text again (stands for Re Find).

CHANGE aaa bbb   Change the string "aaa" to "bbb." If the strings contain any special characters or numbers, enclose the strings in single quotes.

e.g. ==> CHANGE princ print
                           Change the string "princ" to "print."

CHANGE aaa bbb all   Change all occurrences of "aaa" to "bbb" from the current cursor position to the end of the file.

e.g. ==> CHANGE 'PROC ANOVA' 'PROC GLM' ALL
                           Change all occurrences of the string PROC ANOVA to PROC GLM from the current cursor position. Note the single quotes are needed because of the blank in the strings.

PROBLEMS

B-1. What three windows first appear on the screen when you enter the SAS Display Manager?

B-2. What is the command to "toggle" between the three-screen display and the display where one window fills the screen?

B-3. How do you interrupt a SAS program that is running?

B-4. You are on the command line of the program window. What command will bring in a file called XYZ.SAS on the floppy diskette in the A drive?

B-5. You want to save the output from a SAS run to a file called XYZ.LST on a floppy diskette in drive B. You are currently on the command line of the PROGRAM window. What command(s) will accomplish this?

B-6. You have submitted a SAS program, found an error, and want to run it again. You return to the PROGRAM window and find it empty. What command (or function key) will bring back your program so you may edit it?

B-7. You are on the command line of the PROGRAM window and forgot the filename of the ASCII file you previously wrote with your word processor (although you do remember it has a .SAS extension). Without using the BYE command to return to DOS, how would you get a list of files with the extension .SAS?

APPENDIX C

SAS ERROR MESSAGES

This appendix deals with some of the most common error messages generated by SAS programs and how to find and correct the error.

1. **Variable not found.** This error message can result from a variety of errors. Most common is the **misspelling** of a variable name, either on the INPUT statement or elsewhere so that the names do not agree between the data step and a procedure that uses them. An example is shown below:

```
    4      *COMMON ERRORS;
    5      DATA ONE;
    6      INPUT X Y Z;
    7      CARDS;
    8      PROC MEANS;
NOTE: The data set WORK.ONE has 2 observations and 3
variables.
NOTE: The DATA statement used 8.00 seconds.
    9        VAR X U Z;
ERROR: Variable U not found.
```

2. **Syntax error detected.** This is another very common error caused either by misspelling a keyword or statement, or by using a statement that is not valid for a particular procedure. Below is the result of misspelling a keyword in a data step:

```
   11     DATA TWO;
   12       INTPU A B C;
INTPU A B C;
        -
ERROR: Syntax error detected              (cont.)
```

(Continued from previous page)
```
NOTE: Expecting one of the following :

; NAME NAME.NAME + : = ABORT ARRAY ATTRIB BY CALL
CARDS CARDS4 DELETE DISPLAY DO DROP FILE FORMAT GO
GOTO IF INFILE INFORMAT INPUT KEEP LABEL LABLE
LENGTH LINK LIST LOSTCARD MERGE MISSING OUTPUT PUT
RENAME RETAIN RETURN RUN SELECT SET STOP SUBSTR
UPDATE WINDOW [ {
```

3. **Invalid data error.** The most frequent problem here is a character value in a numeric field or an invalid number (such as 6.4.77). The SAS LOG will display the offending error line and substitute a **missing value** for the invalid data. It will then proceed with the following procedures:

```
    17    DATA THREE;
    18    INPUT SEX HEIGHT WEIGHT;
    19    CARDS;
NOTE: Invalid data for SEX in column 1 :
RULE: ----+----1----+----2----+----3----+----4----+----5----+----6
    1> M 63 166
```

4. **Semicolon missing.** This is probably the **most common SAS program-ming error.** The error messages resulting from a missing semicolon can be **very strange indeed.** Look at the example below:

```
    23    DATA FOUR;
    24    INPUT SBP DBP HR
    25    CARDS;
    26    130 80 55
          130 80 55
    ---
ERROR: Syntax error detected
```

Notice that the error message refers to the first **data** line! The reason for this is that the missing semicolon on the INPUT line causes the word CARDS to be read as a **variable name.** Then, when the first data line is encountered, the SAS compiler is looking for a SAS statement since it did not recognize the CARDS statement. The only advice we can give you is, **"If the error message doesn't seem to make sense, look for a missing semicolon in the previous line or two."**

PROBLEM SOLUTIONS

CHAPTER 1

1-1. (a)
```
DATA COLLEGE;
   INPUT ID AGE SEX $ GPA CSCORE;
   CARDS;
   1 18 M 3.7 650
   2 18 F 2.0 490
   3 19 F 3.3 580
   4 23 M 2.8 530
   5 21 M 3.5 640
```

(b)
```
PROC MEANS;
   VAR GPA CSCORE;
RUN;
```

(c) Between the "INPUT" and "CARDS" lines insert

```
INDEX = GPA + 3*CSCORE/500;
```

Add to the end of the program

```
PROC SORT;
   BY INDEX;
RUN;
PROC PRINT;
   TITLE 'STUDENTS IN INDEX ORDER'; (optional)
   ID ID;
   VAR GPA CSCORE INDEX;
RUN;
```

1-2. (a)
```
DATA TAXPROB;
   INPUT SS SALARY AGE RACE $;
   FORMAT SS SSN11.;    (See chapter 3 about FORMATS)
   CARDS;
   123874414 28000 35 W
   646239182 29500 37 B
   012437652 35100 40 W
   018451357 26500 31 W
RUN;
PROC MEANS N MEAN MAXDEC=0;
   TITLE 'DESCRIPTIVE STATISTICS FOR SALARY AND AGE';
   VAR SALARY AGE;
RUN;
```

(b) Add a line after the INPUT statement:

```
TAX = .30 * SALARY;
```

Add to the end of the program:

```
PROC SORT;
   BY SS;
RUN;
PROC PRINT;
   TITLE 'LISTING OF SALARY AND TAXES';
```

```
        ID SS;
        VAR SALARY TAX;
     RUN;
```

1-3.   1.   DATA MISTAKE;
        2.   INPUT ID 1-3 TOWN 4-6 REGION 7-9 YEAR 11-12
        3.   BUDGET 13-14 VOTER TURNOUT 16-20
        (data cards go here)
        4.   PROC MEANS;
        5.   VAR ID REGION VOTER TURNOUT;
        6.   N, STD, MEAN;

Line 3 – Variable name cannot contain a blank. Variable name too long. (Actually, if we had two variables, VOTER and TURNOUT the above INPUT statement would work, since we can combine LIST input with column specifications. However, for this problem, we intended VOTER TURNOUT to represent a single variable.) Semicolon missing after TURNOUT 16-20.

Line 5 – We probably don't want the mean ID. Also, would be more meaningful to use PROC FREQ for a categorical variable such as REGION.

Line 6 – Options for PROC MEANS go on the PROC line between the word MEANS and the semicolon. The options must have a **space** between them, not a comma.

```
     PROC MEANS N MEAN STD;
     VAR ---- ;
```

1-4. We have a SAS data set with the variables AGE, SEX, RACE, INCOME, MARITAL, and HOME (homeowner vs renter).

Code Book

Variable Name	Col(s)	Description and Formats
AGE	1	Age group of subject 1=10-19 2=20-29 3=30-39 4=40-49 5=50-59 6=60+
SEX	2	Sex, 1=male 2=female
RACE	3	Race, 1=white 2=black 3=hispanic 4=other
INCOME	4	Income group, 1=0 to $9,999 2=10,000 to 19,999 3=20,000 to 39,000 4=40,000 to 59,000 5=60,000 to 79,000 6=80,000 and over
MARITAL	5	Marital status, 1=single 2=married 3=separated 4=divorced 5=widowed
HOME	6	Homeowner or renter, 1=homeowner 0=renter

```
            DATA CEO;
            INPUT AGE 1 SEX 2 RACE 3 INCOME 4 MARITAL 5 HOME 6;
            CARDS;
            311411
            etc.
            RUN;
            PROC FREQ ORDER=FREQ;
            *NOTE, THE ORDER=FREQ OPTION WILL LIST THE FREQUENCIES IN
             DECREASING FREQUENCY ORDER, i.e. THE MOST FREQUENT FIRST;
                TITLE 'FREQUENCIES AND CONTINGENCY TABLES FOR CEO
            REPORT';
                TABLES AGE SEX RACE INCOME MARITAL HOME;
                TABLES AGE*SEX*RACE  INCOME*AGE*SEX MARITAL*HOME;
                *OR WHATEVER OTHER COMBINATIONS YOU ARE INTERESTED IN;
            RUN;
            PROC CHART;
                VBAR AGE SEX RACE INCOME MARITAL HOME / DISCRETE;
            RUN;
```

1-5.
```
            DATA PROB1_5;
            INPUT ID RACE $ SBP DBP HR;
            CARDS;
            (data go here)
            PROC SORT;
                BY SBP;
            PROC PRINT;
                TITLE 'RACE AND HEMODYNAMIC VARIABLES';
                ID ID;
                VAR RACE SBP DBP;
            RUN;
```

1-6. Add the following line after the INPUT statement:

```
            ABP = 2*DBP/3 + SBP/3;
```

or

```
            ABP = DBP + (SBP-DBP)/3;
```

CHAPTER 2

2-1.
```
            PROC FREQ;
                TABLES SEX;
            RUN;
```

2-2.
```
            PROC FREQ;
                TABLES RACE;
            RUN;
```

2-3. (a)
```
            PROC CHART;
                VBAR GROUP;
            RUN;
```

(b) ```
PROC PLOT;
    PLOT Y*X;
RUN;
```

(c) ```
PROC SORT;
    BY GROUP;
RUN;
PROC PLOT;
    BY GROUP;
    PLOT Y*X;
RUN;
```

Don't forget that you must have your data set sorted by the BY variables
before you can use a BY statement in a PROC.

2-4. Program to read liver data and produce statistics.

```
DATA LIVER;
INPUT SUBJ DOSE REACT LIVER_WT SPLEEN;
CARDS;
1 1 5.4 10.2 8.9
2 1 5.9 9.8 7.3
      etc.
RUN;
PROC SORT;
    BY DOSE;   *NOTE, OPTIONAL SINCE ALREADY IN DOSE ORDER;
RUN;
PROC UNIVARIATE NORMAL PLOT;
    TITLE 'DISTRIBUTIONS FOR LIVER DATA';
    VAR REACT -- SPLEEN;
RUN;
PROC UNIVARIATE NORMAL PLOT;
    BY DOSE;
    TITLE 'DISTRIBUTIONS FOR LIVER DATA BY DOSE';
    VAR REACT -- SPLEEN;
RUN;
```

2-5.
```
1  DATA;
2  INPUT AGE STATUS PROGNOSIS DOCTOR SEX STATUS2
3       STATUS3;
4  (data cards)
5  PROC CHART BY SEX;
6      VBAR STATUS
7      VBAR PROGNOSIS;
8  PROC PLOT;
9      DOCTOR BY PROGNOSIS;
```

Line 1 – Not an error but a good idea to name your data sets.

Line 2 – PROGNOSIS has 9 letters.

Line 2 – Not really an error, but it would be better to list SEX with the other
demographic variables.

Line 2 – Again, not an error, but an ID variable is desirable.

Lines 2 and 3 – Boy, we're picky. If you have STATUS2 and STATUS3, STATUS should be STATUS1.

Line 5 – Two things wrong here: One, If you use a BY variable, the data set must be sorted in order of the BY variable; two, a semicolon is missing between PROC CHART and BY SEX.

Line 6 – Missing a semicolon at the end of the line.

Line 7 – In case you thought this was an error, it isn't. You **can** have two (or more) VBAR statements with one PROC CHART.

Line 9 – Missing the keyword PLOT before the plot request. Also, the plot request is of the form Y*X not Y BY X.

2-6. (a)
```
DATA SALES;
  INPUT PERSON $ TARGET $ VISITS CALLS UNITS;
  CARDS;
Brown      American  3    12  28000
Johnson    VRW       6    14  33000
Rivera     Texam     2     6   8000
Brown      Standard  0    22      0
Brown      Knowles   2    19  12000
Rivera     Metro     4     8  13000
Rivera     Uniman    8     7  27000
Johnson    Oldham    3    16   8000
Johnson    Rondo     2    14   2000
RUN;
PROC SORT;
  BY PERSON;
RUN;
PROC MEANS N SUM MEAN STD MAXDEC=0;
    BY PERSON;
    TITLE 'SALES FIGURES FOR EACH SALESPERSON';
    VAR VISITS CALLS UNITS;
RUN;
```

(b)
```
PROC PLOT;
    TITLE 'SALES PLOTS';
    PLOT VISITS*CALLS=PERSON;
RUN;
```

(c)
```
PROC CHART;
    TITLE 'DISTRIBUTION OF UNITS SOLD BY SALESPERSON';
    VBAR PERSON / SUMVAR=UNITS TYPE=SUM;
RUN;
```

or

```
PROC CHART;
    TITLE 'DISTRIBUTION OF UNITS SOLD BY SALESPERSON';
    VBAR UNITS / GROUP=PERSON;
RUN;
```

The first PROC CHART in C) above will produce a single bar for each sales person, the height representing the total (sum) of the units sold. The alternate statements will produce an actual frequency distribution of the number of units sold, for each salesperson, in a side-by-side fashion.

2-7. The most efficient program to read this data set and compute means would be:

```
DATA PROB2_7;
INPUT ID TYPE $ SCORE;
CARDS;
1 A 44
1 B  9
1 C 203
   etc.
PROC SORT;
   BY TYPE;
RUN;
PROC MEANS;
   BY TYPE;
   VAR SCORE;
RUN;
```

Remember to sort your data set first, before using a BY variable.

CHAPTER 3

3-1.
```
PROC FORMAT;
VALUE FGROUP 1='CONTROL' 2='DRUG A'
             3='DRUG B';
```

3-2.
```
PROC FORMAT;
   VALUE SEX 1='MALE' 2='FEMALE';
   VALUE PARTY 1='REPUBLICAN' 2='DEMOCRAT'
               3='NOT REGISTERED';
   VALUE YESNO 0='NO' 1='YES';
RUN;
DATA SURVEY;
INPUT ID 1-3 SEX 4 PARTY 5 VOTE 6 FOREIGN 7 SPEND 8;
LABEL PARTY='POLITICAL PARTY'
   VOTE='VOTE IN LAST ELECTION?'
   FOREIGN='AGREE WITH GOVERNMENT POLICY?'
   SPEND='SHOULD WE INCREASE DOMESTIC SPENDING?';
FORMAT SEX SEX. PARTY PARTY. VOTE FOREIGN SPEND YESNO.;
CARDS;
(data goes here)
RUN;
PROC FREQ;
TITLE 'POLITICAL SURVEY RESULTS';
TABLES SEX PARTY FOREIGN SPEND;
TABLES VOTE*(SPEND FOREIGN) / CHISQ;
RUN;
```

3-3. Between the DATA statement and the CARDS statement insert

Method 1

```
IF 0 LE WEIGHT LT 101 THEN WTGRP=1;
   ELSE IF 101 LE WEIGHT LT 151 THEN WTGRP=2;
   ELSE IF 151 LE WEIGHT LE 200 THEN WTGRP=3;
```

```
           ELSE IF WEIGHT GT 200 THEN WTGRP=4;
        IF 0 LE HEIGHT LE 70 THEN HTGRP=1;
           ELSE IF HEIGHT GT 70 THEN HTGRP=2;
```

NOTE: You may use <= instead of LE, < instead of LT, and > instead of GT.

Then add

```
PROC FREQ;
    TABLES WTGRP*HTGRP;
```

Method 2

```
PROC FORMAT;
    VALUE  WTFMT 0-100='1'  101-150='2'  151-200='3'  201-
HIGH='4';
    VALUE HTFMT 0-70='1'  71-HIGH='2';
```

(Insert the following format statement before the CARDS statement.)

```
FORMAT WEIGHT WTFMT. HEIGHT HTFMT.;
```

Then add

```
PROC FREQ;
    TABLES WEIGHT*HEIGHT;
```

3-4.

```
PROC FORMAT;
    VALUE PROB 1='COLD'  2='FLU'  3='TROUBLE SLEEP'
               4='CHEST PAIN'  5='MUSCLE PAIN'  6='HEADACHE'
               7='OVERWEIGHT'  8='HIGH BP'  9='HEARING LOSS';
RUN;
DATA PATIENT;
INPUT SUBJ 1-2 PROB1 3 PROB2 4 PROB3 5 HR 6-8 SBP 9-11
DBP 12-14;
CARDS;
(data lines go here)
RUN;
PROC MEANS N MEAN STD MAXDEC=1;
    TITLE 'STATISTICS FROM PATIENT DATA BASE';
    VAR HR SBP DBP;
RUN;
```

For part (b) add:

```
(Solution without arrays)    (Solution with arrays)
DATA PROBLM;                  DATA PROBLM;
SET PATIENT;                  SET PATIENT;
PROB = PROB1;                 ARRAY XPROB[3] PROB1-PROB3;
OUTPUT;                       DO I = 1 TO 3;
PROB = PROB2;                     PROB = XPROB[I];
OUTPUT;                           OUTPUT;
PROB = PROB3;                     END;
OUTPUT;                       FORMAT PROB PROB.;
FORMAT PROB PROB.;            KEEP PROB;
KEEP PROB;                    RUN;
```

```
RUN;                              PROC FREQ;
PROC FREQ;                            TABLES PROB;
    TABLES PROB;                  RUN;
RUN;
```

3-5.

Line 3 – The formats cannot be assigned to variables before they have been defined. Therefore, move lines 5 through 8 to the beginning of the program (before line 1).

Line 10 – PROC FREQ uses the keyword TABLES not VAR to specify a list of variables.

Line 10 – You cannot use the CHISQ option unless a two-way table (or higher order) is specified. That is, we could have written

```
PROC FREQ;
    TABLES SEX*RACE / CHISQ;
```

Line 12 – You cannot use a BY statement unless the data set has been sorted first by the same variable.

CHAPTER 4

4-1.
```
DATA PROB4_1;
INPUT @1 ID 3. @5 (DOB ST_DATE END_DATE)(MMDDYY6.)
      @23 SALES 4.;
AGE = (ST_DATE - DOB) / 365.25;
*FOR SECTION E, SUBSTITUTE THE LINE BELOW FOR AGE;
AGE = FLOOR ((ST_DATE - DOB) / 365.25);
LENGTH = (END_DATE - ST_DATE) / 365.25;
SALES_YR = SALES / LENGTH;
*FOR SECTION, E SUBSTITUTE THE LINE BELOW FOR SALES_YR;
SALES_YR = ROUND ((SALES/LENGTH),10);
FORMAT DOB MMDDYY8. SALES_YR DOLLAR6.;
CARDS;
001 10214611128012288887343
002 09135502028002049088123
005 06064003128103128550000
003 07054411158011139089544
RUN;
PROC PRINT;
TITLE 'REPORT FOR HOMEWORK PROBLEM 4-1';
    ID ID;
    VAR DOB AGE LENGTH SALES_YR;
RUN;
```

Some notes on this program: 1. The INPUT statement uses formats for all the variables instead of columns. Chapter 10 will give more details on the use of INPUT statements. Briefly, the format N. is a format for a numeric, the value of N being the number of columns the number takes up. We use the pointers (@) to indicate the starting column. When starting column and lengths are given, it's easier to use pointers and formats. By the way, the format for a **character** variable of N columns is $N. We also used a format list in this solution. We can supply a list of variables in parentheses followed by a format (or formats), also in parentheses. So, the variables DOB, ST_DATE, and

END_DATE will all share the MMDDYY6. format. Using the single MMDDYY6. format for these three variables works only because they are contiguous. If there were different numbers of spaces between the three dates, we would have to specify the starting column and a format for each separately.

4-2.
```
DATA RATS;
INPUT RAT_NO 1 @3 (DOB DISEASE DEATH)(DATE7.+1)
      @27 GROUP $1.;
*YOU COULD USE A SIMPLER INPUT STATEMENT LIKE THIS:
INPUT RAT_NO 1 @3 DOB DATE7. @11 DISEASE DATE7.
      @19 DEATH DATE7. GROUP $ 27;
BIR_TO_D = DISEASE - DOB;
DIS_TO_D = DEATH - DISEASE;
AGE = DEATH - DOB;
FORMAT DOB DISEASE DEATH MMDDYY8.;
CARDS;
1 23MAY90 23JUN90 28JUN90 A
2 21MAY90 27JUN90 05JUL90 A
3 23MAY90 25JUN90 01JUL90 A
4 27MAY90 07JUL90 15JUL90 A
5 22MAY90 29JUN90 22JUL90 B
6 26MAY90 03JUL90 03AUG90 B
7 24MAY90 01JUL90 29JUL90 B
8 29MAY90 15JUL90 18AUG90 B
RUN;
*IF THE DATA WERE NOT IN GROUP ORDER, NEED TO RUN PROC
 SORT FIRST, OTHERWISE THE KEYWORD NOTSORTED TELLS THE
 SYSTEM THAT WE KNOW OUR DATA ARE ALREADY SORTED--SAVES
 COMPUTER TIME TOO;
PROC MEANS MAXDEC=1 N MEAN STD STDERR;
    BY GROUP NOTSORTED;
    VAR BIR_TO_D -- AGE;
RUN;
```

4-3.
```
PROC SORT DATA=PATIENTS;
    BY ID;
RUN;
DATA PROB4_3;
SET PATIENTS;
BY ID;
*OMIT THE FIRST VISIT FOR EACH PATIENT;
IF NOT FIRST.ID;
RUN;
PROC MEANS NOPRINT NWAY DATA=PROB4_3;
    CLASS ID;
    VAR HR SBP DBP;
    OUTPUT OUT=PAT_MEAN MEAN=;
RUN;
```

4-4.
```
PROC SORT DATA=PATIENTS;
    BY ID;
RUN;
DATA PROB4_4;
SET PATIENTS;
```

```
    BY ID;
    *OMIT PATIENTS WITH ONLY ONE VISIT;
    IF FIRST.ID AND LAST.ID THEN DELETE;
    RUN;
    PROC MEANS NOPRINT NWAY DATA=PROB4_4;
        CLASS ID;
        VAR HR SBP DBP;
        OUTPUT OUT=PAT_MEAN MEAN=;
    RUN;
```

4-5. Suppose the original data set that contains the ID, GROUP, TIME, WBC, and RBC is called PATIENT. First, use PROC MEANS to create a data set of means per ID.

```
    PROC MEANS NWAY NOPRINT DATA=PATIENT;
        CLASS ID GROUP;
        VAR WBC RBC;
        OUTPUT OUT=TEMP MEAN=;
    RUN;
    DATA PAT_MEAN;
    SET TEMP;
    IF _FREQ_ GT 5;
    DROP _TYPE_ _FREQ_;
    RUN;
```

4-6. Replace the OUTPUT statement of PROC MEANS with:

```
    OUTPUT OUT=TEMP MEAN= STD=SD_WBC SD_RBC;
```

CHAPTER 5

5-1. (a)
```
    DATA PROB5_1;
    INPUT X Y Z;
    CARDS;
    1 3 15              x vs. y   r= .965    p=.0078
    7 13 7              x vs. z   r=-.975    p=.0047
    8 12 5
    3 4 14
    4 7 10
    RUN;
    PROC CORR;
        VAR X;
        WITH Y Z;
    RUN;
```

   (b)
```
    PROC CORR;           y vs. z   r=-.963    p=.0084
        VAR X Y Z;
    RUN;
```

5-2.
```
    DATA PRESSURE;
    INPUT AGE SBP;
    CARDS;
    15 116
    20 120
    25 130
```

```
30 132
40 150
50 148
RUN;
PROC CORR;
   VAR AGE SBP;
RUN;
```

5-3. (a)
```
PROC REG;         int. = .781 prob > |T|=.5753
   MODEL Y = X;   slope=1.524 prob > |T|=.0078
```

5-4.
```
DATA PROB5_4;
INPUT X Y Z;
LX = LOG(X);
LY = LOG(Y);
LZ = LOG(Z);
CARDS;
1 3 15
7 13 7
8 12 5
3 4 14
4 7 10
RUN;
PROC CORR;
   VAR LX LY LZ;
RUN;
```

5-5. (a)
```
PROC PLOT;
   PLOT Y*X;
```

   (b)
```
PROC REG;
   MODEL Y = X;
   PLOT PREDICTED.*X='P' Y*X='o' / OVERLAY;
RUN;
```

You may use any plotting symbol you wish for the two plots; we used P's and o's.

5-6. Sections a-c

```
DATA PROB5_6;
INPUT COUNTY POP HOSPITAL FIRE_CO RURAL $;
CARDS;
1  35  1  2   YES
2  88  5  8    NO
3   5  0  1   YES
4  55  3  3   YES
5  75  4  5    NO
6 125  5  8    NO
7 225  7  9   YES
8 500 10 11    NO
RUN;
PROC UNIVARIATE NORMAL PLOT;
   TITLE 'CHECKING THE DISTRIBUTIONS';
   VAR POP HOSPITAL FIRE_CO;
```

```
RUN;
PROC CORR PEARSON SPEARMAN;
    TITLE 'CORRELATION MATRIX';
    VAR POP HOSPITAL FIRE_CO;
RUN;
```

Because of the outliers in the population variable, we prefer the Spearman correlation for this problem.

(d) We can use the output from UNIVARIATE to find the medians and do the recoding. In chapter 6 we will see that PROC RANK can be used to produce a median cut automatically by using the GROUPS=2 option. For now, we will recode the variables using formats. You can also create new variables in the data step with IF statements.

```
PROC FORMAT;
    VALUE POP LOW-81='BELOW MEDIAN' 82-HIGH='ABOVE MEDIAN';
    VALUE HOSPITAL LOW-4='BELOW MEDIAN' 5-HIGH='ABOVE
MEDIAN';
    VALUE FIRE_CO LOW-6='BELOW MEDIAN' 7-HIGH='ABOVE
MEDIAN';
DATA PROB5_6;
INPUT COUNTY POP HOSPITAL FIRE_CO RURAL $;
CARDS;
(data lines)
PROC FREQ;
    TITLE 'CROSS TABULATIONS';
    FORMAT POP POP. HOSPITAL HOSPITAL. FIRE_CO FIRE_CO.;
    TABLES RURAL*(POP HOSPITAL FIRE_CO) / CHISQ;
RUN;
```

5-7.

Line 1 – Incorrect data set name, cannot contain a dash.

Lines 3-5 – These lines will recode **missing values** to 1, which we probably do not want to do. the correct form of these statements is

```
IF X LE 0 AND X NE . THEN X=1;
```

or

```
IF -999999 LE X LE 0 THEN X=1;
```

Line 10 – The options PEARSON and SPEARMAN do not follow a slash. The line should read

```
PROC CORR PEARSON SPEARMAN;
```

Line 11 – The correct form for a list of variables where the "root" is not the same is

```
VAR X--LOGZ;
```

Remember, the single dash is used for a list of variables such as ABC1-ABC25.

CHAPTER 6

6-1.
```
DATA HEADACHE;
INPUT TREAT $ TIME @@;
CARDS;
A 40 A 42 A 48 A 35 A 62 A 35
T 35 T 37 T 42 T 22 T 38 T 29
RUN;
PROC TTEST;
    CLASS TREAT;
    VAR TIME;
RUN;
```

Not significant at the .05 level (t=1.93, p=.083).

6-2.
```
PROC NPAR1WAY WILCOXON;
    TITLE 'NONPARAMETRIC COMPARISON';
    CLASS TREAT;
    VAR TIME;
RUN;
```

Sum of ranks for A=48.5; for B, 29.5. Z=1.45, p > .146.

6-3.   Use a paired t-test. We have
```
DATA PAIR;
INPUT SUBJ A_TIME T_TIME;
DIFF = T_TIME - A_TIME;
CARDS;
1 20 18
2 40 36
3 30 30
4 45 46
5 19 15                              T=-3.00  p=.0199
6 27 22
7 32 29
8 26 25
RUN;
PROC MEANS N MEAN STD STDERR T PRT MAXDEC=3;
    VAR DIFF;
RUN;
```

6-4.
```
PROC FORMAT;
    VALUE GROUP 0='A' 1='B' 2='C';
RUN;
DATA RANDOM;
INPUT SUBJ @@;
GROUP = RANUNI(0); *NOTE: CAN ALSO USE UNIFORM FUNCTION;
CARDS;
001 137 454 343 257 876 233 165 002
RUN;
PROC RANK GROUP=3;
    VAR GROUP;
RUN;
PROC SORT;
```

```
   BY SUBJ;
RUN;
PROC PRINT;
   TITLE 'LISTING OF SUBJ NUMBERS AND RANDOM GROUP
ASSIGNMENTS';
   FORMAT GROUP GROUP.;
   ID SUBJ;
   VAR GROUP;
RUN;
```

6-5.

Line 2 – Variable name HEARTRATE too long.

Line 10 – Correct procedure name is TTEST.

CHAPTER 7

7-1.
```
DATA BRANDTST;
DO BRAND='A','N','T';
   DO SUBJ=1 TO 8;
      INPUT TIME @;
      OUTPUT;
      END;
   END;
CARDS;
8 10 9 11 10 10 8 12
4 7 5 5 6 7 6 4
12 8 10 10 11 9 9 12
RUN;
PROC ANOVA;
   CLASSES BRAND;
   MODEL TIME = BRAND;
   MEANS BRAND / DUNCAN;
RUN;
```

$F=28.89$, $p=.0001$ N is significantly lower than either T or A ($p < .05$).
T and A are not significantly different ($p > .05$).

7-2.
```
DATA BOUNCE;
DO AGE = 'NEW', 'OLD';
   DO BRAND = 'W','P';
      DO I = 1 TO 5;
         INPUT BOUNCES @;
         OUTPUT;
         END;
      END;
   END;
DROP I;
CARDS;
67 72 74 82 81 75 76 80 72 73
46 44 45 51 43 63 62 66 62 60
RUN;
PROC ANOVA;
   TITLE 'TWO-WAY ANOVA (AGE BY BRAND) FOR TENNIS BALLS';
   CLASSES AGE BRAND;
```

```
      MODEL BOUNCES = AGE|BRAND;
      MEANS AGE|BRAND;
RUN;
```

NOTE: A simpler INPUT statement could have been used: INPUT BRAND AGE BOUNCES;

With the data listed one number per line such as:

```
W NEW 67
P NEW 75
```

Both main effects (AGE and BRAND) are significant (p=.0001, and .0002 respectively). The interaction is also significant, p=.0002.

7-3. (a)

```
DATA SODA;
INPUT BRAND $ AGEGRP RATING;
CARDS;
C 1 7
C 1 6
C 1 6
C 1 5
C 1 6
P 1 9
P 1 8
P 1 9
P 1 9
P 1 9
P 1 8
C 2 9
C 2 8
C 2 8
C 2 9
C 2 7
C 2 8
C 2 8
P 2 6
P 2 7
P 2 6
P 2 6
P 2 5
RUN;
PROC GLM;
    TITLE 'TWO-WAY UNBALANCED ANOVA';
    CLASSES BRAND AGEGRP;
    MODEL RATING = BRAND|AGEGRP;
    MEANS BRAND|AGEGRP;
RUN;
```

(b) Use the values from the MEANS statement in (a) to plot the interaction graph, or use the program below:

```
PROC MEANS NWAY NOPRINT;
    CLASS BRAND AGEGRP;
    VAR RATING;
```

```
        OUTPUT OUT=MEANS MEAN= ;
    RUN;
    PROC PLOT;
        PLOT RATING*AGEGRP=BRAND;
    RUN;

(c) PROC SORT;
        BY AGEGRP;
    RUN;
    PROC TTEST;
        BY AGEGRP;
        CLASS BRAND;
    RUN;
        VAR RATING;
    RUN;
```

7-5.

Line 4 – Since this is a two-way **unbalanced** design, PROC GLM should be used instead of PROC ANOVA.

CHAPTER 8

8-1.
```
    DATA SHIRT;
    INPUT JUDGE 1 BRAND 2 COLOR 3 WORK 4 OVERALL 5;
    INDEX = (3*OVERALL + 2*WORK + COLOR)/6.0;
    CARDS;
    (data cards go here)
    PROC ANOVA;
        CLASSES JUDGE BRAND;
        MODEL COLOR WORK OVERALL INDEX = JUDGE BRAND;
        MEANS BRAND / DUNCAN;
    RUN;
```

8-2.
```
    DATA WATER;
    INPUT ID 1-3 CITY $ 4 RATING 5;
    CARDS;
    (data lines)
    RUN;
    PROC ANOVA;
        CLASSES ID CITY;
        MODEL RATING = ID CITY;
        MEANS CITY / SNK;
    RUN;
```

8-3.
```
    PROC FORMAT;
        VALUE CITY 1='NEW YORK' 2='NEW ORLEANS'
                   3='CHICAGO' 4='DENVER';
    DATA PROB8_3;
    INPUT JUDGE 1-3 @;
        DO CITY=1 TO 4;
     INPUT TASTE 1. @;
     OUTPUT;
     END;
        END;
```

```
        FORMAT CITY CITY.;
        CARDS;
        0018685
        0025654
        0037464
        0047573
        RUN;
```

8-4.
```
        DATA RATS;
        INPUT GROUP $ RATNO DISTAL PROXIMAL;
        CARDS;
        N 1 34 38
        N 2 28 38
        N 3 38 48
        N 4 32 38
        D 5 44 42
        D 6 52 48
        D 7 46 46
        D 8 54 50
        RUN;
        PROC ANOVA;
            CLASSES GROUP;
            MODEL DISTAL PROXIMAL = GROUP / NOUNI;
            REPEATED LOCATION 2;
        RUN;
```

Although the main effects are significant (GROUP p=.01, LOCATION p=.0308) the interaction term is highly significant (GROUP*LOCATION interaction F=31.58, p=.0014). We should look carefully at the interaction graph to see exactly what is going on.

8-5. The DO loops are in the wrong order and the OUTPUT statement is missing. Lines 2 through 8 should read:

```
        DO SUBJ=1 TO 3;
            DO GROUP='CONTROL','DRUG';
                DO TIME='BEFORE','AFTER';
                    INPUT SCORE @;
                    OUTPUT;
                END;
            END;
        END;
```

There are no other errors.

CHAPTER 9

9-1.
```
        DATA TOMATO;
        DO LIGHT=1 TO 3;
            DO WATER=1 TO 2;
                DO I=1 TO 3;
                    INPUT YIELD @;
                    OUTPUT;
                    END;
                END;
```

```
        END;
    CARDS;
    12 9 8 13 15 14 16 14 12 20 16 16 18 25 20 25 27 29
    RUN;
    PROC REG;
        MODEL YIELD = LIGHT WATER;
    RUN;
```

9-2.
```
    DATA LIBRARY;
    INPUT BOOKS ENROLL DEGREE AREA;
    CARDS;
     4   5  3   20
     5   8  3   40
    10  40  3  100
     1   4  2   50
    .5   2  1  300
     2   8  1  400
     7  30  3   40
     4  20  2  200
     1  10  2    5
     1  12  1  100
    RUN;
    PROC REG;
        MODEL BOOKS = ENROLL DEGREE AREA / SELECTION = FORWARD;
    RUN;
```

9-3.
```
    DATA PROB93;
     INPUT GPA HS_GPA BOARD IQ;
     CARDS;
     3.9    3.8        680        130
     3.9    3.9        720        110
     3.8    3.8        650        120
     3.1    3.5        620        125
     2.9    2.7        480        110
     2.7    2.5        440        100
     2.2    2.5        500        115
     2.1    1.9        380        105
     1.9    2.2        380        110
     1.4    2.4        400        110
     RUN;
     PROC REG;
        MODEL GPA = HS_GPA BOARD IQ / SELECTION=MAXR;
     RUN;
```

9-4.
```
    DATA PEOPLE;
    INPUT HEIGHT WAIST LEG ARM WEIGHT;
    CARDS;
    (your data)
    PROC CORR;
       VAR HEIGHT--WEIGHT;
    RUN;
    PROC REG;
        MODEL WEIGHT = HEIGHT WAIST LEG ARM /
              SELECTION = STEPWISE;
    RUN;
```

(You may also use FORWARD, BACKWARD, or MAXR instead of STEPWISE)

9-5. Ha! No errors here. As a matter of fact, you can use this program for Problem 9-4.

CHAPTER 10

10-1.

(a)
```
DATA PROB10_1;
   INPUT GROUP $ SCORE;
   CARDS;
P 77
P 76
   ...
D 80
D 80
   ...
RUN;
```

(b)
```
DATA PROB10_1;
   INPUT GROUP $ SCORE @@;
   CARDS;
P 77 P 76 ...
D 80 D 84 ...
RUN;
```

(c)
```
DATA PROB10_1;
   DO GROUP='P','D';
      DO I = 1 TO 12;
         INPUT SCORE @@;
         OUTPUT;
         END;
      END;
   DROP I;
   CARDS;
77 76 ...
80 84 ...
RUN;
```

(d)
```
DATA PROB10_1;
   DO GROUP='P','D';
      DO I = 1 TO 12;
      SUBJ+1;
         INPUT SCORE @@;
         OUTPUT;
         END;
      END;
   DROP I;
    etc.
```

10-2.
```
INPUT @1 ID 3. SEX $1. @10 (DOB VISIT DISCHRG)(MMDDYY6.)
      @30 (SBP1-SBP3)(3.+5) @33 (DBP1-DBP3)(3.+5)
      @36 (HR1-HR3)(2.+6);
```

CHAPTER 11

11-1.
```
LIBNAME A 'A:\';
DATA A.BILBO;
INFILE 'A:FRODO' MISSOVER;  *(Don't forget the MISSOVER!);
INPUT ID 1-3 AGE 5-6 HR 8-10 SBP 12-14 DBP 16-18;
AVEBP = 2*DBP/3 + SBP/3;
RUN;
DATA A.HIBP;
SET A.BILBO;
IF AVEBP GE 100;
RUN;
```

11-2 (MS-DOS solution)
```
LIBNAME INDATA 'C:\SASDATA';
LIBNAME LIBRARY 'C:\SASDATA';
PROC FREQ DATA=INDATA.SURVEY90 ORDER=FREQ;
   TITLE 'Frequencies for ICD_9 codes from the 1990
Survey';
   TABLES ICD_9;
RUN;
PROC MEANS DATA=INDATA.SURVEY90 N MEAN STD STDERR MIN MAX
MAXDEC=2;
   TITLE 'Descriptive Statistics for 1990 Survey';
   VAR AGE;
RUN;
```

11-3.
```
LIBNAME ADRIVE 'A:\';
PROC DATASETS LIBRARY=ADRIVE;
   CHANGE MESTAKE=MISTAKE;
RUN;
```

CHAPTER 12

12-1.
```
LIBNAME D 'D:\SASDATA';
PROC DATASETS LIBRARY=D;
   MODIFY HTWT;
        RENAME COL1=ID COL2=AGE COL3=SEX COL4=HEIGHT
               COL5=WEIGHT;
RUN;
```

CHAPTER 13

13-1.
```
DATA PROB13_1;
INPUT (HT1-HT5)(2.) (WT1-WT5)(3.);
ARRAY HT[*] HT1-HT5;
ARRAY WT[*] WT1-WT5;
ARRAY DENS[*] DENS1-DENS5;
DO I = 1 TO 5;
```

```
              DENS[I] = WT[I] / HT[I]**2;
              END;
          DROP I;
          CARDS;
```

13-2.
```
          DATA OLDMISS;
          INPUT A B C X1-X3 Y1-Y3;
          ARRAY NINE[*] A B C X1-X3;
          ARRAY SEVEN[*] Y1-Y3;
          DO I = 1 TO 6;
              IF NINE[I] = 999 THEN NINE[I] = .;
              END;
          DO I = 1 TO 3;
              IF SEVEN[I] = 777 THEN SEVEN[I] = .;
              END;
          DROP I;
          CARDS;
```

13-3.
```
          DATA TOAD;
          SET FROG;
          ARRAY XX[5] X1-X5;
          ARRAY YY[5] Y1-Y5;
          DO TIME = 1 TO 5;
              X = XX[I];
              Y = YY[I];
              OUTPUT;
              END;
          DROP X1-X5 Y1-Y5;
          RUN;
```

13-4.
```
          DATA NEWSTATE;
          SET STATE;
          ARRAY XSTATE[*] $ STATE1-STATE5;
          DO I = 1 TO 5;
              IF XSTATE[I] = 'XX' THEN XSTATE[I] = ' ';
              STATE = XSTATE[I];
              OUTPUT;
              END;
          DROP I;
          PROC FREQ ORDER=FREQ;
              TABLES STATE;
          RUN;
```

13-5.
```
          DATA NEW;
          SET BLAH;
          ARRAY JUNK[*] X1-X5 Y1-Y5 Z1-Z5;
          DO J = 1 TO DIM(JUNK);
              IF JUNK[J] = 999 THEN JUNK[J] = ,;
              END;
          DROP J;
          RUN;
```

APPENDIX A

A-1.   1C, 2A, 3D, 4B

A-2.   `C:\> DIR B:`

A-3. (a) `DEL *.*`

    (b) `DEL *.TXT`

    (c) `DEL P*.*`

    (d) `DEL PROG?.SAS`

NOTE: DEL PROG*.SAS will also delete PROGRAM.SAS.

A-4. (a) `COPY B:RON.CDY A:`

    (b) `C:\> MD BIOSTAT`
        `C:\> COPY A:KERMIT.FRG C:\BIOSTAT`

A-5.   `FORMAT B:`

A-6. You will be attempting to format your hard disk. Under most operating systems, you will be informed that you are about to destroy the contents of your hard disk and need to reply with a Y (Yes) to proceed.

A-7.   `COPY A:MYDATA C:\SASDATA`

A-8.   `CHKDSK/F    (Reply to the request to save lost chains in files with an "n.")`

A-9.   `CD SASDATA`

    or

    `CD\SASDATA`

A-10.   `C:\SASPROG> DEL SASUSER`
        `C:\SASPROG> RD SASUSER`
        `C:\SASPROG> DEL SASWORK`
        `C:\SASPROG> RD SASWORK`
        `C:\SASPROG> DEL *.*`
        `C:\SASPROG> CD \`
        `C:\> RD SASPROG`

NOTE: There are other ways to accomplish this.

A-11.   `C:\> DEL \MYDATA`
        `C:\> RD MYDATA`

A-12.   `C:\SASPROG\SASWORK> CD \OSCAR`

APPENDIX B

B-1.   Output, Log, and Program windows.

B-2.   Zoom (or F7 in MS-DOS)

B-3.   Enter a control-C. (This does not work 100% of the time.)

B-4.   `INC 'A:XYZ.SAS'`

B-5.   `OUTPUT` (or F4 under MS-DOS) `FILE 'B:XYZ.LST'`

B-6.   `RECALL` (or F9 under MS-DOS)

B-7.   Either

```
X 'DIR *.SAS'
```

or

```
X   (Exit to the DOS Shell)
C> DIR *.SAS
C> EXIT
```

INDEX